D1263471

FOLLY BISTRO

BRUNO HUBER

⊓ GRANVILLE ISLAND
PUBLISHING

ISBN 978-1-989467-00-8 (paperback)
ISBN 978-1-989467-01-5 (ebook)

Copy editor: Maureen Phillips
Book and cover designer: Daniel Colmont — brandbig.ca
Cover image: from a poster by © Roger Blachon
with permission by Mireille Blachon

Granville Island Publishing Ltd.
212–1656 Duranleau St.
Vancouver, BC, Canada V6H 3S4

604-688-0320 / 1-877-688-0320
info@granvilleislandpublishing.com
www.granvilleislandpublishing.com

Published July 2019
Printed in Canada

All individuals are constructs of real people

All events are true

All opinions are mine unless stated otherwise

All bills have been paid

Dedicated to my wife Elizabeth (Clare),
who put up with me and my folly

Contents

Essential Players

Aldo, my partner
Clare, my wife
Rudy, the facilitator
Mr. Lee, landlord
Jean, the buyer

Cooks and chefs:

David Steele, our first chef
Rick, sous-chef on speed
Sid, hell bent
Yussuf, the Egyptian chef
BBB, Big Bad Bob
Colin, the young and the best
Billy, former accountant for the mob
Kay, the Taiwanese pastry chef
Chase, the cool Aussie
Kana, the rock from Sri Lanka
The three Marias, dishwashers

The front:

Gino, the Italian from Montreal
Alia, from Riga, the glue who held the staff together
Roy McIntosh, the Scottish server, always ready with a joke
Margo, the Czech Sophia Loren
Melinda, late every day, from Quebec
Alex, the charming kid who always slept in
Mandy, going on eighteen and serving liquor
Viva Sanchez, RIP
Marcel, drunk and gone (self-fired)
Alice in Wonderland
Selena, our own Hollywood model

Hook, Line and Sinker

"The French café on the corner, I don't think it's gonna last," Aldo said to me one night, sipping his white Pinot Grigio at the pub just two doors down from said French café. I perched on my bar stool.

"Really? It looks so successful and busy all the time."

"Appearances never tell the whole truth," he said, looking at me over the top of his new, gold, wire-rimmed glasses. "I hear things," he mused, and when I didn't respond, he added: "from the waiters, the cooks, even some of the guests. I used to have a restaurant. We all know each other."

My wife Clare and I walked by the lovely French café many times, since it was an integral part of our neighbourhood. We looked in at the white tablecloths, the upscale diners, checked out the fancy menu and the even more elaborate wine list. The restaurant looked like it was transported whole from some small French country town, plunked down here at the edge of Stanley Park, in the heart of Vancouver's West End. However, we always chose to dine a few doors down at the Italian restaurant, where the prices were more within our reach and the atmosphere was always welcoming and the food tasty and filling.

Over the years we'd become good friends with Aldo, the owner. Harking back to the weeks immediately after 9/11, the streets and most restaurants were left deserted. Some nights we were the only guests and thus ended up chatting with him.

When I asked Aldo which part of Italy he was from, he cryptically replied, "the far eastern part."

Having grown up in Switzerland, I had some idea of local geography. "Near Udine? Or maybe from the Italian Alps, the Dolomites?"

"No, much further east," Aldo said, a twinkle in his eye.

"You got me stumped. What's the town's name?"

"Lahore," he said grinning, "from the far, far east of Italy."

Now it was my turn to feel stupid. "Lahore, Pakistan? Then how did you come by your name, Aldo?"

"It's short for Abdullah and sounds Italian, don't you think?"

Aldo and I had some other traits in common besides both being transplants and first-generation Canadians who had immigrated in our early twenties. I left to escape Swiss mandatory military service and Aldo arrived seeking opportunity and a golden future. We both thought of ourselves as entrepreneurs and were always putting our heads together, scheming and dreaming up new ventures.

Aldo, who was twenty years my junior, sold his restaurant in the early 2000s and we became partners in a couple of profitable real estate and reno projects. We complemented each other perfectly, like yin and yang. Two halves of a whole. We were both pragmatic: he the better businessman, me the more practical minded. He the shrewd negotiator, me the organized facilitator. He the experienced manager, me the bleeding-heart nice guy. He: bad cop; me: good cop. He would be the aggressive frontman, offering to buy for next to nothing, renovate, or rent for top dollar, while I would follow up and smooth things over — explaining the difficulties of the project and promising Swiss honesty and quality.

We did okay, but Aldo always talked about opening another restaurant. Secretly, I also nursed this fantasy — being my own boss, in charge of people's good times, hanging out at my own bar and lording it over my own pleasure palace. So whenever the conversation with Aldo revolved around the topic, I voiced a latent interest in a possible joint venture. But it was all talk, usually late at night, usually after a few drinks. Beer dreams.

For the past couple of years, Aldo had kept a keen eye on the French Ccafé, noticing its steady decline. There were fewer bums in the seats, the opening times changed arbitrarily, the daily menu remained the same for weeks, and staff rotated like tourists on one of those step-on, step-off tour buses. Sometimes the restaurant just remained closed for no apparent reason. The writing was on the wall, as the saying goes.

"It's over," Aldo said. We were both pressing our noses to the glass, staring through the streaked windows of the now-closed bistro on a blustery October afternoon. "It's a fantastic opportunity for somebody!"

I swallowed the bait instantly. "Location, location, location. It's prime."

"A stone's throw from Stanley Park and a skip from Coal Harbour."

"None better!"

"The best."

The restaurant appeared more abandoned than terminated. An old menu dangled askew in the window, still advertising "Table d'hôte: Magret de canard and cassoulet classique."

"You know anything about French cooking?" Aldo asked, then instantly held up both hands, trying to forestall my predictable response.

"French fries, French onion soup, French desserts, French wines," I quipped.

"Stop it. You can just say no, I won't hold it against you."

"French cooking is haute cuisine, Aldo, alchemy for the senses; secrets of French cooking are only known to the initiated, acquired after many years of culinary training at establishments with names like Le Cordon Bleu and Culinary Academy. They even have something akin to a bible, the revered book of recipes by Auguste Escoffier. It's not spaghetti and meatballs."

A call to the landlord confirmed the status of the bistro as officially closed, but since the former owner could not be located — he had somehow left town or indeed the planet — it had yet to be listed for lease. The mysterious disappearance of Jean-Claude, owner for the past five years, baffled everybody, including his family and eventually the police.

On November 1, the sheriff put his seal on the door. A couple of days later, Aldo obtained permission from the landlord to have a look at the premises.

We entered through the back door, our blood pressure up, throats dry and guts queasy. I fumbled for a light switch and we slowly advanced along the dimly lit hallway toward the restaurant. A musty smell enveloped us and I instinctively held my nose. It felt like walking into a tomb of sorts, back in time. Cobwebs dangled from the dark T-bar ceiling lit by suspended light globes dating back to the seventies. Parisian prints and various French booze posters, one next to the other, decorated the mustard-coloured walls. The bathroom doors stood ajar; old discarded aprons and a couple of waiter's waistcoats still hung on wardrobe hooks. A swing door led into the kitchen, which seemed small. Flickering fluorescent tubes illuminated the stainless steel dish pit and prep tables with a greenish light that made it look more like a morgue than a gourmet kitchen. All the utensils and dishes were wrapped in cellophane like on a crime scene or abandoned movie set. But it was all there: blenders, mixers, pots and pans, cutlery and glasses, even red napkin rings.

The restaurant itself consisted of a long red bench along the wainscoted wall on one side, a wood and glass divider with red upholstered benches on both sides, a red-topped stand-up bar with a genuine brass foot rail, and half a dozen wooden upholstered bar stools. A couple of dozen square, white marble-topped tables were stacked against the wall, a few left abandoned on the worn parquet floor, along with the many classic wooden bistro chairs.

"Look at that coffee machine," I said to Aldo. "It's vintage."

"Check out this wine cabinet. There's space here for a few hundred bottles."

"I wish they would have left some behind."

Those that remained were practically empty, the kind of booze nobody drinks anymore — crème de menthe, peach schnapps and Bols cocktail mix.

Suddenly something flickered across my field of vision.

"Did you see that?" I asked, scanning the scuffed, old floor. "There! There it goes again!"

"Fucking mice," Aldo said with an air of resignation. "They've taken over. That will be a challenge — once they're in, they're hard to get out."

We poked around the back of the bar. I thought about all the work that needed to be done — first and foremost cleaning and painting. I looked across from the kitchen at the mirrored walls, the many colourful plates mounted there, the stuffed birds, the old French posters and the chalk menu board.

"It's a golden opportunity," Aldo proclaimed with a little too much enthusiasm. "It's the chance of a lifetime"

I gave him a sceptical look. "More like resurrecting a ghost."

"But we don't have to buy the business, just take over the lease. I already know the landlord; it's practically a cinch."

I couldn't resist the lure of an adventure. This might just be my ticket to retirement, I thought to myself. I already pictured myself the restaurateur: visions of counting money, drink in hand.

"Let's do it!" I said, and we clinked a couple of empty wine glasses.

Rolling the Dice

On Monday, we had a deal.

Aldo and I shook hands with Mr. Lee, the landlord, at his upscale office overlooking False Creek. Aldo nervously chattered on about what a great success this was going to be, how we were going to resurrect the restaurant and make it twice as good as ever before. Unable to process what had just taken place, I remained mute, staring out at the stunning view of the False Creek towers and the already white-capped North Shore mountains framed against an unusually blue sky for this time of year. The corpulent Mr. Lee sat behind his equally massive mahogany desk, his small hands on the green felt pad in front of him, an inscrutable smile behind his black-rimmed glasses.

We arranged to meet later in the week to sign the documents. As far as Aldo and I were concerned, we were now the proud owners of one of Vancouver's most coveted and established restaurants, a landmark for over thirty years. The perfect bistro built by a former French Foreign Legionnaire some two generations ago. A little piece of Paris in the West End.

On the following Wednesday, the deal blew up.

At 3:00 p.m., we had an appointment scheduled with Mr. Lee to sign the lease — a mere formality.

We were ushered into Mr. Lee's opulent office and left waiting, surrounded by gold-framed Chinese prints, a bronze Buddha in his little shrine and the spectacular view. Aldo and I avoided looking at each other, not saying a word. Something didn't feel right. Why were we kept waiting? After a few minutes, Mr. Lee entered, meekly shook our hands, and planted himself behind his fortress of a desk.

"Well, here we are," I said, "ready to sign the lease."

"Some things have come up," Mr. Lee said, staring not at but through us.

"What do you mean?" Aldo asked.

"I have grave doubts about the whole deal. If I were you boys, I'd stay as far away from this restaurant as I could. There are so many liabilities and debts owing to different people — including me — that it's going to be more trouble than it's worth."

"I don't understand," I said. "We have the bailiff's invoice," and I pointed to the clause that clearly absolved everybody of all liens and encumbrances. A mere flicker of surprise registered on Mr. Lee's face.

"We didn't come here to defend our plan but to sign the lease, Mr. Lee," I said.

"I'm worried that you boys are going to flip this place to make a quick buck."

It finally dawned on me what was going on. "You have some bigger offers in your back pocket. Isn't that the real problem?"

"Naturally there's a lot of interest in this location. Let us not be so hasty."

"Hasty?" I cried. "We don't have a lot of time if we want to open before the Olympics. I don't understand."

I looked over at Aldo, who just sat there chewing his lower lip.

"I need to go over the details again. I will call you." Mr. Lee stood up and headed for the door. We were dismissed.

It was obvious: He wanted us to go away. He had bigger fish on the hook.

When I recounted the development to Clare, she was equally taken aback. "Fucking snake," she cursed uncharacteristically, which summed up the day's proceedings nicely.

Aldo and I were miserable. "We've done nothing wrong, Aldo," I kept repeating. "We're the ones who were screwed over."

That's where it stood at the beginning of December. The dream was over, gone — just another fantasy that hit the wall of reality. I was depressed. Clare tried to cheer me up, dangling the carrot of an impending holiday down south. A week later, I started to feel kind of relieved. The pressure was off. No responsibility, no more sleepless nights, no debts, no worries. Still wounded and disappointed, but free as well. Free to do nothing but to go on holiday to Mexico, free to take a job, free to contemplate the wide-open future.

Three weeks later, Aldo called me on my cell. "You better get over here as soon as possible."

"Sure. What now?"

"The deal is back on," he said. "Lee called and offered basically the same terms we had in the first place, except we have no time to decide since he's off to Hong Kong and wants a quick answer. We have two hours, tops."

"What made him change his mind?"

"Who knows, maybe something in his horoscope. Or the deal he thought he had in his back pocket disappeared."

I called Clare and after a pause that lasted a few heartbeats, her response was supportive. "If you really want to do it, I'll be behind you. Whatever you decide, dear."

I felt dazed but was emotionally levitating. Depressed at being jilted, then relieved at being free, I now had to swing back around another 180 degrees or forever live with the regret of not seizing this opportunity.

Aldo had no such qualms. To him, the deal was back on and just as good as the month before.

"Let's go for it," he said. I nodded numbly.

An hour later we were sitting back in Lee's opulent office, handing over a fat cheque for the first and last months' rent. Then we drove out to Surrey to pay the bailiff, and that sealed the deal.

Next, we found ourselves across from our stylish thirty-year-old bank manager, who assured us we'd get all the help we needed, except no overdraft, no credit card for the first two years, no loans, and no lines of credit. Great, I thought. Here goes my fifty grand. Aldo's followed thirty seconds later. The bistro account was now flush, and I felt giddy with excitement. Or was it trepidation? After all, this was all the money I had. It included RRSPs and savings. When I pointed this out to Aldo, he clapped me patronizingly on the shoulder. "Don't worry, my friend, it's just like priming the pump. The money isn't gone, it's breeding, and there is a certain gestation period."

Really, I thought. Gestation, golden calf, breeding money. I liked that concept.

Aldo suggested we meet with Rudy. "He's a lawyer and an architect and he could be our man," he said.

Rudy was full of inspiring confidence and promised to facilitate jumping all the hurdles — for a substantial fee, of course. "I'll be your puppet master who holds all the strings: to city hall, to the liquor board, to the health and fire departments," he assured us in his booming, slightly accented voice. "All the licensing will be in place before the Olympics, five short weeks away. Don't worry, boys. Trust me. It's practically a done deal." I lapped it all up like milk for a kitty cat.

A couple of days before Christmas we were working the phones like telemarketers. Aldo made inquiries with regards to computer systems and credit card scanners, held preliminary chats with wine and food merchants, called linen, security, phone and Internet providers, while I concentrated on the renovation aspect of the enterprise. We needed to change the awning, redo the floors, paint, reconfigure the bar, improve the lighting.

The first big surprise came from Rudy, who casually pointed out, "You need to install a handicap bathroom."

Oh shit, I thought, there goes a few thousand dollars.

Our lawyer, Morris, also a good friend of Aldo's, looked into setting up a company, but the name was turning out to be a headache. We couldn't use the current one since there were too many liabilities attached to it. We racked our brains, asked our friends, and searched the Internet for inspiration. Aldo was not in favour of a French name and I didn't think an English name would be suitable for a French restaurant. In the end, we settled on the most basic and easiest solution. We simply called it Le Bistro.

We needed to hire a chef, a first cook, prep cooks, servers and a couple of dishwashers. We also hired the maître d', who had worked for the restaurant for several years before its implosion. Kendrik, or Ken as we called him, knew everybody and everything.

"He's going to be a real asset," Aldo said, assuaging my doubts. "He'll bring in all the old-money customers."

Through Craigslist, we found our chef, who was thrilled to join the team. He came with glowing references, stellar culinary skills, and a mountain of enthusiasm. "I can't wait to start. We'll make this into the finest restaurant in the Lower Mainland. Heck no, in the whole province."

"How about just on this street," I said, thinking of the tailor allegory. (Three tailors on the same street boast about their shop. The first claims to be the best in the land, the second the best in the world, and the third one the best on the street.)

I was to be the all-round in-house manager, while Aldo, who already had restaurant experience, would oversee the business side and be my mentor.

"There is so much to take care of," he said. "Staffing, advertising, menus, payroll, scheduling, ordering, banking. You'll be fine."

I wasn't so sure, being a bit of a worrier, but on the surface it all looked good. We had the money, a name, the landlord's handshake, the bailiff's invoice, and the keys to the establishment. Somehow the news leaked out to some of our friends. I didn't deny, but coyly said that we were working on something exciting.

Throughout these initial frenzied days, Clare remained passively supportive — she didn't want to stand in the way of my dreams but didn't want to be involved in the operation. "It's your baby, and I'm looking forward to taking advantage of having a French restaurant in the family."

Then the fear set in, and the doubts. What the hell did I know about running a French restaurant? How was I going to generate enough money every month just to cover the bills and overhead?

"No problem," Aldo laughed, dismissing my concerns. "You'd be surprised how much money you can generate. Fifteen lunches and forty dinners will cover the bills. The rest is gravy."

Looking at it like that sounded simple enough. Perfectly doable.

On New Year's Eve, Clare and I celebrated with our friends. That's when I announced to the world at large that I had indeed entered the glamorous restaurant business and was about to reopen an iconic French bistro.

Outwardly casual, I answered a flurry of questions while Clare held on to my sweaty hand. "Yep, it's a done deal, my friends. It's called Le Bistro and yes, we'll be open before the Olympics."

"Wow, that's incredible! It must feel so thrilling," somebody said.

Others thought I was crazy. Most just shook their heads in wonder.

"A toast to Le Bistro," someone else yelled, and we all drank to that.

I grinned until my face hurt, trying to be nonchalant, but inside I was in a sort of suspended stupor, not at all convinced that I had done the right thing. When Clare and I walked home, long after midnight, tipsy and tired, I waxed philosophical.

"This could be the best thing I've ever done in my life, or the worst thing."

Clare didn't say a word, just squeezed my hand and steered me home.

Setting the Stage

There was no time to waste. I arrived ten minutes early and Aldo followed, his customary half hour late. Every hour and every day now counted. We fumbled with the door lock — needed to be fixed — and stepped into the abandoned restaurant for the first time as the rightful owners. We just stood there, inside the back door, overwhelmed and in shock.

A musty smell permeated the air, a mix of mould, mouse shit and filthy floors. The original parquet floor in front of the bar was black with years of grime, and all along the rear corridor, dirt had been trampled into the oak floor. In the kitchen, all the implements, plates and cutlery had been wrapped in cellophane. The washrooms were grimy, the sinks cracked, the paint faded and the vanities rotten and falling apart. The most surprising discovery were dozens — no, hundreds — of jars, bottles, containers and boxes filled with little greasy plastic bags tied with rubber bands, containing screws, angle brackets, springs, electrical gizmos, locks, nails, numerous pieces and parts of hardware, equipment and discards.

We stood at the bar in the front and looked in at the kitchen. Yes, it was all there, more or less cleaned up by the bailiff's crew. The cookware — numerous dented pots and pans, crockery, and glasses — all mummified in cling wrap. We were also the proud owners of the twenty-two square, white marble tables and sixty-five French bistro chairs, haphazardly stacked along the wall.

"Where should we start?" asked Aldo.

I wanted to say at the beginning, but this was not the time to be cynical. "Let's just get rid of all the crap we don't want or need, starting with these crazy jars," I said.

They were stacked row upon row on shelves built along the walls of the bathrooms and, bizarrely, up into the sixteen-foot-high ceiling of the storage/electrical room. We filled boxes and garbage bags and hauled them out to the dumpster. We discarded an unbelievable pile of crap, all of it assembled and collected over a twenty-five-year period by a character named Philippe, who, as it turned out, had made his home three metres above the floor in the ceiling of the electrical room. I climbed up among the pipes and conduits until I reached a plywood platform still containing an old "foamy," a mouldy sleeping bag, a collection of useless umbrellas, an old chandelier, more makeshift shelves — some filled with tired, dusty books — and more jars of widgets and gizmos.

We later found out from a former waiter that Philippe still had a key to the electrical room and was tolerated by successive former managements due to the fact that he fixed blenders, meat cutters and stove doors, and fabricated all manner of implements. In turn, he was allowed to sleep on his lofty platform and receive the occasional meal at the back door, out of sight of the customers.

"What about these birds?" I asked, referring to the half-dozen stuffed and mounted game birds that adorned the restaurant walls. Golden and silver pheasants and wild ducks in flight with open beaks and glassy eyes stared down from the mustard walls, reminiscent of another era, all of them smelly, dusty, and full of mites. Aldo found them fascinating and was loath to chuck them in the bin.

"The birds have got to go!" Clare declared with absolute certainty when she dropped by after work. "Who wants to eat below a stuffed carcass? It's positively medieval and they're certainly not going to attract any customers."

Her verdict left no room for discussion. To pacify Aldo, we had the carcasses examined by a taxidermist, who dismissed the dusty flock as "so much garbage — cheaper to get new ones than to restore these relics." Aldo stored them in plastic containers and took them home.

The floor presented a challenge. The original parquet in front of the bar and down the back hallway was worn thin by thirty-five years of traffic. It was grimy, and many of the slats were loose or missing. Among Philippe's jars we also found a box of oak slats, which I carefully glued into place where pieces were missing. We endlessly discussed how to refinish it.

"It needs doing, no question," Aldo said.

"We can do it ourselves or hire somebody," I replied, pointing out the obvious.

"It's going to be expensive to contract it out."

"Well then, let's just do it ourselves," I said. "We'll rent a sander at Home Depot and go for it."

It was the only proper solution, but a very unpleasant one. I operated the sander while Aldo, his knees being twenty years younger than mine, worked in the corners and along the walls with the edger. The whole operation was noisy and dirty, and the fine dust infected every surface and crack and cranny for weeks to come. But after a long day of sanding, we were happy with the progress. The oak looked new and blonde, and heaps of sawdust filled a couple of garbage bags. Still, the fine dust clung to everything.

For a varnish, we selected a marine product: an oil-modified urethane that smelled nasty and poisonous. Drying time was about eight hours. We applied the finish with foam mops that night and painted ourselves out the back door. We congratulated ourselves for a job well done.

The next morning, we arrived early to inspect our floor. It was dry, but something was wrong. Instead of a shiny finish, as we'd expected, it seemed dull and gritty. I kneeled down to inspect it up close. "Ah fuck, I can't believe this," I groaned.

"What? What the hell happened?" Aldo asked, mystified.

It was obvious to me in a flash. "The dust that was still in the air from all the sanding settled overnight into the wet varnish and now the whole floor feels like sandpaper."

"What are we going to do?" Aldo asked, mortified.

"We're going to buy some sandpaper and get down on our hands and knees and sand."

The rest of that day we did just that, painstakingly hand-sanding the whole floor and mopping up the resulting dust. It worked. We decided to add another coat of varnish that night, and this time it turned out shiny, like new.

Over the next couple of weeks, Clare showed up every night after work and cleaned, scrubbed, and polished all the copper ornaments, kitchen utensils, wine glasses, picture frames, mirrors, shelves, chairs and surfaces. "There's sawdust and grime everywhere," she commented dryly, "just like after Mount St. Helens."

"Just check out the new floor," I said, very proud of our handiwork. One of the first strategic discussions we had was whether or not to paper over the windows. Aldo wanted to cover them, but I argued against it. "Let the public see that we're fixing the place up. Maybe that will create some interest. We can put out a sign saying 'Opening Soon' or something like that. It's a bit like theatre. People like to look in and check out what's happening."

"Yeah, but if they can't see anything, they will be curious, and suddenly like magic we rip down the paper and there is a brand new restaurant."

In the end we compromised and covered the windows with the original lace curtains. From the outside it still looked like a restaurant, and we had people walk right in asking for a table even though they stepped straight into a construction zone.

"Not today, but soon. As you can see, we're in the middle of a renovation."

Back when we were doing the floor, Aldo had walked in with Chuluun, who hailed all the way from Ulan Bator in Mongolia.

Chulu, as we called him, turned out to be a jack-of-all-trades and a tireless worker. He never did anything twice, he always got it right the first time and he didn't need to be reminded of anything. He hardly spoke any English but somehow always understood what the problem was and how to fix it.

We ripped out shelving, replaced T-bar ceiling panels, plastered and painted. Chulu installed new bathroom vanities, steel shelves in the kitchen, and more shelves wherever there was space. Often he worked past midnight, but he never complained. The one thing lacking was storage, even after we removed most of Philippe's jars. I made countless trips to Home Depot and rode my bicycle to the hardware store up the street at least once a day. One whole morning I spent with a putty knife removing fossilized bubble gum from underneath the chairs and tables. Hundreds of them. It put me off chewing gum for the rest of my days.

In mid-January we met Stewart, the dreaded city health inspector. He arrived suddenly, like an apparition. I blinked and there he was, an inch or two over five feet tall, a polite, pedantic English fellow. Skinny and wiry and somewhere between thirty and fifty years old. He spoke in clipped, precise sentences without verbs, pointing with his clipboard or his flashlight: "Clean working surfaces. Exhaust fan maintenance. Grease and food residue equals rodents. Mouse droppings, here, there, and over here! A sanitation plan a necessity. Daily maintenance essential."

Stewy, as we named him, had the uncanny ability to point his annoying, high-powered flashlight exactly at the small holes along the floor under the appliances, behind the fridges, and anywhere in the kitchen where potential mice could slip through. "Holes here, here, and there. Steel wool does the job."

"Vigilance!" he said, holding up his index finger for emphasis. "Vigilance is the enemy of all things unclean, like rodents and mould." I nodded in total agreement, numb from all the discrepancies he so accurately spotted. All of them blemishes on our score sheet. He marched through the restaurant and headed straight behind the bar. His flashlight illuminated the improper drain plumbing and pointed at the cooler's thermometers, which showed too high a temperature. Stewy did not judge; he lectured and admonished. He made notes in perfectly printed, tiny writing. He handed over his score sheet: we were an abysmal failure.

"I'm very busy with all the temporary food vendors and beer tents springing up all over the city. I will be back one more time, and if you don't comply with all my recommendations, you will not be able to open the doors before the Olympics."

He snapped his clipboard shut, politely shook mine and Aldo's hands, and was gone just as fast as he'd appeared, like a bad dream.

"We're screwed," I said, looking despairingly at the long list of things to do.

"No worry." Aldo shrugged, the eternal optimist. "Piece of cake. We'll put Chulu on it. He'll plug all the holes and clean behind the stoves and fridges and the bar. I'll call the cooler guys to recharge the refrigerant lines and check all the coolers and freezer. Nothing that can't be solved with a couple of phone calls and a few bucks."

The event that promised to bring thousands of tourists and hordes of potential customers to our fledgling restaurant was but a couple of weeks away and still we had no name, no liquor license, no health permit, and no menu. On the other hand, we had already hired and committed to our chef and a maître d', as well as promised employment to cooks and dishwashers, waiters and assistants. Up front, we acted as though there was no question that we would be open for business once the torch was lit in the Olympic Plaza, but out of earshot we pestered Rudy, our man pulling all the strings in Victoria, about the agonizing delays.

"No need to up the blood pressure," Rudy assured us. "The wheels of bureaucracy turn slowly and mysteriously and the process is whimsical, dependent on the weather, the mood of the clerks, even the time of day the paper arrives on the desk. Be ready, boys, to open up and feed the masses."

All through January we worked on our new look, menu designs, and logos. I wanted something more upbeat and modern, to get away from the former elitist, stuffy atmosphere with the dead birds and starched white linen and napkins. We settled on golden yellow tablecloths and napkins, to match the walls. With the white bistro paper on top of the golden covers, it looked still classy but affordable. "We need to be more of a bistro, inclusive, not exclusive. We need to bring in new and young customers as well as the old and rich," I said.

Aldo, who didn't have as good a sense of décor, was fine with my choices. He instead concentrated on who to advertise with and how much we should spend on food and booze. We staged a few tables, complete with wine grasses, cutlery, and dishes, and paraded Clare and Aldo's wife and kids past the prototype table set.

Clare slowly walked around the two tables. She sat down at one and raised the empty glass of wine. "These colours will go well with red wine," she said.

We even asked a couple of strangers who popped their heads in, looking for donations to their various causes, for an opinion. All agreed that the golden yellow against the dark oak floor and the red upholstered benches looked warm and inviting, classy but not exclusive.

For a menu cover, we needed something fun and upbeat, and like magic, it presented itself in the form of the pastel poster of a Parisian café on the north wall. For the wine list, we chose the painting of a girl with a glass of wine that adorned the wall by the entrance, and for the dessert menu we picked a small framed print by the kitchen depicting a poire belle Hélène, a poached pear in vanilla cream with chocolate drizzle, succulently arranged in a V-shaped glass against a bright red background.

While Aldo worked the phones for advertisers, suppliers and services, I either laboured with Chulu, fixing, painting, or installing, discussed the menu with the chef, or brainstormed with Jude, our graphic designer, on the logos, fonts and menu designs.

It was already the end of January and still the crucial liquor license eluded us. Without that license, we had no official name, and without a name, we couldn't paint the awning, get a proper phone number, take out any ads, or print the menus, the letterheads or the invites for the opening. We pretended that all was going according to plan and kept forging ahead. Every time the phone rang I leaped up, hoping it was Rudy on the other end with the good news from Victoria.

David Steele, our chef-in-waiting, spent hours figuring out our menu (on his ancient laptop) while I tried to match menu items with fair pricing, a fine balancing act. We endlessly discussed dishes like coquilles St. Jacques — should they be served in a shell-like dish or just on a plate? Should the escargots be presented in real snail casings or plain, just on a dish? And then of course, over and over, the pommes frites.

"David, the frites were a trademark at this restaurant and we want to keep it that way. We'll serve them in those wire baskets in a coffee filter cone. It'll look great."

"Yes, absolutely, the frites are most important, as are the Béarnaise and peppercorn sauces!" David would exclaim with enthusiasm, while pecking away with his two index fingers on his laptop, and then, without fail, follow up with an expletive. "Fuck this piece of shit!" His curser had frozen again.

Rudy called around 4:00 p.m. informing us that our liaison at the liquor board had taken a sick day. That was Wednesday.

On Thursday, Mr. Bureaucrat took a flex day, and on Friday, to everybody's chagrin, he signed up for a desk day, which meant that he didn't work on any of his current files. I couldn't believe it; the absolute arrogance of a small-time civil servant could very well cost us thousands of dollars in lost business if we didn't get that darned permit.

"Imagine such shenanigans in the real world," I said to Clare when I came home that night, discouraged and depressed. "A sick day, a flex day and then a flipping desk day! Only working for the government is that possible. Anywhere else a simple bribe would have solved the impasse. It's driving me crazy."

"Best not to think about it. Nothing you can do," Clare pointed out, pouring herself a glass of wine. "You don't even want to hear about my day," she said, and proceeded to commiserate in detail what happened at the hospital where she worked.

I joined Clare and we emptied the bottle, which made me only more morose but at least helped me fall into a fitful sleep. I ran along an endless corridor, knocking on doors and shouting, "I want my name, I want my number!" Definitely Kafkaesque.

At the beginning of February, the whole city vibrated in a state of latent euphoria, punctuated with street parties, torch relays and parades. Large screens projected flags and sports events onto the tall glass office towers around Robson Square. Hourly updates on the incoming celebrities and athletes preceded the news of the day over the airwaves, while the hotels, restaurants and bars flooded with thousands of cosmopolitan, multicultural visitors, all flocking to the largest tribal gathering of nations and spectators.

The Olympics is more than a winter sports competition. It involves every facet of the best of every nation: food, dance, exhibitions and of course, the people. Every country had its flagship house, offering TV channels in their respective original languages, culinary treats, and souvenirs sold by pretty girls and boys in traditional costume. Hundreds of temporary food outlets opened up all over the downtown core, in direct competition with existing restaurants and bars. Beer tents, each able to hold a thousand people, were scattered throughout in strategic locations. There was only one venue missing: Our little bistro still didn't officially exist.

I proudly surveyed the new staff washroom, stood behind the bar with the newly installed sink, and listened to the clinking of the brand new ice machine. But above it all, I was waiting for the darn phone to ring. Over the past two weeks we had replaced all the drainage under the bar and the dishwasher and even installed a new grease trap.

"What the hell is a grease trap?" I asked our plumber, Sunny. He pointed at the large, rusty metal box, the size of a milk crate, submerged in the ground under the kitchen sink, full of, yes, rancid grease.

Aldo found Sunny, the bionic plumber, in Surrey. I have no idea how Aldo finds people like Chulu or Sunny, but I was happy he did. A wiry little Vietnamese fellow who spoke bad English (very loudly), there was nothing in the world of plumbing that Sunny wouldn't tackle. Nothing scared him. True to his name, he had a sunny outlook, even in the face of utter misery. He worked methodically and was fully absorbed in his task. Not only did he fix our drains, toilets, sinks, and the grease trap, but he also rerouted the broken and crumbling drain pipe from the dishwasher, a massive physical and logistical challenge in itself. There was only an eight-inch space between the bottom of the machine and the concrete floor in which to jam the pointy end of a jackhammer and dig out a shallow trench leading toward another drainpipe in the wall; no fat white guy could have done what Sunny did. He twisted himself into a pretzel and worked for ten hours straight to do a job others would never even have attempted.

I found Ken, the Iranian cooler specialist. He condemned every piece of equipment we had and offered to sell us new used "deal-of-the-century" fridges and coolers. I made the mistake of having him install one compressor, which for the next two months needed constant adjustments and/or parts to make it work.

Aldo fired Ken and conjured up Fabio, the Korean refrigeration specialist, who always showed up with his tiny and wrinkled old father in tow, who couldn't speak a word of English and just stood there, nodded, and watched everything with animated interest like he had fallen out of the sky onto an alien planet.

Fabio himself spoke perfect English, having grown up here, and he turned out to be a very capable and diligent worker. We came to rely on him for all our coolers and fridges.

While Sunny was plumbing, Chulu painted, the chef tried fixing his computer, Aldo talked on his cellphone, Clare polished silverware, Jude (our graphic designer) tweaked her logos, and I tried my best to keep calm amidst the chaos. Throughout the day, sales reps, people looking for jobs, prospective customers, and the curious walked in and out of the door; wine merchants offered their portfolios (with appropriate tastings, at least); Joe the linen supplier, alarm providers, Max, who was in charge of the awning, and even the florist came by, dropping off a complimentary bouquet of flowers that looked oddly out of place. Most of this fervent activity was costing us money and none was coming in.

Next came the utility people — gas, hydro, and finally Telus, your friendly phone service provider. First, they installed a defective program that could only phone out and not receive calls. It took them eight days to even admit that it was their fault that our phones only worked one-way. Who knows how much business we lost in those first few crucial days because potential customers couldn't get through to make a reservation. (Yes, we were taking reservations even though we weren't open yet.)

It had now been five weeks and still we had no name or number. The Olympics were ten days away. The clock was ticking and I was by all accounts close to a nervous breakdown. I yelled at the poor guy from Telus, even though he was just the technician. I almost tossed the chef's computer into the trash, and I made sarcastic remarks like "I guess we can just hold a party for all the workers, bring our own wine, and instead of a menu board install a big-screen TV."

Clare and I often went for a late evening walk around the lagoon in Stanley Park to escape the buzz of the city and the mayhem at the bistro. We talked things over, I lamenting and stressing out, she calmly telling me what a good job I was doing and that everything would be all right. When my cellphone buzzed for the hundredth time that day, I lost it and hurdled it into the trees. Clare quietly retrieved it while I was kicking the shit out of an innocent garbage can.

Folly Bistro

I kept waking up in the middle of the night in a sweat. "Just like menopause," Clare wryly observed.

I conjured up ways to torture the man in charge of our file at the liquor board — how to take away his pension, stigmatize his offspring with shame, provide him with a posting in charge of picking up dog shit. We desperately needed that name and number like we needed air to breathe or the sun to come up in the morning.

"If you don't pass my next inspection, I will not be able to come back before the Olympics," Stewy the health inspector had warned us. We enlisted everybody to ferret out and plug every hole, hoover up every mouse turd, remove every bit of grease and grime and scrub, seal and sanctify the whole restaurant. The kitchen proved to be a nasty mess. This should have been the chef's job — it was his domain — but he was still busy trying to back up or fix his failing computer.

"David, this is your kitchen, your responsibility," I pointed out to him.

"I don't have my crew here yet. It's usually their job. I create the dishes and delegate the work," he said, his nose up in the air. "I have to go to the computer shop now. My screen froze."

Chulu came to the rescue, methodically scraped inch-thick layers of grease from behind the stove and the coolers and used copper mesh to plug several access holes for rodents. It was an arduous but necessary task, and afterwards we were certain we now had the cleanest and most rodent-proof restaurant in all of the West End.

And then, like a bad dream, Stewy, infallible rodent sleuth, appeared in the middle of the restaurant. Nobody heard or saw him come in. Like a rodent himself, Stewy, with his pointy, powerful flashlight unwavering like a guided missile, shone his sharp beam of light at the one hole we had missed in the furthest corner under the dishwasher. A collective groan went up from all of us, and like an athlete I thrust myself under the dishwasher, armed with a wad of copper mesh, and with the stick end of a broom, jammed the mesh into the hole with such determination that even Stewy was impressed. He bestowed his seal of approval on the report and we almost shouted with joy. We overcame a major hurdle. This would surely help us in our quest for our holy grail — the elusive permit. But still we remained nameless.

The ads were ready to go. Max, from East Germany, as he pointed out to me (even though the wall had been down for twenty years) and his two Mexican labourers were ready to paint the signs and the awning; our menus were lingering in the outbox of Jude's computer, and we answered our phone as if we had a name. Eight days to go until the Olympic cauldron was lit, and time was wasting away. The kitchen gleamed. All the ovens and coolers were fixed and ready for food. The chef still cursed his laptop daily, and we brought in Ken, our maître d', to work on the wine list and interview prospective servers and assistants.

Rudy called and assured us that if not today, tomorrow was surely and absolutely the day. We also received our municipal business license, which was dependent on the health report from Stewy, and those permits were immediately forwarded to Rudy and the liquor board in Victoria.

"No more flex or sick days, no holidays or accidents, no births or deaths or natural disasters, please!" I said to Rudy.

"Don't worry, everything will be fine. You boys need to relax," he said jovially, without a hint of doubt in his voice.

I'd become quite sceptical of Rudy's assurances, since none of them had materialized. But Aldo just looked at me over top of his glasses. "Rudy's on it. He's pulling all the strings he can."

I just wanted to shout, "Stop the world and deal with our application!"

Even Rhonda, the local liquor inspector, a large, stout woman with a loud guffaw and a belly laugh that could shake buildings, was on our side. She promised to drop by the minute she had the magic number from the demigods at the liquor board. She would have the final word. We were one phone call and one mouse click away. For them, a simple routine. For us, life or death.

Then the unforeseeable happened. According to our pedantic, phlegmatic bureaucrat in Victoria, one of my initials on form 47B was not satisfactory and could possibly be a fake.

"A fake?" I cried. "How could it be a fake! Who on earth could be interested in faking my initial on an obscure liquor licensing form?" I became more desperate by the minute, balancing dangerously on the fine edge between madness and sanity, ready to snap and go on a murderous rampage of liquor board bureaucrats.

A flurry of phone calls and faxes ensued, additional copies of form 47B were printed, photocopied, initialled, signed by witnesses, notarized, addressed, sealed, faxed and e-mailed, all within a couple of frenzied hours before 4:00 p.m. when the office in Victoria closed. Following up with phone calls and polite, subservient inquires, even rock-steady Rudy started to waver. But at 3:55 p.m., we got word back from Victoria that yes, all the forms were now satisfactory, but alas, it was too late in the day to obtain the number. Sorry, we had to wait until tomorrow. I almost croaked. Aldo just sat there his eyes darting around the room, biting his lower lip.

A sense of doom settled over the gleaming, ready bistro, and we all sat around, some silently cursing, others, like me, not so silently ranting about the bizarre farce being played out by some lowly pen-pusher with more power than the Pope. I had to be restrained and calmed down with the help of several beers.

At home that night, I was quiet and morose, moping and cursing the day I ever set eyes on the restaurant. I felt like I was fighting a losing battle, tilting at windmills with my bare hands, and meanwhile the money was flowing out like a waterfall.

"It's going to happen tomorrow, I know it," Clare said, pouring me a glass of wine. "You've done all you can and you better get ready to open your restaurant." Clare, always the optimist even in the midst of calamity and disaster, could see the light on the other side of the tunnel, which to me looked like an oncoming train. She was right of course. Looking in from the outside gave her a more objective perspective.

The moment we got our health permit we were allowed to cook, serve and sell food. Just no liquor yet. We used this interim period for trial-and-error in the kitchen. I asked David to exchange his laptop for a knife and a spoon.

"Let's try some of those creations of yours, David." I was dying to taste the poulet de Paris or the coquilles St. Jacques, by far the most discussed dish. Aldo had never heard of it, but David insisted it be on the menu. "It's a classic French dish and everybody loves it." But by far our biggest arguments were over the darn pommes frites.

I'd made it crystal clear right from the beginning that they'd be handmade on the premises. Initially, I was met with quite a lot of opposition from the chef, and even Aldo was sceptical.

Apparently, pommes frites are a lot of work, but I could not tolerate a French restaurant worth its name that served McCain frozen fries. That was anathema to me. Also, the frites had been iconic at the location for two generations — the one tradition we needed to continue.

"I would much rather add the labour here and buy the potatoes than pay somebody else to prefab them in some warehouse" went one of my arguments. "This is not rocket science."

The rescue came from an unlikely quarter: Kana, our cleaning lady and prep cook from Sri Lanka, who very quietly and stoically worked and did her job. "I've been preparing the fries for the last two years," she said in her quiet voice, with an almost imperceptible sideways shake of her head.

I looked down at Kana — she was about five feet tall, if that — and then over to the chef, who towered over her with his lanky six-foot frame.

"You know how to prep the fries, Kana?" I asked.

"Yes," she said simply. "I know what to do."

"Well, I think you two better talk," I said, looking at the chef. "And thank you, Kana." She just nodded her head with the tiniest hint of a smile on her broad, inscrutable face.

Aldo told me later that he had hired Kana because she had worked for the former owners and he thought she would be an asset, knowing the place and some of its quirks. "I forgot to mention it," he added.

"It doesn't matter, Aldo, she just saved our pommes frites!"

Chef called me into the kitchen the next morning to observe Kana prepping the legendary frites. She deftly peeled the Kennebec potatoes and cut them (with our special manual cutting press) straight into a bath of cold, salted water. Next, she spread them on tea towels, dried them, and then blanched them in the deep fryer until a pale yellow. She then spread the golden batch out on large baking sheets and stored them in the cooler for several hours. "Now they cool down and will be ready," she said.

When the customers were seated, she retrieved the pale frites and deep-fried them for a second time until golden brown, then left them to drip, salted them, and served them piled high in our special wire baskets lined with #4 brown coffee filters. It was an art in itself, and the fabulous results settled all arguments once and for all. They were crisp on the outside, creamy on the inside, and ever so succulent.

"These are the most delicious fries I've ever tasted," I exclaimed, and my compliments were echoed by all who tried them. "Our future reputation depends on our french fries," I proclaimed. "We're ready to go! Let the games begin!"

Exactly a week before the games started, Rudy arrived just before noon with Rhonda the liquor inspector in tow. She greeted us with a bombastic "Good morning all! We have good news!"

We filled out more forms, initialled and signed them, and Rhonda declared with a big toothy grin, "Boys, you'll have your official number by the end of the day."

Then we waited, eating more fries, trying out the crème brûlée and the chocolate mousse until we were ready to explode. Aldo chewed his lower lip and his eyes zipped around like in a pinball machine.

At a quarter to four, the phone call came from Rudy, who gleefully announced a fax he was about to send.

"That's it. We got it!" I cried, and did a drumroll with my hands on the counter while Aldo danced a jig behind the bar. Everybody high-fived. We'd done it. In just under six weeks.

"In record time," as Rudy reminded us.

A frenzy of phone calls ensued and everybody raced off their starting blocks. Jude pushed "send" and the menus were at the printers; Max and his gang started on the awning; David called the food suppliers; I called the local newspapers and told them the ads were ready to go; and most importantly, Ken called his buddy at the liquor store and gave them the go-ahead.

We rented a two-ton U-Haul and met at the liquor store. Ken knew all the guys and walked in like he owned the place. There was a large stack of boxes labelled "Le Bistro," ready and waiting for us. I handed over a big fat cheque and we loaded over two dozen cases of wine and liquor into the truck. Back at the bistro, we unpacked the treasure and I went gaga at all the fancy bottles of fine wines and liquors I suddenly owned.

"Wow, what's this?" I asked, holding aloft a magnum bottle of 2005 Châteauneuf du Pape Beaucastel like a schoolboy holding a trophy.

"Be careful with that — it's a $400 bottle," Ken said patronizingly.

I gingerly put the bottle down and wondered who in the hell would order a $400 bottle of wine. We did let Ken, who also proclaimed himself a sommelier, create the very eclectic wine list. Definitely not aimed at the Walmart-and-burger crowd.

The bistro sure looked great with all the liquor displayed on the new glass shelves and the full wine rack waiting for discerning customers.

I opened the first bottle, a Côtes du Rhône, one of our designated house wines, and the chef surprised us with a bowl of delicious gratin Lyonnais, a classic French onion soup, accompanied by our signature pommes frites.

"Bon appetit!" David announced with a flair, setting the steaming crock bowl, with melted cheese overflowing the rim, in front of us like an offering.

"This is good," I said to Aldo, taking a healthy swallow of wine from one of our burgundy glasses. For just a fleeting moment, time stood still and I felt like a rich guy living the good life, until Aldo broke my reverie with a nasty dose of reality.

"How much money is left in our bank account?"

We planned for a soft opening on the following Saturday night and invited our friends and all the workers that had laboured so diligently over the past six weeks.

"We're ready!" the chef yelled over the noise coming out of the steamy kitchen. The coolers were packed, the ovens lit, the draught beer hooked up at the last minute. The wine bottles stood like little soldiers, labels all pointing out, ready on the bar counter. Ken, the maître d', with his hands folded behind his back, assured us all was in place up front.

Every seat was taken, and Aldo and I stood at the bar with grins like Cheshire cats, surveying the party. Clare stood beside me and squeezed my arm affectionately. "I'm so proud of you guys. You really did it." I felt like we'd already won the Olympics.

We didn't charge anybody and the compliments came freely, ranging from simply fantastic to outright spectacular. Some had to wait a bit longer and stuffed themselves with our delicious fries until their steak or duck breast arrived. For the first time, Le Bistro was filled with laughter and conversation, happy sounds of contented diners. Life at its best. We served the whole menu, including the desserts, and it was a feast to behold. Surely no other restaurant served such fabulous food, at such bargain prices, prepared from scratch by professionals. Definitely not on this night.

After everybody had left and the tables were cleared, only the kitchen still remained active. Aldo and I thanked everybody for a job well done and joined in a staff meal of leftovers and free beer for all.

2

Showtime

Le Bistro officially opened its doors to the public at 11:00 a.m. on Monday, February 8th, 2010. Just four days before the official start to the Winter Olympics. We drew back the curtain and let the show begin.

Ken the maître d', resplendent in his green apron, white pressed shirt and black vest, stood by the door. Gino, our head waiter, with his hair slicked back, dressed all in black, lingered by the bar with Margo, our Czech busser, a cross between Sophia Loren and Julia Roberts, tall, doe-eyed, with full lips and jet-black hair pulled tight into a ponytail. Ken, who hired her, could have been her father and tried very much to be her friend, teaching her how to set a proper table, forks and knives perfectly lined up across from one another.

"Just like this, Margo," Ken said, pulling the golden napkin through the red ring with an exaggerated flair and placing it diagonally between the cutlery. He leered at her when she bent over, slowly and methodically setting the tables.

"Wine glasses on the right, my dear, just above the fork, and always make sure they're spotless, like this." He held up the glass against the light and gave it a perfunctory wipe. Ken's a bit over the top, I thought, a bit too much snobbery and not enough joviality. He's also a know-it-all and regards me, the owner, with disdain, as if I'm always in his way.

"You don't have to be here," he told me. "Why don't you just stay home."

"Well, Ken, I have every intention of being useful, and it's our opening day. Just watching you, I learn so much," I added, trying not to sound sarcastic.

He just looked at me with his superior air, chin thrust forward, lips slightly puckered below his grey pencil moustache, hands folded behind his back. "Thank you," he said.

We didn't know what to expect. All we were hoping for was that some of the half million people descending on Vancouver would wander into the bistro.

And they did. And sat down just like it was the most natural thing to do, as if we had always been open.

"There will be lineups around the block," Aldo predicted, rubbing his hands with glee, already counting the money in his mind. I was a bit more sceptical.

"I'll be happy if we fill the place for dinner," I said, worried that we'd overstaffed or hadn't bought enough supplies. The mantra we repeated over and over to the kitchen staff was simply "Be ready for anything." Better to have and not need than to need and not have.

The stampede didn't happen, but customers did come in at all hours, mostly bleary-eyed Olympic tourists from all over the globe. It was certainly a great time to try out our menu, fine-tune our service, and actually make a bit of money for a change.

Some locals came in and identified themselves as such: "I just live around the corner and used to come here, but not in the last couple of years," said one, and "We never knew when they were open and the food was never the same," an older woman told me, while her companion, who could have been her sister (both had the same grey bob), just nodded. "We really liked the pommes frites."

We knew we had a hill to climb just to get back to the popularity the restaurant had enjoyed until just a few years earlier, when you had to have a reservation just to get in. But in the last five years, the place had lost its former status. Ken, who had worked for a couple of the former owners (the reason we hired him), painted an ugly picture of the decline and fall of the venue. He couldn't seem to help but pontificate.

"A restaurant is all about the food and the service. The service was not the problem, since I was in charge, but the food, my god, what were they thinking? They regularly ran out of dishes, the chef changed every second week, and sometimes there was no chef, so the dishes were never consistent, and many times they just changed the items. Chicken for duck, strip loin for filet, and no soup or crème brûlée, or they didn't have the wines that were on the list. Many times they didn't have the homemade fries, so they just used frozen product. A total disgrace. And when the customers stayed away, the money wasn't there to pay the bills. Then came the shortcuts and the blame games that deteriorated into infighting, rip-offs, lies, and deceit, to its eventual implosion and the subsequent closure."

"That sounds very dramatic," I said.

"It's the short version," said Ken, dismissing the subject with a wave of his manicured hand.

A history we didn't want to dwell on; we wanted to recapture old-fashioned values like excellent food, a fair price, a new and fresh look, classy but not snobbish. We wanted to appeal to the next generation of people with disposable incomes, as well as bring back the original patrons, the old, idle, and rich. But there were too few of them left over from the old days. These were lean times and we had to reach out to a broad spectrum of customers, even though Ken kept harping about the good old days when he used to serve an exclusive class.

"We need to bring back the people who know good food and wine, not the hamburger-and-hot-dog crowd; they don't know the difference between Béarnaise and béchamel sauce, couldn't tell steak tartare from hamburger, champagne from Henkel," he said, with his superior disdain for the common folk.

It was a balancing act, and I knew that Ken was right about one aspect of a successful eatery: The consistency in the food and service would eventually result in spreading the word, the driving engine behind every good gastronomic enterprise. We had the location and the classy French country-style interior: old-fashioned but modern, comfortable and cozy, warm and inviting. What could possibly go wrong?

Folly Bistro

During the games, the suppliers only delivered between midnight and 6:00 a.m., which meant that one of us, Aldo or me, had to be at the back of the bistro at 3:00 or 4:00 a.m. I volunteered to camp in my Westy van behind the restaurant on delivery days. Of course this turned into a complete mess, since some night drivers didn't have my phone number or I passed out and missed the truck that idled for half an hour right beside me while I slept blissfully.

The fantasy of lineups around the block also did not materialize. Instead, people came in at all hours for food or drink. The best time was after 10:00 p.m., when the Olympic broadcasts were over, with the media people leaving their headquarters at the Westin Bayshore Hotel, dropping by and sitting around until 2:00 a.m., mostly drinking. That was okay with us and the servers — no labour costs in booze.

Most of the dedicated Olympic venues concentrated the crowds within a four-block radius around the Art Gallery. The day's highlights were projected onto the office towers, which served as gigantic screens. The beer tents and fast food stands catered to the masses and those restaurants and pubs within those four blocks made a killing. Some of the traffic spilled over into our neighbourhood but nowhere near the hordes that everybody expected. For us, this two-week period was a perfect time to try out our menu, train the staff, and sort out the labour schedule. We found out how it all worked under unusual circumstances. We even installed a TV despite Ken's pompous protests.

"A French restaurant is a place for drink and food, talk and relaxation. TVs belong in sports bars and beer parlours. It's a disgrace and an insult to the intelligence of our customers."

"Ken, it's the Olympics. People want to watch it. There is no getting away from it, not during the Olympics," Aldo said.

"He's right, you know," I echoed, and to calm Ken down, lamely added, "It's only going to be temporary."

On the afternoon after the Russians lost to the Canadians in the semifinals, some of the Russian hockey players wandered into the restaurant and headed straight for the bar. They stayed for over six hours and cleaned us out of vodka. Ken actually felt sorry for them and served up some free pommes frites to go with the booze. They tried to sell their tickets to the final game for astronomical prices, but since there were no takers in the bistro crowd they kept on drinking and toasting each other, Mother Russia and Margo, our star busser, who got invited all the way to Russia several times.

"They're so cute when they're drunk," she said, "like lost puppies."

When Sidney Crosby scored the winning goal in the gold medal game against the US, the whole city erupted in an all-encompassing explosion of mass euphoria, and everybody spilled into the streets, embracing each other, high-fiving, and converging on the city centre. All of downtown was awash with people celebrating not only the win but a very successful Olympic Games. Clare and I joined the throng and let ourselves be carried along toward Granville Street, the cultural entertainment hub of the last three weeks.

"This almost feels like we won some kind of war," Clare said at one point, when a convertible with several shirtless fans, enthusiastically waving the Canadian flag, weaved its way through the celebrating crowd.

The Vancouver Olympics were called the "friendly games," and they were. Canadians are polite and proud of it, and the Vancouverites lived up to the accolades. We Canadians even apologize for our collective virtue. Time seemed to stand still for two weeks and everybody I came into contact with enjoyed the party atmosphere, even if they disagreed with the politics, and despite having to put up with all sorts of impositions, traffic pattern changes, and late-night revellers. A lot of locals left town to avoid the circus, but the visitors loved the unusually balmy weather, the cosmopolitan but intimate city and what it had to offer — including fine dining for a fair price at Le Bistro. It was certainly a fun time and a great opportunity for our opening. The past six weeks had been frantic, exciting, and certainly unusual. We had our own race to win and succeeded just in time. Kick-starting a restaurant out of a coma and imbuing it with new energy and live blood was not something I had any experience in. In the end, it was about managing work, time, bureaucrats, and the miscreants who work in the restaurant industry the world over.

Folly Bistro

"We did it," Aldo said over a glass of Bordeaux after the closing ceremony featuring Nickelback, Neil Young singing "Long May You Run," Avril Lavigne, and even William Shatner. Epic.

"Yes, we did it," I nodded, "and now that the games are over and the crowd is leaving town, it's going to be a whole new ball game."

"You two should be proud. You've pulled off the impossible and it's going to be a great bistro. I just know it," Clare said, always the optimist. "I'll leave you two alone to lock up."

We did indeed feel very proud of what we had accomplished. It felt like the future was ours to seize. We basked in the moment of glory and toasted each other late into the night, putting a minor dent into our fully stocked bar.

Sometime at the Beginning

Renovating a restaurant and running a restaurant are two completely different kettles of fish. Everybody knows that. I'm pretty confident at fixing a plumbing problem or hanging a light fixture or a painting on a wall, but I knew nothing about who to order the meat from or what ingredients go into a peppercorn sauce or even how to align the cutlery on the tables. That's why we hired a proper chef and an experienced maître d'. Nobody said they had to be friends. Just get along while on the job, please. As it turned out, Ken, the maître d', didn't like David Steele, the chef. In some past life they'd had a run-in and shared some unpleasant history. Ken cryptically alluded to this by calling David a "doper," almost something not quite human.

"A doper?" I asked, but Ken turned his back and dismissed me, probably including me in that same subhuman category.

Ken thought of himself as God's gift to the restaurant industry, the highest authority on every subject and not just in the restaurant business. Pick any topic and he knew it better. One day Ken overheard me talking to Aldo about possibly buying an apartment close to the restaurant.

"To get the best deal, you need two people. When buying, you," and he pointed a knowing finger at me, "make a lowball offer with a twenty-four-hour window. The same day, you Aldo," now pointing at Aldo like we were part of a two-man sports team before a big match, "go in with an even lower offer. Now the seller panics and thinks that the first offer might be a good one after all and will more than likely accept it. Bingo."

"Isn't this kind of risky, Ken? If not illegal, then for sure unethical?" I asked. "What if a third offer comes in which is more realistic and actually fair, and I sit there with my lowball offer, out of the running. But I really want this apartment. Now somebody else might get it for a great deal."

Ken looked down at me from his perch behind the bar and sneered.

Ken knew every rich patron, had worked at the best establishments, was renowned for his skills and connections, and there wasn't a thing in all the restaurant industry he didn't know or hadn't done. "Just ask him," Gino, our head waiter, said.

This translated into the simple fact that Ken wasn't about to learn anything new or listen to anybody. Ken did not suffer from low self-esteem or modesty. To the contrary, he had delusions of grandeur and was a bit of a prima donna. Just like all the young girls, he could never walk past the large mirror on the back wall without looking at himself sideways. Because I was a newbie in the biz, he regarded me as a travesty and a waste of space. I was basically in his way and best off invisible. He wanted to run the bistro by himself.

"Just let me worry about the schedule, the customers and the staff. You don't need to be here." Except for the fact that I wanted to learn and keep an eye on the operation. It was, after all, my money and my business.

Aldo and I were primarily concerned about the here and now and the immediate future, not the murky past, especially when it was all based on hearsay and self-aggrandizing. We were only interested that the kitchen produce the menu and the waiters serve it to the customer's satisfaction. That's all. Does that sound complicated?

Philippe, the phantom of the electrical room, dropped by a couple of times during those first few weeks. He rode in on a World War II bicycle with a milk crate full of electronic junk strapped behind the seat, wearing every stitch of clothing he owned. We informed him politely that his days as a resident were over. I handed him a few envelopes, since he still used the restaurant as his mailing address.

"Can I keep the address for now since I can't receive mail where I live?"

"Where is that, Philippe?"

"I live in Stanley Park now," he said, as if the park was the most normal place of residence.

At a loss for what to say, I reluctantly agreed to keep any mail for the next couple of months. He got on his unwieldy bike and pedalled off in the direction of Stanley Park.

Sometime at the Beginning

I didn't realize that restaurants are territorially divided up into little fiefdoms. Militaristic hierarchy rules behaviour in the kitchen. The chef is the general, the loyalty of his lieutenants and serfs paramount to the functioning of the kingdom.

"A kitchen is not a democracy, it's a dictatorship," David informed me matter-of-factly, with no room for discussion. This included Aldo and me, apparently. We had no say, and woe to us if we made changes to the kitchen schedule or the menu without the chef's consent or knowledge.

Whenever Aldo or I wanted menu items changed or the look of the plates adjusted, we had to go directly to the chef. If we didn't follow the proper chain of command, we were scolded like schoolboys.

Much the same protocol applied to the front of the restaurant. With Ken in charge, it seemed we had little or nothing to say in terms of hiring and scheduling, and when we tried to interfere we were harangued that we'd overstepped our mandate.

"But I am the owner and I would like Alia to have more shifts; otherwise she's not going to be able to make a living here and we're gonna lose her!" I'd hired Alia because she was smart and attractive, with a serious work ethic, thanks to her Latvian upbringing, and a smile that could melt icebergs.

"If I have more shifts to give out, I certainly will," Ken barked. "We all want more, but there is only so much to go around." I felt chastised and taken aback. But Ken wasn't done yet. "You hired me to run the restaurant, which means you must let me do my job." He looked and acted like he'd just stepped out of a Humphrey Bogart movie, peering over the top of his bifocals, down his prominent nose, hands folded behind his back. "I know what I'm doing and we'll do it my way," Ken told me in no uncertain tone of voice, like a father reprimanding his confused child. "You'll thank me for it later."

"I can't believe he talked to me like that," I complained to Aldo. "I know we hired him, but he acts like he's the owner. I haven't been dressed down like that since the third grade when I broke my teacher's glasses."

"How did that happen?" Aldo asked, looking at me over top of his glasses, stroking his moustache.

"How did what happen?"

"The glasses, how'd you break them?"

"Oh, well, she'd left the classroom for a minute and left her glasses on her desk. Being the class clown, I put them on and paraded around. They were too big for my face and fell down and broke just when she came back in. Anyway, Ken is pushing his luck."

Aldo just laughed and told me that I'd better get used to this. "If you want any kind of change, you just have to tell Ken or David in no uncertain terms. We are the owners and we'll tell them what we want and they have to deliver. Don't discuss it, just demand it. David is right, restaurants are not a democracy but a dictatorship — but we decide the menu, the specials, the opening hours, and the kind of food we want to serve, and at what price. We design and set the stage, the props, and the food and they — the chef, the maître d', the servers, the cooks, the bartender and the bussers — act their part just like actors do, as waiters, greeters, hosts and food- or drink-delivery players. We, on the other hand, have to make sure the bills get paid and nobody robs the place blind. As you've already noticed, once we put these guys in charge they want to take over. We let them believe that's what they're doing. We just watch them carefully and hopefully they deliver. We will know how the restaurant works when the accountant tells us the bottom line." This was the longest speech I ever heard from Aldo. Amen.

The restaurant venture proved to be a steep learning curve for me. I was used to working within a team framework, altogether bigger than the sum of the parts, everybody working as one rather than a whole group of individual specialists — artists — defending their own little patch of territory, which is the murky reality of the restaurant subculture. I had this idealistic concept, a fantasy really, of a fully cohesive team, everyone helping each other, working together to create a whole. I still believe this to be a good theory, but maybe for a hospital or a co-op, apparently not for a restaurant.

Ken, the dinosaur, wanted to recreate a bygone time capsule of the heady days of power drinking lunches and rich patrons splurging like bank robbers. He wanted to emulate a certain look which I didn't agree with. For one thing, he wanted every server to wear a green apron, a white shirt and a black waistcoat or vest.

"Ken, this is way too formal," I said, trying to sound strong and no-nonsense, like Aldo. "We're a bistro, not a rich men's club, therefore we need to look and act more relaxed. We want a casual, easygoing but still classy look. You can wear your green apron and vest with the pocket watch if you like, but the servers are free to wear white shirts and black pants or all black. Also, the girls need to look and feel comfortable. No tight-sleeved dresses, no high heels. They can wear ties or not, as they like, as long as they wear a smile."

"You want me to work in a cafeteria? You want this to look like a disco?" Ken asked, aghast and disgusted.

"No, but I want this place to look attractive to a broader spectrum of customers than you are used to. Times have changed. The same goes for the customers. We can't just cater to the suits — we serve jeans and shorts as well." I turned on my heel and left.

I repeated the conversation to Clare, who agreed with me wholeheartedly. "Young people don't care about stuffy appearances, and you do want young people to come in. Ken is a fossil. He has his merits, but you're the boss."

"Absolutely." I said. "Ken is just like those stuffed birds we got rid of, and I have the distinct feeling that he and I are not going to grow old together."

The secret of a successful restaurant is really simple: You have to have bums in the seats. That's it. An empty restaurant is a black hole. A full restaurant might not make a lot of money either, but it turns over the food and money and looks busy, and busy places attract customers while the empty eatery remains vacant. I've often wondered why there will be a lineup at one place while the place next door looms empty, even if both sell the same food. Right across the street, every day at lunchtime, I can observe this exact phenomenon between two Korean noodle joints. Ramen

One is always full, while Ramen Two is deserted. Why? I think it's a crowd thing, elusive and illogical. Something to do with the herd mentality. It's not the food or the location. I tried both and could discern no difference, except one was loud and full of energy while the empty one felt depressed and, as a result, looked a bit dumpy.

How to put bums in the seats? That's the strength of my partner Aldo, illustrated by this nugget: "Before I bought my previous restaurant," he said, pointing across the street, "I planted myself over there for several days, counting the passersby. Judging from the walk-by traffic, I knew the odds before I made an offer."

Rudy suggested that we should put a banner outside proclaiming the bistro was under new management.

"How about 'Under new Swiss-Pakistani Management'?" Aldo chimed in, and we dropped the idea right there and then.

Over the years, Aldo had tried every form of advertising. "But even the best advertisement means nothing if you don't keep rule number one in mind," he said. "Rule number one is: consistency. First and foremost the product has to be of consistent quality. Return customers want their steak just like the last time. That's why they're back, because they remember what they liked."

Aldo took out ads in newspapers, magazines and flyers, and we even paid for expensive jingles on the radio. We tried every form of advertisement short of a billboard. Aldo found out what people wanted not by thinking and rationalizing but through sheer trial and error. One fact eventually stood out. Even though it was so blatantly obvious, it took a while to bubble to the surface: Everybody loves a deal! Everybody wants something for free! Even if it's not really for free. As long as they think they're getting a bargain — that alone brings them through the door.

"So I came up with an $8.95 special on Tuesdays, the slowest day of the week," Aldo said. "That brought in some customers, but not enough. Eight dollars and ninety-five cents happened to be half of $17.95. I changed tactics and just called it Half-Price Tuesday. Bingo! The place was packed on Tuesdays."

In an Italian restaurant that meant half-price pasta but full price for everything else: the meat dishes, the salads, soups, desserts and the drinks. In other words, it didn't really cost Aldo anything, but the patrons were convinced they were getting away with a super deal. Slowly but surely that Tuesday night grew into a frenzied feeding with lineups out the door and every seat filled at least three times during the course of the night. Aldo hit on a winning formula simply by tapping into a basic human instinct.

We had to come up with a similar deal at the bistro.

Which night was consistently the slowest of the week? We already knew the answer. Wednesday, for some reason, was always slow. Now the hard question: What should the deal be? Being a French restaurant, the choice wasn't that easy. French food is steak, chicken, and duck breast, wild salmon fillets, creamy and buttery sauces, bisques and lovely fresh desserts, meaning most items had a large food replacement cost. We agonized over this and decided to ignore the food and labour costs for now and offered 50 percent off all main courses on Wednesday nights. Damn the torpedoes! We advertised in the local papers, added a large red banner to the awning. And lo and behold, it worked — at least for the customers. This time around people really were getting a bargain. Filet mignon for half price is a fantastic deal. Once people were in the restaurant, they got to know and love the food and the atmosphere, and they became comfortable with a French bistro. We assumed these customers would return on other days of the week. Wrong. That lofty theory didn't pan out; we would see the same people only on Wednesdays. The other thought was that if people were getting such a smoking deal on the food, they might spring for a good bottle of wine or get a couple of appies or a dessert. We urged the waiters to upsell, meaning, "Push the darned desserts and the better wines."

We also attracted the proverbial families of four who ordered four filet mignons, no soups, no appies, no drinks except water all around and "with lemon, please." Some even asked for hot water and then produced their own tea bags. Of course they always wanted more free stuff like bread and butter and the complimentary fries. I croaked when I saw the bill for those tables. But a lot of other customers did have an extra drink, a salad, or a dessert — at full price. The indisputable fact was that everybody loved our crazy Wednesday nights at the bistro — and they became legendary in no time.

Right from the first Super Wednesday, the place would always fill up starting at 5:00 p.m., and by 7:30 p.m. it was packed to the rafters and the kitchen rocked. Ken refused to work in a "factory atmosphere," so I took over as the meeter, greeter and seater in charge of the door. My challenge was to not turn anybody away. (The trick was offering half a glass of [cheap] wine, and with glass in hand, everybody patiently waited their turn.)

The kitchen resembled a pressure cooker. Mayhem and chaos reigned supreme, but the crew always managed to somehow pump out up to 140 covers with a six-burner stove and three people working the line, sharing a very tight space. In the excessive heat and steam. Tempers flared and half the kitchen crew — including the chef, who looked like he was about to have a heart attack any second — was ready to quit every Wednesday night. It took a lot of backstroking, free beer and the promise of improvements to calm everybody down.

Another benefit of those Wednesday sellouts was the fact that the larder was always emptied — we got rid of all the food and were able to start Thursdays with fresh produce and meat, just in time for the weekend.

Rick was our overweight, hyperactive sous-chef, who denied a rapidly receding hairline with a comb-over but couldn't hide the dark rings under his bloodshot eyes. In stark contrast to Rick, April, our new busser, was as fresh as mint and as flighty as a ladybug. Rick tried to keep it a secret, but it was obvious to everyone that he fantasized about more than just going out for drinks with April. And since this was Fool's Day, Rick apparently was alone in his passionate feelings.

"I never promised," she said.

"I never asked," he answered.

As Rick confessed to me out back of the restaurant while frantically smoking a cigarette, he had taken her to hockey games, the casino, to lavish dinners and drinks, "and then I always put her in a taxi because she wanted to go home."

Every morning after these so-called dates, he came in to work more tired than he left the night before — and that after a hot, sweaty shift in the kitchen.

"I can't sleep," he confessed. "I think I'm going crazy."

"Hookers would be cheaper," David, the chef, laconically pointed out.

Rick's preoccupation proved to be a handicap for the bistro. We couldn't function with a worn-out, lovesick sous-chef. He needed to be in charge when the chef was absent (as he often was these days, trying once again to get his computer fixed).

Rick's constant fatigue evolved into erratic mood swings. Mental instability eclipsed by frantic work immersion and overshadowed by nightly insomnia was a precarious cocktail. Rick skated close to the edge of a mental and physical breakdown, and when it happened, it was not going to be pretty. He started nagging and bitching about everything: the chef, the schedule, the work space, the constant heat, even the time of day was never right, and he lamented the utter lack of compassion from his co-workers. The fun went out of him and so did his initial enthusiasm for the job, which culminated in his getting violently sick to the point where one afternoon I finally had to send him home. Some April Fool's Day.

We had to fill Rick's position and immediately posted an ad on Craigslist. By the end of the day, we had over fifty resumés and responses. Aldo vetted them and narrowed the list down to ten, interviewed five the next day, and hired one while keeping another on hold. As long as the food looked and tasted the same and came out through the pass-through as ordered, we were all right. Nobody had to know what went on behind the scenes.

Just one day later, April suddenly went on holiday, apparently with her boyfriend (not Rick), and never returned. Just like a moth. Two weeks went by until Rick showed up pleading with us to take him back.

"I'm so over her, it's like she doesn't exist," he insisted, and being the bleeding heart Clare claims I am, I gave him a second chance. To do so, we had to let the new guy go, which was no loss, since

Dewar had even more problems than Rick. His personal difficulties stemmed from the fact that he lived in Surrey, about an hour and a half away, and had six kids, a sickly wife, and several other family members living with them. Most days he couldn't make it or came in so late that he might as well have stayed home. During the interview, none of this had come to light.

"He seemed like the perfect knowledgeable and well-balanced candidate," Aldo had insisted.

Everything returned to normal. Which meant the usual frantic chaos, a common environment in a restaurant kitchen. When it's busy, the crew work like mules. The steamy heat and the incessant shouting and banging sounds chaotic but is apparently the normal noise of a well-functioning kitchen. It wouldn't be long before the next drama started to take shape, however.

We desperately needed food pictures for our ads in a couple of tourist brochures. Luckily for us, my friend John, who is a director of photography and makes his living lighting for film and TV, offered to help us out. David prepared the best-looking filet mignon this side of France and flanked it with a basket of succulent pommes frites. We spent the best part of the morning finding a good spot for the shoot. Too dark in the back, too much light in the front, too many shadows in the centre. In the end, we opted for the front, and I used my body and our menu board to block out the sun. We ended up with a few decent-looking pictures which I thought represented the bistro perfectly.

"You're welcome to use these shots, just as long as my name isn't on them. Otherwise, I'll never get another job."

I have to say that all the so-called professionals who would shoot rolls of food pictures for our various ads over the next two years would not come up with a better display of our signature dishes. It goes to show that all the fancy equipment and hoity-toity bluster of the young photographers sent out by the various papers does not compensate for a good eye and experience. Here is John's picture that defined the food and atmosphere at the bistro.

Late at night after all the customers had left, the staff would sit down to a meal, usually prepared by the sous-chef, since the

chef had already long gone. (He hightailed it out the back door the second the last order was filled.) Sometimes a few beers on the house were also in order. The end of the day is never an ideal time to solve problems, but it seems to be when pent-up issues come forward; tired minds and spirits spill over, propelled by a few drinks and voiced with shifty sideways glances and mumbled whispers so as to not upset the management.

"David isn't doing his job," Kay, our sensitive pastry chef, mumbled.

"He's never on time, either," Chase, our new prep cook, added.

"David's on fucking drugs, I swear," Rick said. "It's so obvious. Red, beady eyes, twitchy, falls asleep in the middle of a sentence, always borrowing money."

"Yeah, he's no good," Kay said.

Since these nightly bitch sessions happen when the chef is not around, he himself often becomes the target of everything that is wrong with the kitchen. "We're taking out the chef" was a common joke referring to the thirty-gallon garbage bin, which took two people to haul out to the dumpster. The fact that the customers loved the food, which the chef, along with his disgruntled team, delivered night after night, seemed to elude the resentful cooks. For Aldo and me, the food was really the primary issue.

It seemed that Rick had other ideas and ambitions, making the chef out to be the source of all real and imagined trouble and himself the saviour of the proverbial sinking ship. "His ordering is erratic, he has hissy fits over nothing, spaces out, leaves at unpredictable times — mostly when the heat is on — he comes in late, leaves too early, yells at everybody and makes everybody wonder what the fuck is up."

"Who is everybody?" I wanted to know.

"Everybody in the kitchen," Rick answered, nervously fumbling for his cigarettes.

"Everybody?"

"Yeah, just ask them. And also ask Ken, he really wants him gone. I second that."

"Really?"

We knew Ken didn't like the chef because of their long-ago shared history, but we didn't think he would egg on the kitchen staff to near mutiny.

The next day, Aldo and I took a discreet poll to gauge the popularity of the chef, and the responses were unsettling. There seemed indeed to be something not quite right with our star player. There was too much whining from his underlings, too many complaints about his shoddy treatment of them, which all added up to a lot of disrespect and poor leadership.

I asked Kana, our stalwart and most solid and dependable pommes frites prep cook, cleaner, and all-around kitchen helper. She only talked when directly addressed and answered the question quietly with a sideways shake of her large head. Large because she wore her waist-long hair tied in a bun and wrapped in a hairnet. "Chef always yell at everybody."

"Does he yell at you?"

"Sometimes."

"Why?"

Kana just shrugged her shoulders, her dark brown eyes looking at me unblinking.

"Oh, well, thank you, Kana."

She gave me a little bow, almost like a curtsy, and went back to work.

"If you don't have respect from your staff, you're not performing at your best," I pointed out to Aldo. "Leadership is about trust and integrity, not who wields the biggest stick or yells the loudest."

We promised Rick we'd do something about the situation. Worst-case scenario: We'd change chefs. Of course this was what Rick wanted to hear.

"All options are on the table!" Aldo and I said, sounding like politicians.

I had a couple more beers, Aldo topped up his glass of Pinot Grigio, and altogether we thought we'd handled the situation competently. Yet somehow we missed the whole point. Which was, at the end of the night, after a few drinks, concerns are generally misunderstood, situations exaggerated, and inebriated solutions should not to be confused with sober judgment.

I told Clare about our dilemma before I crawled into bed, hoping she was still awake.

"You should never talk about work at the end of the night," Clare said, rolling over. "Talk about sports, cars or politics."

"How about girls?"

"I hope not."

I tossed and turned all night, and early the next morning I called Aldo.

"We can't just fire the chef," I said. "We need to talk to him and get his point of view, at the very least let him answer the allegations. Even a murderer gets his day in court to tell his side of the story." Aldo agreed. The same thoughts had troubled him during the night. "And another thing. We can't make Rick the chef. He's way too unstable."

"I know. We have to tell them to just shut up and do their job," Aldo said.

"And no more business talk at the end of the day," I added.

Aldo and I sat down with our chef at the Starbucks next door. We talked amiably about the food and the lousy weather and joked about the crazy Wednesdays.

"Giving it away always works," David said.

"Yeah, but it sure puts bums in the seats," I said.

"And money in the till," Aldo added.

An awkward pause ensued. All of us knew that we weren't just having coffee and shooting the breeze.

I finally broke the loud silence. "Well, chef, we've received a number of complaints, uh, from your crew, that we need to address. The ordering seems to be sporadic, to the point where Rick or Kay will have to fill orders on the spot or somebody has to run off to the store in a panic, and there doesn't seem to be any control on pricing. No comparative shopping, from what we can tell. We need to get the food costs under control."

"Yeah, I've been a bit distracted lately due to some personal problems," David admitted. "Hey, guys, I'm on your side, and I'll make some phone calls. My computer also crashed again. I lost a whole bunch of data."

David promised to concentrate on the job at hand and regain control of his crew. "They better get in line," he said. "I need some respect around here. They need to know who's the boss. Just watch me. I'll put the fear of God in them." He winked at us. "Just kidding."

I wasn't so sure.

An hour and several coffees later we left, somewhat satisfied that we had done the right thing and gotten the progress we'd desired without taking any drastic and unnecessary action.

"I'm still the best cook in that kitchen," David said, just as we were leaving. Both Aldo and I agreed.

We informed Rick that we had indeed tackled and solved the problems with David and that we would be watching closely and take action in the future if the situation required it. We could tell that Rick wasn't altogether happy with us, but he grudgingly agreed that we did the right thing.

"We had to talk to him, Rick," I said. "We can't just fire people on rumours and innuendos. To do that, we need hard evidence, like if someone comes in drunk or attacks a co-worker or shoots up in the bathroom. We can't just ruin somebody's career and life because he didn't order any eggs or over-salted the sauce. Even a murderer gets a fair hearing."

Rick stomped off, desperately needing a smoke.

"He's after the chef's job," Aldo said to me when we were alone.

"It's obvious," I agreed. "But he's dreaming. The guy is nuts."

During lunchtime, I was going over the evening's reservations. This happened to be a crazy Wednesday, also known as "fight night." I casually mentioned to Ken, our crusty and snobby maître d', that we had indeed calmed the waters and talked to the chef, who promised to pull up his socks and get his mind back to the job at hand. Ken stopped polishing a glass, gave me a withering look, and walked away. He was in the middle of serving a table of four and I gave it no further thought. Two minutes later the phone rang and Aldo, on the other end, cried, "What's the matter with Ken? What the hell did you say to him?"

Puzzled, I told him that I had just informed him that everything was okay and that we had talked to David. "That's all."

"He told me to call him when we make up our minds," Aldo said, "and then he hung up."

"Where the hell is he? He's got a table of four to serve."

"I think he left. Go check if his car is still there in the back."

I ran to the back door, and sure enough Ken's car was gone. I was totally flabbergasted. I called Aldo right back and confirmed the facts. "He's gone, ran away like a schoolboy in the middle of lunch. What an idiot!"

I told Alia, our dependable but shy server, to take care of Ken's table, and we switched immediately into damage control. This was surreal. The wrong guy had jumped ship. That morning we had thought that the chef might be gone by lunch, and instead the maître d' had run away. But when the fact sank in that Ken was gone, I actually felt relieved. One less problem to tackle in the future. Ken hated serving ordinary people in jeans and T-shirts, he loathed our discount nights, and he hated David. He wanted three-piece suits and the days of the $300 martini lunch back. He refused to acknowledge that times had changed and these were the new good old days! Good riddance, I thought.

Sometime in March, just after the Olympics, I read a review in the *Globe and Mail* that totally trashed an unsuspecting restaurant. It went something like this:

For instance, I only order spaghetti alla Norcina ($19) and yet the pasta we receive is a mix of spaghetti and linguine; the noodles are clumped in sticky wads. The pasta is tasteless, with copious chunks of oily, puréed truffle in which the dish drowns. If these are fresh truffles (not the inferior, jarred variety), I'll eat a wild boar's snout for breakfast.

The bone-in pork chop is unusually thick, about 1½ inches, and edged with an inedible layer of chewy gristle and fat. The breadcrumb batter is chunky and greasy. The vegetables only add insult to injury – the chop is laid over a starchy mound of lumpy turnip and mushy pickled purple sauerkraut. Roast potatoes are cold and hard; baked wedges of (whitish) tomato and (bland) golden beet are so overcooked they look mashed. The service and food was lousy, the dessert from a bakery down the road.

This review basically annihilated the establishment, and I'd be surprised if they recovered from that stinging criticism.

What the hell, I thought, why don't I invite the reviewer to our humble restaurant? We serve good food for a fair price; in fact, that's our mantra. And we have nothing to lose. I wrote the reviewer an email inviting her to come and dine at the bistro and taste our delectable frites. To my surprise, she wrote back, a bit taken aback herself by my forward invitation, and promised to take me up on it.

When I told Aldo, he was appalled. "Are you crazy! You just invited the butcher to a vegan party. It's courting the devil, inviting disaster. What if she comes on a bad night? What if we run out of fries that night? What if she comes on a Wednesday?"

"Hold it right there, Aldo. There are too many ifs, and what the hell is wrong with you? If she likes it, it's fantastic free advertising. The best we can get. I have faith in our food and service. Don't worry, it will be fine." That's what I said, but inside, yeah, I had my doubts.

When I told Clare about it, she looked at me sideways, pursed her lips, and then nodded. "Good on you," she said. "You know the saying: no guts, no glory."

We didn't hear from the food critic for three months, until out of the blue I got an email announcing her impending visit. Oh boy! I decided to call her, and we had a long chat about the varied history of the restaurant, the recent mystery of the vanished owner, the fact that we researched and made our own fries — served free to every table — and the difficulty in pricing and attracting new customers; in fact, we talked about everything, even what kinds of books we were presently reading, which turned out to be the same trilogy by Stieg Larsson. On the whole, it was a very amiable conversation.

I put everybody on high alert: Aldo, the chef, the servers, even Kana, who, after all, prepped the famous frites. Not one of us had a clue as to the food critic's identity. Everybody knew her name, but what did she look like? Was she old, young, tall, short?

"Maybe she is a man," Aldo said.

Speculation ran wild, and then we waited. A week went by, ten days, and then one morning I got an email telling us that she had been to the restaurant, loved the atmosphere, inhaled the frites, and basically gave us a thumbs-up. She went further and asked if it was all right if she wrote a feature article about us and if she could send in a photographer. Absolutely!

In the following week's *Globe and Mail* we were prominently featured as the best French restaurant in town, along with a glowing review of our chef and his food. So much for letting David go. She made him a star, and all talk of changing the kitchen staff ceased. Suddenly everybody in our kitchen was proud to be working in the unique and instantly famous bistro.

The following night, Friday, the place was packed. So was Saturday. Many people had read the article. We of course made no secret of it and flaunted the piece on the back of the wine list.

One good review begat another. Millions of people google, tweet and blog. If you did a search for our bistro, it suddenly popped up as the number one French restaurant in all of Vancouver. How did this happen? All I know is that we tried to serve a good product for a fair price in a comfortable setting. The ultimate goal was to be everybody's favourite. I took a gamble and it paid off.

At the end of the busy night, I poured Aldo a full glass of his Pinot Grigio, drew a pint for myself and a pitcher for the kitchen.

Folly Bistro

"To the best French bistro this side of Paris!" I toasted.

"Hear, hear! And a special toast to you, my friend," Aldo said. "You made believers out of doubters, practically turned vegans into meat lovers."

This is probably as good a place as any to mention the unusual previous history of our iconic establishment. This mystery no doubt inspired the *Globe and Mail* food critic to cover our humble bistro's resurrection.

The former owner, Claude, had a reputation as an eccentric, but was well liked. He had adopted a trendy French accent and always wore a black beret at a jaunty angle over his shoulder-length black hair. One day a Ludova started working at the restaurant as a waitress, and not long after that Claude left his wife and kids and shacked up with her.

"He was besotted with her," Ken said when I asked him about it. I knew Ken had worked with them right to the end (or at least until they forgot to pay his wages.) "He couldn't keep his eyes or his hands off her. They were like a couple of teenagers, chasing each other through the restaurant, and one day, you won't believe it. Well I better go no further."

"Ken, come on, now. Let's hear it," I said. "Let the cat out of the bag."

"Well, one day after we finished the service and were just about to lock up, uh, it was just me, Claude, and Ludova. We'd all had a few drinks. Claude was very generous with the wine. Oh well, you don't want to hear this."

"Yes, we do," Rick said from behind me. Everybody wanted to hear what Ken had to offer.

"He bonked her right there, at table one, two feet from the sidewalk right by the window. Bent her over the table while I was polishing glasses behind the bar. No lie, I swear, but you didn't hear it from me."

"Damn right, we did," Rick grinned. "You're telling us that he fucked her right here in the restaurant. That's awesome, man."

"Kind of cathartic," I said, shaking my head. "He really lost his head over her."

"Right about that time, things slowly started to go downhill," Ken said. "The quality of the food became inconsistent. The chef spent all his time upstairs in the office and left the cooking to whoever was in the kitchen. Every night, the drinking went on until the wee hours and the customers started to stay away. Everything of any value disappeared out the back door, including some antiques and all of the booze and wine. And then one day Claude vanished without a trace. The police found his passport, driver's licence and wallet, but no trace of him. Ludova was the last person who'd seen him before he vanished, but she claimed complete ignorance as to his whereabouts and state of health — which was rumoured to be bad.

"Claude's family launched a media campaign and hired a detective agency to find him, but to no avail. I got questioned, as if I had any clue as to what had happened. His sudden disappearance remains inconclusive and riddled with speculation. It's a tragic mystery."

"I'm sure Ludova knows more than she lets on," Aldo said, and his feelings were echoed by everybody.

One day Celine, our classy French waitress from Aix-en-Provence who was in Canada on a one-year work visa, suddenly quit on us, along with her boyfriend, Giles, who had been helping Kay with the desserts and prep.

"Why so suddenly?" I asked Celine.

"We want to travel," she replied vaguely.

"Just like that? You want to leave tomorrow?"

Furtive looks between Celine and Giles told me she was simply lying. Two days later, Gino, our head waiter, told me that both were working for another upscale French restaurant in the city.

"Miserable traitors," I cursed.

On the same morning, Sara, the busser who'd replaced April, revealed that her grandma was on her deathbed in Saskatoon and needed Sara to be near her.

All of a sudden we were left with an acute labour shortage. Unbelievable. We immediately posted on Craigslist and had over 100 hits in just one day. We applied the same elimination process as with the cooks, and Aldo settled on a professional waiter who came with excellent references and a wealth of experience. What luck! The first two shifts, Carl performed beautifully — we had ourselves an ace, a keeper, a good find.

Even Clare liked him. "He's a smart man and knows his job. You guys have yourselves a winner here."

On the third day, Carl was booked for our discount Wednesday to hold down the bar and help out where he could. He arrived at 6:00 p.m., half an hour late, and immediately Margo noticed something odd in his behaviour.

"I ask him five times for a martini, but he make too much and then he drink from the glass. I cannot serve that. Then I ask him to open a bottle of wine. He take the wrong bottle and break the cork. And he talks like he is underwater. I cannot understand him."

I took one look at Carl and, no doubt, he was completely pie-eyed. He could barely stand up. I had no choice. "Carl, what's going on?"

"Nothing," he burped, looking at me through watery eyes, his comb-over flopping off to the side over his ear.

"Carl, you need to go home now," I said, taking him by the arm and leading him past the bar to the back of the bistro and out the door. He didn't protest and followed me, docile as a puppy dog. No wonder the server with the best resumé had no job.

At the same time we hired Alice as a busser. Actually, Gino hired her. She walked in through the door without a resumé, but Gino was so enamoured by her "lovely personality and rapturous smile" that he signed her on the spot. When I talked to her later, I noticed that her baby blue eyes didn't focus and seemed to look into the distance, but she made up for the lack of concentration with her angelic smile. That, and her two blonde ponytails perched on either side of her head like Pippi Longstocking, made it easy to forgive her for many things. When I told Clare about our new busser, she said, "Maybe Alice in Wonderland is short-sighted and just needs glasses."

Whenever Margo worked the shift, the boys in the kitchen worked twice as hard, but they often got the orders mixed up and put the wrong sauce on the fish or the steak. Between Alice in

Wonderland and Margo, the Princess of Prague, it was paramount that I be there as the token adult, just to supply an element of stable responsibility in the restaurant and keep the boys from tripping over each other.

We decided to give Carl another chance, but this time Aldo baited a simple trap. We arranged with Margo that she would take off at 4:00 p.m. under some pretext and come back a couple of hours later. This left Carl all by himself during the quiet, late afternoon — with all that tempting booze behind the bar. Aldo bet me that Carl wouldn't be able to control himself and would take a snort or two, just to steady the nerves.

Margo loved the intrigue and discreetly marked all the vodka, rum and gin bottles. If we couldn't smell it on his breath, the proof would be in by the discrepancies in the bottles.

It was so predictable and kind of sad at the same time. When Margo got back, she called me. "He is so drunk," she whispered into the phone.

I immediately went to the restaurant. "Carl, we had a deal. No drinking on the job."

"I know, I know," he said, turning away from me so I couldn't smell his breath. "I have a bit of a cold."

I walked behind the bar and took the first vodka bottle off the shelf. It was so obvious that it was pathetic. Two fingers were missing. When I pointed this out to Carl, he folded. "I'm sorry," he said, picked up his belongings, and walked out.

"Me too," I said, but I doubt he heard me. I felt sorry for Carl's wife and kids.

Our next server walked in off the street at exactly the right moment, just when Carl had slunk out the back door.

Melinda was small and wiry, full of nervous energy, and had a lilting French accent. She hailed from Montreal, she was fluent in French, and she came with good references and a greedy hunger for work. As it turned out, too hungry. She wanted to work seven days from morning to night. When I insisted she take two days off, she was bitterly disappointed and sulked for days. And she was notoriously late. Though she was supposed to be at the bistro at 10:00 a.m., she always flew in the door half an hour behind, scarves and hair flying, her eyes bulging from the long stressful commute by bus and SkyTrain from Burnaby. At least her tardiness was predictable. I told her that for every half hour she was late, I would dock her an hour's pay. She was fine with that.

Melinda had constant boyfriend problems. One day she came in with hickies on her neck, which I asked her to cover up. But she was in a good mood that day, at least, with a certain swagger in her narrow hips. The next day, she slouched into work through the back door looking dejected, dragging a battered old suitcase along behind her.

"I hate him, I hate him. He is so stupid. He stop making love when his phone ring. Imagine that!" I didn't want to.

The rest of that day she was depressed and lethargic, which did nothing for our customer service. This state lasted until numerous frantic phone calls on her cell straightened matters out.

"We made up! I love Luc so much!" she exclaimed, almost in tears, she was so overwhelmed.

Melinda wore her emotions wide open for all to see, but due to her erratic rollercoaster life she always needed to shift or change her hours at the last minute, which drove me crazy.

Aldo just shrugged it off. "Tell them to make their own arrangements. That's the way it is, buddy. Restaurants are insane asylums and the inmates are unpredictable."

Reality Check

We'd only been in business for five months, but it felt like I'd always done this. It never let up. We'd solve a staffing issue and then there would be a food problem; we'd just get over a surprise visit from Stewy, the poxy health inspector with his lightsaber flashlight pointing out hidden holes and telltale mouse turds, and right away we'd need to deal with one of the cooks who had a drug problem. Whenever I'd walk in the back door, I'd count to three and then somebody would bring up a problem or an issue.

"Oh, did you know that the thermostat isn't working?"

"I can't make this Saturday's shift because I've got to go to a wedding."

"We're out of cranberry juice and the pop dispenser is on the fritz."

"All part of running a restaurant," said Aldo, pointing out the obvious. "And you just have to deal with the issues one by one, one after the other. Never look at them all together, it's too overwhelming."

"Aldo is right," Clare said after I debriefed my woes during one of our few dinners at home. Usually I spent suppertime at the restaurant, and once or twice a week Clare would come in for her favourite: gratin Lyonnais (French onion soup with Gruyère cheese) accompanied by our classic salade mimosa (butter lettuce and grated egg with vinaigrette), along with a glass or two of our Côte du Rhone house wine.

"I love the fact that you have a restaurant," she confessed over our solitary home-cooked dinner.

"You're welcome."

I have sailed on the BC coast, tacking back and forth all day, never making any headway but just enjoying the fact that we were sailing. The restaurant felt a bit like that. Moving all day long, but at the end of the day we were no further ahead. The money that painstakingly came in the front left out the back faster than it arrived. Whenever I thought we were ahead after a good night, I'd get an unexpected bill the next day that took care of that — the yearly insurance bill or the quarterly fire-suppression system check or a tax adjustment.

I loved our atmosphere — warm, welcoming, even homey, but classy at the same time. The mustard-yellow walls and tablecloths offset by the red bar counter and brass rails, the parquet floor and the authentic wooden bistro chairs, all bathed in diffused light from the spherical low-hanging globes, gave the place a cozy feel. A home away from home, a place to relax and enjoy good food and company. That was the ambition and that was the kind of restaurant I wanted the bistro to be.

Restaurants are like theatres: The stage sets the mood; the actors bring the stage alive; and the food, well, that's the music and the dance, that's for the senses. It elevates anticipation into well-being and satisfaction and even mild ecstasy, inspired, for example, by our simple mimosa salad or the homey poulet de Paris (roast chicken with peppercorn sauce). Customers' eyes would light up and some would coo and smack their lips when the aromatic bowl of gratin Lyonnais with the Gruyère cheese melting over top was set before them.

What I lacked, though, was a callous business sense. Unlike Aldo, I was a total pushover, always trying to accommodate, trying to please everybody. I needed to learn from my partner not to put up with the bullshit and ignore the whining and pining. Aldo gave me heck one day, once again, for being too nice to the staff.

"Don't ask them how they are. You don't want to hear their problems, which always either have to do with money or love. You just need to ask them about their work. Are the orders done, are the desserts ready, or is the kitchen clean. Nothing else. You're not their friend, you're their boss. Just tell them to do their darn job and to shut up. Don't listen to their daily bullshit, because it never stops. They should be happy to have a God-darned job."

I supposed he was right, and Clare tended to agree with Aldo. "You can be nice and polite without being personal. You offer your little finger and they take the whole hand. Every time."

Case in point: the weekly schedule. Every week I had to make a schedule for fourteen shifts and slot everybody in, trying to dispense the shifts evenly, be fair and accommodate preferences, and then put up with the whining and excuses.

"Oh, I can't do Friday night; it's my cousin's stag."

"By the way, I think Margo is getting all the good shifts. I do all the slow lunches and she's getting the better section."

"I don't want to do Sundays."

"I want more evening shifts. Lunches are boring and I can't make any money."

I always tried to accommodate everybody, but it was a battle I couldn't win. "I can't do it, Aldo. They're all driving me crazy."

Aldo took the schedule from me and told me to go have a coffee or a beer. Ten minutes later he was done.

"Here is the schedule and this is what you tell the staff: If you want changes, sort them out among yourselves. Remember, all the shifts need to be covered. No excuses. And the schedule stays the same, every week. Go print out a dozen of them. Everybody gets one and then you post it for all to see."

It wasn't the perfect solution, but it worked. There was a lot of grumbling and whining, but I stuck to my guns and told them in as stern a tone of voice as I could, "Everybody has their shifts, and if you don't like it, sort it out among yourselves or go talk to Aldo." They knew better than that, and Aldo never got bothered by anyone.

I was more concerned with the food. As long as the dishes looked and tasted great and the customers were happy, I was happy. We started with a very ambitious French-only menu, which nobody but the sophisticated Europhiles and foodies comprehended. So we anglicized the menu, or at least added the English version — i.e., gratin Lyonnais = French onion soup, magret de canard = duck breast, potage du jour (as I assumed everybody knew) = daily soup. Of course there were some purists, like our chef, who got offended, but we needed to reach the common people, the ones who didn't speak French or had no idea who Auguste Escoffier was.

How about the times when nobody showed up at the restaurant? Depressingly empty seats all around. The kitchen full of food, two servers and two bussers lounging at the bar, me pawing through bills in the back, trying to appear unconcerned and optimistic when all I wanted to do was scream. Should I send somebody home? Do I tell the kitchen to shut down? Do I yell at somebody? Or should I just go for that pint of beer, even though it's only 7:30 p.m.? The night was young, but as far as I was concerned we were already skunked.

And then, out of nowhere a deuce walks in, then right behind them a four, and suddenly there is life in the place. I rush to turn up the music, maybe turn it down, hide that beer, straighten out, pretend I'm answering the phone, taking a reservation: "Yes, absolutely, a table for six for tomorrow, certainly, Madame. We'll expect you at seven and have your usual place for you." Who was I trying to impress? Nobody is who. All I knew was that we had to make another twelve grand before month's end to meet the bills, to pay the wages, the lease, the taxes, the suppliers, the utilities, the ads, the printers, the liquor store, the repair man, the laundry guys, the stove repair guy, the fishmonger. A never-ending avalanche of bills cascading through the mail slot and out of our bank account. Aldo and I were happy when we didn't have to put any money in at the end of the month. Another month with all the bills paid is a successful month in the restaurant business. Of course, there was always the future, the summer, the tourist season, when we'd serve 150 customers every day, as Aldo optimistically prophesied.

"Just you wait and see. It will happen," he assured me. I was waiting for that day.

Success or failure simply came down to the whims of the customers, or patrons, as we liked to call them. One wrong impression — a mistake in the order, not being able to supply the wine they ordered, the music being too loud, their favourite waiter not being on shift — could trigger a switch in their brain which would prevent them from returning. The old cliché that the customer is always right fits the restaurant business perfectly. No matter how they like their steak or their sauce, or on which side of the plate the veggies should be arranged, or how much is too much and how much too little, the staff and cooks can never please enough. It's where the clichés become the truth: Happy customers make a happy restaurant, and a happy restaurant is a full restaurant. A full restaurant makes money, an empty one loses money, and the essence of success is having money left over at the end of the month. Amen.

Patrons

We catered to a fair crop of difficult clients, the ones you could never fully satisfy no matter what you dished out or poured into their glasses. They were the real challenge. Like Paddy, the seventy-five-year-old Irish obsessive-compulsive prizefighter millionaire who stopped in every Tuesday and Sunday after walking the ten-kilometre seawall around Stanley Park. Winter or summer, rain or shine, he'd be in before 11:30 a.m. He was as strong as an ox, with a ruddy face stuck forward on his thick neck, one step ahead of his body, like he was always ready to fight. His head was topped with a shock of unruly white hair, while his steely, unblinking blue eyes stared straight into a mean old world that could never measure up to his demanding and high standards. He'd spend over $100 for each lunch, an unusual occurrence in those tight-fisted times, and he ate lunch every day in one of his favourite restaurants. He would have his bottle of rosé to the right of him, uncorked in an ice bucket. He hated soup, so he started with a mimosa salad, not too much egg, not too much dressing. Then he'd have the poulet de Paris, peppercorn sauce on the side, and the frites had to arrive at the same time. He never had any cooked greens like beans or asparagus. He liked bread but hated butter, hated even the sight of butter. Margo once served him a dish of butter with his bread. Paddy gave her a withering look, then stood up and stormed out of the restaurant, to the extreme horror of the poor girl.

"It's not your fault," I explained, trying to lessen the shock. "Somebody should have warned you."

It took a couple of phone calls from both Aldo and me to placate the old codger, assuring him that it would never happen again.

Next week Paddy was back, and then the calamity occurred. "We're out of rosé," Margo whispered. "We just sold the last bottle to a couple first thing." She was panic-stricken.

Gino glanced over at the Irish codger and led Margo behind the bar, out of sight. "There is just one solution,' he said. "It's an old server's trick in case of just such an emergency. A bit of alchemy usually employed at weddings, late at night, but it will have to do here. Get me the empty rosé bottle."

Margo did as told while Gino fetched a Sauvignon Blanc, a Beaujolais and a funnel. He poured three-quarters of the white into the empty rosé bottle and added one-quarter of the red wine until the mix was a pink, blush rose colour. Margo, who followed the procedure with wide-open eyes, served the "homemade" rosé in an ice bucket and then set it down on Paddy's right-hand side, just as he liked it.

"The rosé is quite tart," Paddy commented, smacking his lips. "I always thought it was sweeter."

"Must be a new vintage," Gino said, winking at Margo, who was busy polishing glasses.

And then came Monsieur Duvalier, with his bejewelled wife gliding ahead of him like a showboat. They insisted on their table, always table three in the alcove facing the street. Woe to us if we did not stock his favourite wine, a Puligny-Montrachet by Joseph Drouhin, an elusive white from France that was not always available. We'd go to great pains to get it in, knowing full well that Doc and Jewel — as we called them — would show up sooner or later. They had been honouring the establishment with their divine presence long before Aldo and I took it over. It was worth the trouble to cater to customers like them, because one of their lunches made up for a dozen walk-ins.

It was a weekday evening — not a Wednesday — when Gino and Margo were sharing the floor. Since it was the chef's day off, Rick, looking tired and stressed, was in charge of the kitchen, with Kay nervously prepping vegetables and desserts. Kana had just left, after telling me in her quiet voice that the potatoes were not up to the usual standard. I made a mental note to check into this the next day. Just after 6:00 p.m., two women walked in. They looked like a mother-daughter team — the mother wanting to look like the daughter — both in high heels, both artificial blondes. The minute they sat down, they started bitching.

"Is there any service in this place?"

Gino was surprised because although he had just seated them, he was going to wait the usual couple of beats before approaching them with menus.

"Is this the best table you got? The chairs are uncomfortable."

"Would you like to sit on the bench?" Gino asked.

"No, we like to sit by ourselves," the older of the two replied testily, "and I want to speak to the manager."

I happened to be in the restaurant and overheard the exchange. I warily sauntered over and introduced myself while Gino walked by me rolling his eyes.

"How can I help you?" I inquired politely.

"I don't like the way your waiter just brushed us off. He is supposed to wait off to the side until we're ready."

"I will let him know."

I walked over to Gino and quietly said, so they couldn't overhear but still saw me talk to him, "You need to pretend they're royals, Gino, and you can't let them see what you think."

During the whole meal, the bitching never stopped. "The music is too loud," although it was hardly audible; "The wine is cold," although it was at room temperature, and if anything, too warm; "The bread is too old," although delivered fresh from our bakery that morning; "The fries are limp," which Gino confirmed. But it didn't stop there. The salad was much too oily, the filet mignon too thin, and the dessert too large — and on and on it went.

Gino, who had served customers for the past thirty years and thought he had seen everything, could hardly keep his cool. At one point, the daughter put the basket of bread on the floor, indicating that it was now time to clear it. I told Gino just to humour these freaks. Either they hadn't taken their meds or had taken too many. It was kind of entertaining to a point, because they were so outrageously rude. They paid by Visa, left a meagre tip, and eventually marched out, the mother first, their heads held aloft — but they weren't done yet. The daughter turned around at the door and lashed out at us: "It's a custom at any self-respecting restaurant to hold the door for the guests and not let it slam behind them."

Gino held himself together and just asked, "Isn't that your mother standing out there in the rain?"

She gave him a withering look and said, "We won't be back!" then did a dramatic 180° turn on her heels and bolted out the door.

"Go back to hell," Gino grumbled, looking disgustedly at his puny tip.

I confronted the chef the next day about the fries, which had come out of the fryer limp, tasted different, and were not the golden, crusty and creamy frites everybody loved and expected.

"We can't get the Kennebec potatoes, so I used Yukon Gold instead," David said, dismissing the issue.

"But the customers are complaining, David. Did you try other suppliers?" I asked, knowing that I was treading on dangerous territory.

The chef stopped stirring and turned around to face me. "When I said we can't get any Kennebecs, then I mean there are none available, not in Vancouver, not this week, not today. Since you don't charge for the frites, I can't see what the problem is."

He had a point, but it was not his to make. I then realized that the frites were all about the right kind of potato. The Kennebec potato was developed in the forties by the US Department of Agriculture, mainly cultivated in Maine, and destined to make the perfect pommes frites. No other lowly tuber would do.

We experienced two encounters of the pregnant kind. The first one sat with her significant other at table seven, and I remembered her because she was quite loud and demanding — as if the world had better pay attention since she was now bearing the future of mankind in her belly. She was a large girl, even before she'd gotten pregnant, with a wild shock of curly black hair held back with a pink headband. She ate like a boxer and drank like a sailor. Her boyfriend was a swarthy, uncouth fellow in a black T-shirt with a skull print that showed off his vulgar tattoos. They started drinking martinis with their steak tartare, devoured a basket of bread, then progressed to a bottle of white wine with their poulet de Paris, emptied two portions of pommes frites, and then opted for crème brûlées for dessert, an extra nine-ounce glass of white for her, and a double brandy for him. Finally done, she sailed out of the restaurant with her lucky boyfriend paying the bill and staggering behind trying to catch up.

The next morning, just after we opened at 11:30 a.m., I received an agitated phone call.

"We ate there last night and we have both come down with massive food poisoning. We intend to make an official complaint to the health board."

I remembered her well. They were Melinda's customers and she couldn't get over how much food and booze they'd had. "She eat like pig and he is pig," she had pointed out after they were gone.

I was easily able to retrieve the bill, which showed quite clearly that the complainers had consumed enough food and alcohol to make anybody sick, never mind if they were pregnant. They were obviously looking for money. I offered the bimbo a full refund on their dinners if she'd come in with the doctor's report. Needless to say, we never heard from them again.

The second pregnant encounter took place on a very busy Wednesday night. We were hosting the entire West End Seniors' Association. Wednesday was our craziest night even without special parties, but they'd reserved well ahead, just after the Olympics, and we felt obliged to honour the commitment. They'd booked for fifteen, and twenty-five showed up. Separate bills for everybody and musical chairs until they all knew where they were going to sit — across from who, beside who, and close to the bathroom.

Gino and Melinda served the seniors while Margo, with her hair piled up, revealing two large hoop earrings, and her sultry eyes ringed with mascara, took care of the walk-ins. We had Sanchez manning the bar, as on every Wednesday. People mistook him for Cesar Millan (the dog guy on TV), and he loved the attention. With his big, infectious grin, he made the perfect bartender. Selena, our new busser who could not walk by the mirror without checking herself out, and Alice in Wonderland, whose mind was always somewhere else but on the job, were bussing. Alice did have one special talent, though: She had lovely handwriting, and we got her to do all our blackboard menus, a task she loved.

I manned the door and managed the tables and reservations, which was a challenge, as we had over-reserved due to all those extra seniors — ten more than expected — and some tables were staying longer than anticipated, pushing the next seating to the bar for drinks. The place was hopping by 7:00 p.m. and there was a joyful noise in the bistro.

The skinny blonde with a pinched look on her face was a walk-in and, without waiting to be seated, sat down at a table that was already reserved. I politely tried to move her but she refused to sit at the bar where we usually placed singles and early birds.

"I'm pregnant and I wouldn't be comfortable at the bar," she said with an annoying whine to her voice. She left me no choice but to believe her. We were here to serve, not to judge. I let her have a table for two. I wanted Gino to look after her, rather than Margo, who was busy with a table of six guys who couldn't tear their eyes off her.

Gino took the anaemic-looking pregnant woman under his wing. With her exasperating voice, she inquired about every dish: Did it contain alcohol? Was it organic? Had it been previously frozen? She eventually settled on a salade mesclun and poulet de Paris with no fries. "I can't eat deep-fried foods."

She was well past her salad, which she'd demolished, and was lustily tucking into her chicken while reading the menu one more time, when she suddenly yelled and gasped as if about to die on the spot. Gino rushed over to see what the commotion was all about or if he would have to employ the Heimlich manoeuvre.

"Oh my God," she cried. "I need to call my doctor and my fiancé! You didn't tell me that there was alcohol in the salad."

"In the salad?" Gino asked, perplexed.

"Yes, yes, here it says 'Beaujolais poached pears,' and I ate all of them."

"Well, yes, but there is at best just a hint of alcohol in the pears. It's mostly for flavour, and the alcohol has long evaporated."

There was no way to placate her, and in his wisdom, Gino asked one of the West End Seniors women to come over and talk some sense into the girl.

After having listened to her tale of woe, the grizzled, stout senior, with her hands on her hips, told the girl to get a grip and a life. "You have to relax, girl. Get out and have some fun and stop the silly whining."

Folly Bistro

Not at all the sensible approach Gino was hoping for. He quickly intervened and led the feisty elder back to her table, thanking her profusely, then ran back to the girl and assured her that no harm would possibly come to her from just the wine-soaked pears. It did no good. The girl was on her feet by now and, as if in a dream, steered for the door with outstretched arms and bulging eyes, gulping and crying, and conveniently forgot to pay, stiffing us for the bill and Gino for his tip. She was either genuinely messed up or just a very good actress, but either way we lost.

The night was young yet, and we still had two dozen owly, demanding seniors to please. When the old curmudgeons finally settled their bills one by one and left amid a flurry of mixed-up coats, hats, walking sticks and purses, we were finally able to clear the tables for a second round of bargain-hunting diners, some of whom had been waiting patiently by the bar, nursing their drinks. Just one old biddy remained, steadfastly sitting at the head of the long table, apparently not in any hurry to leave. She was holding up the whole section. I walked up to her and politely inquired if she was waiting for somebody.

"I'm waiting for somebody to help me with my coat," she said with an air of exasperated finality.

"I'll help you," I offered, taking hold of the fluffy old faux-tiger fur that matched her pillbox hat. She stood up and put her left arm into the sleeve and then stopped. I looked, and noticed her right arm just dangling, limp and thin by her side. Shit, what now? Being a practical man, I gently took hold of her inert arm and quickly shoved it into the coat sleeve, which prompted her to turn around and whack me across the head with her good hand. "Don't you touch me like that!" she squealed.

"Whoa, hold it, girl," I replied, taking a step backwards. "You're quite the feisty tiger lily," I said from a safe distance.

She cackled and then demanded, "Button me up, young man!"

I liked the "young man" bit but declined her offer. Instead, I requested Margo's assistance for the delicate job.

Now all buttoned and coated, Tiger Lily was almost ready to move on.

"Don't forget your suitcase," I said, trying to wheel her suitcase ahead of her out the door.

"Don't touch that. Give it to me," she demanded, indignant. Okay, I thought, have it your way. She grabbed the suitcase and wheeled it ahead of her with her good arm, pushing and leaning on it while she walked. "It's my walker, silly boy," she said with a twinkle in her eye, "and my name is Hazel."

I got it — a disguised walker. Very ingenious. "What's in there, Hazel?"

"None of your business, but I'll tell you anyways." She leaned close to me and whispered, "My survival gear — diapers, Kleenex, and toilet paper."

"You look like a girl on the move, Hazel," I said, trying to ignore her comments.

"You bet I am, young man," she replied with authority, and out the door she wheeled, with her good hand steering her suitcase full of treasure.

Our favourite customers were the ones that stayed for hours, wining and dining like it was their first date, complimenting us on the food and the service, thanking us for providing them with such a pleasurable dining experience, and then tipping like kings. Most often those patrons consisted of older gentlemen in groups of two, four, or even six — retired, polite and incredibly exuberant about their dining experience. It's no secret that the West End is home to men and women of every persuasion, and we loved the ones who went out on a regular basis.

There was Colette, a spry eighty-five-year-old who looked and moved like she was twenty years younger, accompanied by her son, Peter, who was (and looked) sixty-five. They came in at least once a week and preferred to sit in one of the alcoves. They invariably stayed at least two hours, shared a bottle of Château Rousselle, and were continually engaged in animated conversation as if they had just met. They always seemed to be celebrating, toasting their glasses with every refill.

"What are you celebrating?" I had to ask one night when not much else was happening.

"We're celebrating Albert Einstein's birthday. It's March 14, you know."

"Really? I didn't know that," I said.

"Here is one for old Albert." Colette raised her glass and they happily toasted.

A couple of weeks later they sat at table three and ordered half a bottle of Veuve Clicquot. Gino and I quickly checked the Internet for celebrity birthdays.

"It can't be Lady Gaga," Gino said.

"How about Anheuser Busch, the famous brewer?"

"Who is it today?" I asked sheepishly. "Lady Gaga or Anheuser Busch?"

Collette giggled. "Silly, it's my birthday. I'm eighty-five."

How about Harry and Herby, the retired couple who came every Wednesday for their steak 'n' frites and half a litre of Pinot Noir? Both used to be schoolteachers and had lived together for forty years. One busy Wednesday, Harry showed up by himself because Herby was back East dealing with a family problem.

Harry wanted his usual table, but I didn't want to lose a table for two. There was another young, single guy at the bar waiting for a table. In the heat of the moment, I wasn't thinking clearly and said to Harry, "I'll set you up with the young man at the bar," meaning I wanted to seat both of them together at his usual table — but somehow this hadn't come out right.

Harry thrust out his chest and said, "You've got the wrong impression of me. I've been with Herby for forty years now." He indignantly threw his napkin on the table like it was a gauntlet, got up, and stalked out of the bistro.

I had no idea what I'd said to offend him. It took several phone calls from Aldo and Gino to set things right with Harry, but he always avoided me after that, pretending not to see me.

Calvin was a lawyer who came in regularly for dinner, always with his mom and sometimes one or two of their friends in tow. We all called her Mom, and she always ordered the salmon, cooked to oblivion, while Calvin preferred the steak, rare of course. They liked to come in late, usually after 8:00 p.m. Mom loved to talk about the old times, the good old days, when they lived in Moscow during the sixties as part of the embassy staff.

"Those were the real party days," she chortled. "We used to drive around in a chauffeured limo to all the clubs and never went to bed before the sun came up. Not like today when everybody goes home at ten o'clock."

The staff were well aware of these special customers and their peculiarities, and would let the kitchen know when they came in. Only once did Mom's salmon come out perfectly cooked, still moist and pink in the middle, and we nearly lost a steady customer. Mom let us know in no uncertain terms, in a voice loud enough for everybody to hear, that she liked her fish cooked, "not swimming in the sauce still half alive."

It was 50 Percent Wednesday and in came the Wangs. They only showed up on Wednesdays and they only called about ten minutes before they arrived, invariably asking for table seven like we owed it to them. They would drive up in a shiny new black Infinity. Mr. Wang was handicapped, so Mrs. Wang drove, but because of her small stature she had to look through the steering wheel at the road. They always parked just by the "No Parking" sign in the alley on the side of the restaurant, where we would have liked to eventually have the patio. Mrs. Wang walked in and, without bothering to stop, steered straight for table seven, sat down, and immediately called for a waiter. Mr. Wang hobbled in with his walker, two minutes behind her. They ordered the same items every time: magret de canard — duck breast with glazed apples and Calvados — for her and filet mignon with our homemade sauce Béarnaise for him. They didn't drink but they did eat dessert. Crème brûlée for him, chocolate mousse for her.

Roy was our newly hired waiter, a jovial, ruddy Scotsman with a proud paunch under his black waistcoat, who always had a joke at the ready and never let his true feelings show. Besides Gino, he was our most experienced and professional waiter and always ended up serving the Wangs, who were in his section, to his chagrin. Roy, during his illustrious career, had served everybody from ex-prime minister Jean Chrétien to Keith Richards, and he hated the Wangs.

"They are rude and think I'm their personal servant and then they don't tip." Nothing irks a waiter more than a wealthy but stingy customer. "They are obviously stinking rich but cheap as Scrooge. They never come in on any other day, just Wednesdays."

Roy had a point. As soon as Mrs. Wang finished, she demanded the bill, paid with her black American Express, then got up and left, while Mr. Wang scrambled after her with his walker as she started the motor.

One tall young man with a shaven head and biceps the size of my thighs returned every Wednesday and always ordered three entrées — then ate them, one after the other, to the last bite.

"He is professional athlete?" Margo whispered to Gino, admiring the guy's hearty appetite.

Gino shook his head. "Professional athletes don't need discounts, and he's a poor tipper."

"Oh, he is hungry, poor athlete," Margo sighed. "But he is gay," she concluded after trying to make eye contact with the hulky young man, who, to her chagrin, only had eyes for his three filets mignons.

Every couple of weeks we'd get a lunch visit from Monsieur Ducat and guests. On most occasions he brought his business associate along, a large, boisterous German who always winked and nudged like everything was a clandestine joke or clever aside. Monsieur Ducat was "the Duke," not just because of his name but because he looked the part — tall and skinny, with long dangling arms, a grey pencil moustache, sideburns, and his longish grey hair combed straight back, covering his neck. We thought he was French because of his cultivated accent, but Melinda, who hailed from Montreal, thought otherwise. "He is a snob from Quebec, I swear! He is not from Paris, that is for sure."

The Duke was a wine merchant and he catered to those restaurants that carried some of his wines. We did, since Ken, our original maître d', had made sure of that, knowing full well that Monsieur Ducat would be grateful.

The Duke always ordered the steak tartare, followed by a rare filet mignon. When he said "rare," he meant blue, the French way: seared quickly on both sides and immediately removed from the grill. Although the filet was not on our lunch menu, we accommodated the Duke because he regularly ordered one of his own expensive wines alongside it, mostly just to make sure we had it in stock.

"Bring me a bottle of Crozes-Hermitage Les Brunelles, s'il vous plaît."

My fear was always that our lunch servers, who we seemed to replace like cheap tools, wouldn't know who the Duke was and would deny him his filet mignon and not know the difference between a Crozes-Hermitage and a bottle of plonk. I told Kana — our most dependable daytime staffer in the kitchen, who saw and heard everything but said little unless prompted — to keep an eye out for our special customers like Paddy or the Duke and sound the alarm when she spotted them so that everybody could snap to attention.

And then there was Rama, who would always turn heads with his flamboyant entrance. It was no coincidence that he came to the bistro on Margo's shift, usually later, after all the customers had already gone. He always offered to drive Margo home, which she coyly refused, citing the fact that she lived just around the corner.

"Me too," Rama said. "I have the penthouse two blocks away. I'd love to show it to you."

"I'm sure you would," she said coyly, serving him a $25 glass of XO Rémy Martin.

Dressed as if for a royal wedding in shiny three-piece silk suits, Rama wore jewellery like Liberace, with glittering rings, a large gold watch and a golden tie pin against a ruffled shirt that would make Prince blush. His loafers were tasselled and gleaming and his hair was coiffed and elevated like Little Richard's, to add an extra inch to his five-foot frame. Rama was born in Vancouver. His mother was of English descent and lived in Surrey, while his dad hailed from Rajasthan and was at large.

"I think I'm the only real Canadian here tonight," Rama said, looking around the mostly empty restaurant with just a few Asian customers finishing their late dinners. "It's like the United Nations in here."

At the time, we had a Filipino cook, an Egyptian chef, a Taiwanese garde manger, a Portuguese dishwasher, and up front, Alice in Wonderland from Germany, Margo from Prague, Gino from Italy, Roy from Scotland, Sanchez from San Salvador, Alia from Latvia, myself from Switzerland, and Aldo all the way from the "far, far east," which did indeed make Rama our token genuine born-and-bred Canadian.

Rama launched into his usual spiel, with which we were all familiar by now: "I'm in the middle of a billion-dollar court battle and I've been advised to keep a low profile." This was to explain the fact that he'd arrived in his mom's old Honda Civic instead of his usual Ferrari or Rolls Royce. Other people talked in thousands of dollars about their deals; Rama talked in millions. With a wave of his hand, he dismissed claims that he'd just lost hundreds of millions due to a change in governors in the state of Hyderabad or Kerala, depending on where he was promoting his latest dream project. "We build cities, not subdivisions. We are the future of India, which has the fastest-growing middle class in the world," he proclaimed, as Margo served him his third XO cognac.

Other than his height, there was nothing small about Rama — not his cars, not his self-aggrandizing claims, not his bar tab, which he paid some of the time and deferred at others. To his credit, he always did pay up, usually after he'd been able to persuade somebody to invest in his dream scams.

I was intrigued when I first met him, until he showed me a brochure of their planned golf course estate outside Bangaluru. The brochure was of an Italian castle somewhere in Tuscany, complete with photos of the pool, the vineyards and the splendid neoclassical villa.

"This is in Italy," I said. "What's this got to do with India and Bangaluru?"

"Exactly," he said, holding up his index finger like a lecturer about to make an important point. "We're building an exact replica of this estate, complete with a golf course designed by Arnold

Palmer, with our own airport, I may add."

"Wow," I said, leafing through the dog-eared brochure, waiting for inspiration of what to say. "This is, uh, fantastic."

Despite his mom's Honda Civic out back, Rama, on this particular day, was flush with cash and pulled a crisp $100 bill from a roll. "Keep the change," he said to Margo, who thanked him for the generous tip with a million-dollar smile and a hand-blown kiss, which almost knocked Rama off his barstool.

There was a time when the hallmark of a successful businessman manifested in extended lunches, commencing with martinis, a couple of bottles of expensive wine with steak, and cognac and Scotch to top it off. Now, those same execs sit at their desks with their iPhones and computers running, wolfing down a sandwich with some bottled water while the restaurants entice customers with cheap specials and cost-effective gimmicks.

Wages are consistent and leases are reflective of overvalued real estate, while food costs and taxes are through the roof. It's tough to make a profit when everybody wants a deal, and even harder to offer consistent quality while maintaining the fine balancing act between barely making it and going broke. Succeeding in the restaurant business depends a lot on return customers and the special patrons who need to be treated not so much as family but as lords and gentry. These people often see themselves as the privileged class, and snobs do patronize French restaurants. Nothing pleases them more than to be treated like the prince or princess of Versailles.

Roy, who treated everybody like nobility, did well by them, whereas Melinda, whose distaste for snobs was palpable in her face and body language, was often spurned and dismissed with a small tip. Margo got away with anything simply due to her gorgeous looks, while Gino was everybody's friend, and Alia everybody's orphan in need of nurturing. As the owner, I had to please everybody, an act which I initially despised but in time perfected. I was able to chat with anyone about everything — generally known as the art of kowtowing.

3

Summertime

It was one of those hot, early summer days when people flock to the beach, hungry for the sun after the long dreary winter and rainy spring. Even Kana stopped for a moment while sweeping the floor and looked longingly out the window at the blue sky.

"Must make you feel just like back home in Sri Lanka," I said awkwardly.

"Is nicer here," she said.

"Really?"

"Better life in Canada, better for my son," she said, continuing to sweep.

It was 50 Percent Discount Wednesday, which always brought in the deal-seekers, as well as the curious, the tight-fisted and the discount cruisers. They would order the main course, no salads or desserts — in other words, no full-price items — and no drinks: "Just water please" or hot water for the tea-baggers. Our servers hated these "bottom feeders," as they left measly or no tips.

"La vida loca," as Sanchez described those Wednesday nights. "Half-price food brings in half-price people," he added with his big, infectious grin.

We served the rich and the poor, the three-piece suits as well as the jeans and T-shirts, tattoos as well as nose rings. We didn't care what they dressed like or where they were from as long as they paid the bill, didn't abuse the staff or the premises, and left a tip, especially when they were getting such a deal. But since the food was discounted, so were the tips. On Wednesdays, the servers made it up in volume, which meant twice the work for the same money. Also they had to give 3 percent of the gross sales to the kitchen staff. That was their bonus. The more we sold, the more they worked, therefore the better the tips. It was our way of trying to have everybody share in the bounty. Not many restaurants do this; some restaurant managers even keep the servers' tips and only hand them out once a week (and always less than expected). Tips are a murky commodity — a lot of it in cash and impossible to control.

Sometimes with tourists or large groups, the servers would include an 18 percent tip on the bill. That was okay if they let the customer know. What we did not want to see, and what happens in many restaurants, is that the waiter conveniently forgets to inform the patrons that the tip is already included in the bill. This is especially easy to do with credit cards. We had one German customer point out to me that not only did nobody tell him that the gratuity was included, they also overcharged him on the wine. Needless to say, Jude, a know-it-all and flamboyant weekend server who had only been with us for a couple of weeks, was looking for another job the next day. I also paid for the customer's meal but took it out of Jude's pay cheque. We couldn't rip anybody off. That was tantamount to high treason in the fickle restaurant world. Word about something like that travels much faster than the fact that we serve real pommes frites.

Summer solstice had arrived, and we were investing our hopes for the season in the elusive patio on the alley side of the bistro. We — that is, Rudy — apparently put the wheels in motion two months before, and we still hadn't heard from anybody, least of all him. We needed this patio, not only because it was a cheap way to add six tables but also because it would make the bistro a lot more attractive, especially during the warm months. We were impatiently waiting, as we had waited for the liquor license and the name, relying once more on Rudy to steer us through the bureaucratic maze of city hall.

I badgered Aldo to call Rudy, and when he finally relented, Rudy's answer was predictable: "It's days away. The permit is practically on my desk, so don't you boys worry."

"Days away from when?" I asked Aldo. "From when we applied? From when we will get it? Or is it just days away from the future?"

The first and fifteenth of the month was everybody's favourite day except mine. Payday! I wrote cheques until my fingers bled. By my last count, we had thirteen people on the payroll. Like a small factory. It was hard to believe. In the kitchen: one chef, one sous-chef, one line cook, one prep cook/dishwasher, one full-time dishwasher, and one cleaning lady/prep cook; up front: one server/manager, three other servers (four before we let Jude go), three bus girls. That didn't include Aldo and me. We were the owners, and we didn't get a pay cheque.

Then I wrote cheques for the monthly lease and the numerous food replacement bills: Cisco, Bosa, various meat suppliers and fishmongers, the bakery. Add to that the Costco and the large liquor store bills. At the end of every month, all the other regular bills were due: utilities, advertisement, insurance, credit card processing, laundry, the OpenTable reservation system, the accountant, the bank charges. On the first of every month, the employee taxes, and once every three months we had to claw 12 percent of our gross sales out of the bank account to pay the much-maligned harmonized sales tax (HST). I wondered a couple of times if all that free beer I got to drink at the end of the day was actually quite expensive.

The temperature in mid-July hit thirty-plus degrees and the masses flocked to the beach. The bistro stood empty and the frites lay limp in their trays, lethargic and pasty like most of the people in these latitudes where the mercury seldom rises to Vegas temperatures. I suggested a cardboard cut-out of a polar bear pointing to the air-conditioned interior of the bistro. How about an ice-cream special for openers, iced coffees, baked Alaska, cool drinks. Even I didn't feel like eating in this heat. If we opened the door, we'd lose the AC, so I put a big sign out front: "Air-

Conditioned Inside!" That brought in a few sweaty customers. What we really needed was that elusive patio, but there was no point calling Rudy again.

And since we had nothing much else to do, we started dickering with the over-ambitious wine list, which dated back to the pre-Olympics time. Hopelessly outdated and cumbersome, the list still reflected Ken's snobby and prejudiced taste, featuring many obscure wines from the Duke.

We now had our own in-house sommelier and self-proclaimed wine connoisseur, Marcel, our new and equally snobby French-Canadian server. What luck for us poor philistines that he was here to help us. We gladly handed Marcel the wine portfolio. He took to it with gusto, armed with highlighter, black Sharpie and several catalogues from other local wine merchants besides the Duke. We wanted a trimmed-down, variety-oriented, modern and sophisticated list, one that reflected our humble establishment, with wines that ordinary people might even recognize.

Slowly but surely we were making progress toward a leaner, more streamlined establishment, one that was relevant for our modern, somewhat less sophisticated customers, who valued price over name recognition.

Summer in Vancouver makes this town the best city in the world. The spectacular view of the North Shore mountains, their two lions against the backdrop of English Bay and the Lions Gate Bridge spanning the harbour entrance from Stanley Park is breathtaking; the miles of public beaches all around the bay up to the University of British Columbia, ending at the famous Wreck Beach, become a never-ending outdoor festival of music, beach volleyball, swimming, sunbathing, boating, windsurfing and family picnics. Summer is the much-anticipated tourist season and all those visitors from around the globe, armed with cameras, sunglasses and floppy hats, were our coveted customers. Cruise ships arrived and departed at regular intervals from Canada Place, catering to thousands of passengers that swarm out over the city, and the popular hop-on hop-off bus tours drove right by our restaurant. That day felt like summer was here to stay.

Aldo and I were poring over accounts, trying to figure out if we had made enough to pay the week's bills when in walked this skinny, small man in a dark suit with a purple tie. His hair was grey and wavy and kind of long, which made his bony head on top of a long neck look small. He purposefully walked over to our table and introduced himself as Mr. Yes.

"Just call me Mr. Yes, since I'm the author and creator of the Yes Campaign." He pointed to a fluorescent green button on his lapel with the word "YES" emblazoned on it.

Aldo rolled his eyes, looking at the scrawny figure over the top of his glasses. Mr. Yes kept on introducing himself, brandishing a binder with newspaper articles and flyers, all apparently lauding the ubiquitous Yes Campaign. We duly congratulated him and nodded in sympathy, which only spurred him on.

"You'll never think or say no again when you join the yes team," he explained. "And you will feel the positive effects on your life immediately. Just say yes. It's that simple."

I couldn't help myself. "Can I poke a burning stick in your eye, steal your money and your girlfriend?"

"Yes, you can!" he immediately answered. "If that makes you feel happy, go right ahead."

Obviously a nutcase, I silently concluded.

Mr. Yes sat down in one of our window seats and instantly engaged Melinda, who had just flown in the back door, half an hour late, her hair flying behind her. She appeared from the staff room with a ponytail, hastily applied makeup, and made her way over to our strange guest. As if on cue, he rolled out his spiel on our young waitress, who was still half asleep. He ordered a bottle of Veuve Clicquot champagne and asked for a filet mignon for lunch. This woke her up.

Mr. Yes wined and dined like an aristocrat and ordered another bottle of champagne. He was feeling no pain. When I walked by his table, he magnanimously invited me to share the next bottle. I politely refused, pointing toward the stack of bills and the time of day. "It's a bit early for me," I said.

"You guys are the best and this is a fantastic restaurant!" he effused, throwing his hands up in an all-inclusive embrace. "I'll invite all of you to my gala opening at the Commodore. Bob Dylan and Tom Hanks will both be there and I want you to meet them."

"Bob and Tom?"

"Oh yeah, they are very much involved in the Yes Campaign." And then he confided in a lower tone, "You'll have to take it easy on Bob — he's not in the best of health."

"Oh really, must be all that smoking and touring."

Then came the coup de grâce of his performance. "Can I pay in advance for a month of — let me see — $100 lunches? Like I give you $3,000 and just come and eat and drink without bothering to pay every time?"

Now Aldo, who was going over bills in the back, pricked up his ears. "Sure you can," he said. "Melinda, can you make out a gift certificate, and every time Mr. Yes has lunch you deduct the amount from the balance until it's gone?"

"You guys are totally awesome!" Mr. Yes gushed.

I had to leave at that point, but not before Mr. Yes wanted to know if I had always been in the restaurant business.

"No, I actually work in the film industry as well, in charge of electrical distribution."

"You have to be kidding, this is unbelievable. I must give Tom a call. You're exactly what he is looking for. Tom absolutely needs you."

"Tom Hanks? I don't think so, but give him my regards."

I left the starry-eyed Melinda in charge of Mr. Yes, feeling a bit uneasy about it all. When I came back later that afternoon Melinda immediately gave me the bad news.

"His credit card denied his $165 lunch bill, which also cancelled the $3,000 gift certificate. He left his bank card and his credit card behind, as well as his campaign folder. I feel so bad; he was such a nice guy and he offered me champagne."

"Shit," I said, my worst suspicions confirmed.

"He promised to come back and clear it all up. He said he was on his way to buy a yacht, which might have tied up his credit card. He was in a hurry," Melinda said, her eyes downcast.

"A yacht?" This was getting even better. What could we do? We couldn't ask the customer during lunch if he had enough money to pay for it. So we had to live with it. Chalk it up to promotional expenses. Maybe make some phone calls about his useless credit cards.

Melinda was all in a tizzy and obviously very upset and close to tears.

"Don't worry, Melinda, these things happen. It's not your fault," I said, but we both knew we were being ripped off, and that never feels right. She should not have been left in charge by herself, but there were no grown-ups around at the time Mr. Yes departed, since both Aldo and I had other things to do. Just the kids left in charge. That's what Aldo always called the staff: "Just a bunch of kids without parental supervision."

A few days later a very excited Melinda ran to meet me when I came in the back door. "He came back and paid!"

"Slow down, girl. Who, what?"

The more exited Melinda got, the worse her accent became. Normally she spoke with perfect diction. "He, I mean Mr. Yes, he come back and pay. He give me $80 in tips."

"Really?" I said. "That's fantastic! Maybe we get to meet Tom and Bob after all."

Unbelievable! Miracles apparently still happened, even in the age of the cynic.

My daughter Jo arrived at the end of July for a summer visit, all the way from Berlin, where she made her living as a writer and part-time English language editor. Her career was like a house of which she was the architect, the builder, and the tenant. Few are the rewards, but her losses and gains, triumphs and defeats are her own. I've always been a passionate armchair supporter of the arts, but it's another kind of advocacy to champion artists in your own family. Since Dad now owned a French restaurant, it was a no-brainer where to go out to eat and drink. We enjoyed dinner together en famille at the bistro at least every second night. Clare joined when she could, and for those few special moments I felt like it was all worth it.

During one such family dinner, the conversation made its way from food to people of the world, and somehow I brought up the superior behaviour of the quintessential archetype of the American asshole when abroad. We all knew the cliché of the cowboy from Texas, belligerently demanding his ketchup and coke in a French restaurant in Paris or a sidewalk café in Florence. We all snickered with superior glee, but Jo took umbrage to this kind of generalization.

"You can't do that, Dad, just lump all Americans into the same pot. They're individuals like everybody else. There are Swiss, Canadian, and German assholes; believe me, some of them are politicians. Just tell me what you mean when you say 'American' like it's a cheap brand name."

"Well done, girl," said Clare, who had known my daughter since she was seven years old. "You're absolutely right, Jo, but I'll tell you a little story to illustrate your dad's point.

"It just happened last week over there, in the hallway by the bar. It had been a busy night and we were sitting with Connie, a good friend of ours, who was in town with an old flame from San Diego. We all sat at the end table close to the washrooms. Gino and Marcel were serving.

"It was late, around 10:00 p.m., and this couple who sat at the front of the restaurant had been enjoying themselves for a couple of hours. It may have been their anniversary or a birthday. The woman, middle-aged and fashionably dressed, was on her way to the bathroom when she sidestepped around a chair, slipped and fell with a thud onto the hard parquet floor. She didn't scream but immediately started lowing like a cow about to calve. We thought the worst — she had broken her back, her hip, at the very least her leg. This was a disaster. I got up and knelt down beside the hysterical woman, who was clutching her left hand with her right one, heaving and hyperventilating. Gino had already called 911. I was able to help her off the floor onto the bench. Her husband meanwhile had joined her, soothing her with his arm around her. The ambulance arrived and the two attendants were eventually able to calm her down enough for her to answer a couple of questions. It looked like she had broken her ring finger, or at least dislocated it. The ambulance drivers offered to drop her off at the hospital and that was that."

"What does this story have to do with Americans?" a confused Jo asked.

"I'm coming to that," Clare said. "The second the woman hit the floor, Dave, Connie's friend, urged me to take a picture of the high-heeled pumps and the floor. 'Make sure you have the date and time function on. Do it,' he insisted with some urgency.

"'I don't have a camera,' I said, perplexed.

"'You have a cellphone, don't you?'

"'Yeah, but the woman is in pain. Excuse me.'

"While I went over to comfort the poor soul, Dave was clicking his iPhone at the floor, the shoes and God knows what else. The rest of us were helping the woman. That's my point."

We all sat nodding in silence.

"That," I said, "is what defines a certain American. No other member of the human race would think 'lawsuit' first and 'help' second. Dave couldn't understand why we looked at him as if he was from Mars, but then again, as far as we know, San Diego is full of Martians."

"What did Connie say?" Jo wanted to know.

"Well, she wasn't too impressed with Dave, I think. They left soon after the incident."

"What about the woman?" Jo asked.

"As a matter of fact, she wrote us a lovely card, thanking us for the care and attention and apologizing for the fuss she created," I said.

"Wow, she was surely a Canadian," Jo conceded, "definitely not a Martian."

"Is that a uniquely Canadian trait? Politeness? Doesn't that smack of generalization?"

"You got me, Dad."

"To assholes and Martians from everywhere, many of them our valued customers," I toasted, and we all raised and clinked our glasses, accompanied by lots of laughter.

It's an old movie cliché that if nothing happens, kick in the door and start shooting from both barrels — that gets everybody's immediate attention. The same is true for restaurants. They need to get the public's attention and, like in a silly western, hype and perception is everything. A busy, bustling restaurant implies popularity and that in turn signifies good food, whereas the empty, quiet restaurant may well serve the better food but nobody knows it. Therefore it is paramount to at least appear to be busy. Look no further than our Wednesday nights. The secret is to create that kind of excitement without giving away the store.

Some restaurants create lineups at the door by simply not opening until a sizable queue has formed, coupled with a no-reservation policy, like Vij's. The ensuing buzz has nothing to do with the quality of the food but everything to do with the hype of a created atmosphere. Of course, at the end of the day the food has to match the hype, otherwise it's over.

Our problem was that a French restaurant does not cater to the mob, nor is it synonymous with frenzied crowds beating down the door to get in. There is a sizable stigma to overcome in a French restaurant. The common perception is still that French food is expensive, exclusive, and out of the common man's league, also snobby, old worldly, and simply too rich. All of these attributes apply to French restaurants. We wanted to be everybody's bistro, but it wasn't easy to project that message. It was working on Wednesday nights, but how to duplicate that energy the rest of the week?

The best strategy is to create a bargain, a gimmick like an irresistible special that draws in the crowds. Either serve up a fantastic deal or create the illusion of one, like Aldo's Italian restaurant, which switched from $7.95 lunch specials to half-price specials. Same thing but different message. It triggers a chemical reaction in the human brain, which instantly translates into motor action and propels bodies through the door into the seats.

In August we hung a big red banner underneath our awning which proclaimed the "Annual BC Salmon Festival!" Sockeye salmon was in season and we featured a salmon pâté, smoked salmon appetizers, a filet of salmon baked in béchamel, a grilled salmon with beurre blanc, and salmon mousse. The tourists loved our BC specialties and flocked in by the droves. It meant that in the late summer months at least we'd break even.

Every chef always wants to add their own touch, their signature dish, their very special sauce, even if it's not on the menu. So when the customer wants his duck breast just like the last time, it doesn't work when this time, instead of a Calvados glaze, it is served with an orange glaze.

Consistency, as the mantra goes, is the secret of every good restaurant. I cannot stress that enough, and I repeated it to the servers, the cooks, and even the chef. But instead of enthusiastic understanding, more often than not I just got a blank look.

In fact, all we really had to deliver was our advertised menu. This doesn't sound that difficult, but apparently it was a challenge, one that surprised me but not Aldo. Come to think of it, nothing much in the restaurant business surprised Aldo.

Changing of the Guards

In the summer our staff changed like extras in a soap opera. The good weather offered very little incentive to work for minimum wage, especially when life seemed cheap and the summer endless. We had to cover fourteen shifts and were down to five servers: Gino, Melinda, Roy, Marcel, and Margo, all of whom wanted the good weekend evening shifts; nobody wanted to do weekday lunches. For bussers, we had our dependable Alia from Latvia, slim and agile, bright blue eyes and short blonde hair in a stylish side-part. Alia was quiet and unassuming, but always working, never idling like some of the others, and alert to what was going on around her. However, she lacked self-esteem and therefore appeared shy. She was never late and never missed shifts. That alone made her invaluable in any restaurant. We elevated her to lunchtime server, which she managed with aplomb. Then there was Alice in Wonderland, whose mind wandered off all day long. She kept missing shifts, calling in at the last minute and pissing off the servers who had to take up the slack when no bussers showed up. I didn't have the heart to fire her; she tried, and everybody liked Alice.

When Selena waltzed in the door and asked for work, I couldn't have turned her down if I wanted to. Long-legged, a regal five-foot-ten without heels; large, doe-like eyes; olive skin, due to her Spanish heritage, which she proudly proclaimed; a full-lipped, wide mouth over a perfect set of pearly whites; and a figure to melt icebergs.

She had an appetite like a tiger and could polish off a platter of fries and a couple of desserts at the end of a shift, unlike the other girls, who preferred salads and low-carb fare. It didn't seem to affect her weight or figure. "I have the metabolism of a race horse," she laughed when I teased her about her voracious appetite.

Wherever Selena walked, all eyes would follow, men and women alike. She was perfectly aware of her alluring presence, and although smart and witty, she could not help but be self-enamoured and vain, which was a very sensitive subject. There was a whole wall of mirrors opposite the kitchen, making the restaurant seem larger and also giving the cooks a view of the front without leaving the kitchen. Whenever Selena walked by the wall of mirrors, her head would automatically swivel and follow her own image, to the detriment of her job. Instead of keeping her eyes peeled for customers' needs, she was continuously distracted by her own reflection and kept bumping into other servers or customers. Because of her stunning presence, she was always forgiven, but behind her back the grumbling and finger-pointing prompted me to intervene.

"Selena, stop looking at yourself, you're just fine. You need to pay attention to what's going on around you."

"I can't help it. Mirrors are my curse. I grew up in front of a mirror from an early age in ballet class, and now that I'm trying out for a modelling career, the mirror is again my nemesis. Mirrors are like a camera lens, did you know that?"

"No, uh, I didn't know that," I said, somehow put in a defensive position.

"Oh yes," Selena pointed out. "Painters always used mirrors to find flaws in their paintings, like perspective or texture. Of course today they use digital cameras, just like a mirror that stores the image."

"Selena, you're a smart girl, but I hired you as an assistant — which includes filling in as a hostess and bussing tables — not as a model or an art critic. Please help me out here," I pleaded.

She rewarded me with a dazzling smile and a coquettish flash of her intense eyes and clapped me on the shoulder like we were old buddies. I couldn't help but like her.

Even Clare saw her potential. "She may not be your best worker, but she sure draws in the boys. And I bet you she can sell a steak to a vegetarian."

The kitchen is an altogether different realm from the front of the restaurant. The two crews dance to separate drummers and "What goes on in the kitchen stays in the kitchen" is the proverbial mantra. There is a never-ending atmosphere of yelling and screaming, "Yes sir, no sir" and "Dessert for five and seven on the double" or "Ready to go on main course on three and twelve," interrupted by bell-ringing, and whenever the printers in the kitchen spit out the orders put in by the servers, they got read out aloud so that everybody was aware of the incoming orders. "I'm going to install a hidden camera in the kitchen and stream it as a live reality-TV drama so all the world can see what goes on in here," I said to the chef when he told me of the latest hirings and firings in the ever-mutating kitchen staff.

"That might be a good idea," David said with a sigh. "The problem is that as soon as they move from the dishwashing pit to the salad and prep side, they think they're cooks, and all cooks think they're chefs."

"And all chefs think they're executive chefs and artists," I said. Then my phone rang. While I answered the call, David gave me a haughty look and disappeared back into the safety of his kitchen.

"It's the same in every kitchen the world over," Aldo explained. "The chef is the general with absolute authority and like every general they report to the government, which in this case is us: you and I. The chef does the hiring and firing of his own staff, or at least he needs to appear thus to his minions. As far as food and menu changes are concerned, he has to listen, consult and inform us. All the other cooks and kitchen staff listen only to the chef. When they step out of line, they create havoc and discord, which can only be reined in by the chef."

"Yeah, as soon as we put Rick, our first sous-chef, on salary, he had his eyes on the chef's job and was ready to usurp the kitchen," I said.

Rick, a recovered addict and alcoholic with the emotional stability of a volcano, was apparently typical of kitchen folk. He was fast and knowledgeable, but totally unpredictable. That day Rick was supposed to be in charge, since it was the chef's day off. He stumbled in the back door after 10:00 a.m., late and already irritable and tired, due to of lack of sleep, I supposed.

"Why are you so tired first thing in the morning?" I made the mistake to ask.

"Because I have too much going on in my head and the chef pisses me off. He makes me do all the work, always goes home early, and I get to clean up the mess." He threw down his headband and banged his fists on the counter in full frustration.

I feared Rick's head was about to explode at any moment, which would leave a nasty mess.

"I can do better for less money and bring in more customers in a shorter time," he stated angrily.

He'd tried to get us, Aldo and me — the government — to fire the chef once before. At that time it had been Ken, the snobby maître d' who'd quit in a huff. The chef stayed on and Rick crept back into his shell for the time being. It lasted until that day, one of the busiest times of the year and the first day of our highly promoted salmon festival.

"Rick, you're late, you bitch like an old woman, and you tell me you're tired first thing in the morning. What am I do?" I asked, getting frustrated myself. I had enough on my plate without being Rick's counsellor.

Rick just looked at me with an unblinking stare, tore off his apron, gathered his knives, and stormed out of the kitchen, down the hallway, and out the door. "I'm out of here!" he yelled.

"Don't come back!" I returned.

Now we were in trouble. I had Kana prepping and washing and Kay working on his desserts and appies, but no chef. I knew Kay had the expertise and experience. "Kay, can you help me out here? We're in trouble. Rick quit."

Kay slowly put down his knife and took a few moments before he turned to me and looked me straight in the eye. "I can make the sauces and prep the salmon, no problem," he said solemnly, and as an afterthought, "I'm glad Rick is gone — he is not a nice man."

I desperately called David and explained the situation, asking him to please cancel his day off and come in.

"What happened? How come Rick quit today of all days?"

"You know how he is. He's tired every day, bitches and complains and keeps up his manic monologue, which gives us all a headache. He packed his knives and clothes and vanished."

"Oh, and that's it?" David said. "I'll kill him if I catch him."

David was not at all pleased to work on his day off.

"As far as I'm concerned we're looking for a new sous-chef," I said. "Meanwhile, Kay is taking over Rick's position for the day."

Folly Bistro

"Just like that," David fumed. "No preliminaries, no warnings, no consults, no talks. Nothing. He just fucks off and leaves us all in a lurch. "

"I'll put an ad on Craigslist right away." I wanted to scream.

We hired two new kitchen staffers. The responses to the ad were not as varied or plentiful as during the winter months, so our choices were somewhat limited. Aldo and the chef conducted the face-to-face interviews and I stayed out of it. I don't think either one of them trusted my instincts in this matter, and they were probably right. I'm not callous enough to sort out human beings, a bit of a flaw in the restaurant business.

They decided on Sidney as the new sous-chef. Sid, as he liked to be called, graduated from the Culinary School in Winnipeg and had held several positions as line cook, caterer and sous-chef in a Belgian restaurant in Brussels. No real way to check that. He arrived to the interview on a bicycle without brakes, fenders, lights, or gears. He was over six feet tall, lean, and self-confident about his abilities. He knew all about peppercorn sauce, Béarnaise and béchamel, knew how to make proper fries and how to plate a good-looking dish.

"When can you start?" I asked.

"I'm ready now," he said.

"You're on. Today is Wednesday, our 50-percent discount night, and you can jump into the deep end of the pool, so to speak," I said.

"Great," he muttered. "I'll just get my shit."

Instead of Rick's manic monologue, Sid muttered and cursed under his breath. You had to ask every question twice, sort of like Tourette's syndrome. It too put everybody else on edge in the very small, confined kitchen. Maybe Sid was nervous because this was his first day.

Kay complained to me at the end of the chaotic night. "This new guy, Sid, is not very nice. He in my way and put meat where I have dessert and he always uses bad language. He no good."

"Settle down, Kay, it's his first night. I'll talk to him. We need him right now. Thanks for helping us out." I knew how much a compliment meant to the sensitive Kay, who was usually quiet and liked to work by himself. Those Wednesday nights taxed him to the maximum, and when Kay was stressed, he always looked like he was about to cry, guarding his fancy desserts with his life against the boorish manners of his co-workers. His sensitivity also made him the butt of some mean jokes. "You are such a girl, Kay," or "You're such a cupcake." Kay bore these taunts like a martyr, outwardly stoic, inwardly suffering.

The other position we filled was a nighttime dishwasher and prep cook. We hired Billy because he was eager to work, full of nervous energy, and didn't care what shifts he was assigned. When I asked him later what made him choose this line of back-breaking employment at his age, he told me that he used to be an accountant for the mob before he had a nervous breakdown.

"Too much pressure, too many sleepless nights, too much drink. This is different and it keeps me out of trouble."

I wasn't sure if he meant the drink or the law. "Are you married?"

He just shook his head and, in his staccato English, said, "Nope, divorced. She got the house, the money, the works." And after a short laugh, "Gotta go to work, boss."

He always called me "boss," which made me feel kind of funny. It was never my ambition to be anybody's boss.

Sid, our new sous-chef, had the exact same ambitions as Rick had. Before a couple of weeks were up, Sid fantasized just like his predecessor that he would be a better, faster, cheaper, and more modern chef for our establishment than the "old-school geezer" who, according to Sid, "doesn't have a clue anymore, is unorganized, temperamental, and basically has done his time."

"He's an old horse ready to be put out to pasture," Meagan overheard him saying to Billy.

Instead of confronting Sid about his ambitions, I went about it the reverse way. As usual, I found Sid out back by himself, smoking frantically. I casually pointed out the chef's positive sides in order to see how Sid responded. Kind of a honey trap.

"I'm basically happy with the chef," I said. "He can serve up to fifty people by himself with only a helper like Billy by his side, his food still comes out consistently good, and his plating is modern and imaginative, don't you think so?"

Sid stared at me like he had just witnessed a killing, butted out his smoke, then lowered his pin head and walked right by me, cursing to himself. "Fucking loser, waste case, stupid restaurant, idiots, everybody . . ." He worked furiously all morning, grumbling, head down, scaring poor Kana.

"He is a devil," Kana said, crossing herself three times to ward off the evil spirit.

During the following Wednesday's hot and steamy shift, the whole place was a chaotic study in confusion to anybody looking in from the outside — people stacked at the bar waiting for a table, more customers in a boisterous line at the door, waiters dancing through the mad throng precariously balancing several plates of food. Selena cleaned and reset tables without any time to check herself in the mirror and Alice for once was forced to focus on her job instead of her fantasy world. The kitchen was the usual cacophony of frenzied mayhem, everyone yelling and cursing in an atmosphere of hellish steam and heat. At some point in the midst of all this bedlam, without a word to anybody, Sid vanished from the kitchen and, as far as we knew, from the planet.

"Maybe he's gone out for a smoke," Billy said, shaking his head. "Crazy fucker."

We never saw Sid again, and as far as I was concerned, he might as well have gone back to hell, where, according to Kana, he spawned from. In fact, I saw her the next morning sprinkling water from a little vessel in all the corners and the staff room.

"Holy water," she said, looking me straight in the eye. I just nodded and said, "Thank you." There is no harm in a bit of superstition, and if it made her more comfortable then the silly ritual was worth it.

On the other hand, we were once again hunting for another sous-chef on Craigslist.

This time we just advertised for line cooks and we found Kyle, a young, passionate man, built like an athlete, recently graduated with honours from the Pacific Institute of Culinary Arts, and incredibly excited to work in a real French restaurant where he could actually apply all the skills he had just acquired. He had great ideas about plating and fusion food, which we had to stifle right away.

"Kyle, we appreciate your creative energy, but we need somebody to cook our menu, listen and learn from the chef, and fit in with the other staff."

"Absolutely," he assured us. "When can I start?"

Our kitchen was a small one and Kyle was a big boy, but we felt he brought the right kind of energy to the place and we were willing to take a chance on him. I warned him about the Wednesday nights, but he seemed okay with that. Of course, he hadn't yet experienced the real thing. It's okay to talk about a battle in theory; it's a whole other ball game to be in the midst of one, fighting in close quarters with no end in sight.

"I love crazy busy. I can cook for a thousand people, " Kyle said, pounding his fist gorilla-like into his chest with great enthusiasm.

Kyle brought along his friend Mac, who was permanently hoarse but displayed exceptional cooking skills. Mac was only to be part-time and fill in as Kyle's sous-chef on the chef's days off. Both Kyle and Mac got on reasonably well with the chef, who liked to be the know-it-all teacher lording over his ignorant pupils. Between the three of them, Aldo and I hoped we might get through the summer. Peace descended onto the kitchen for the next few weeks and we functioned once again like a repaired car after a blown head gasket.

The Wednesday nights kept getting ever more popular and taxed the kitchen to its ultimate limits. One day toward the end of the last couple of orders, overcome by the infernal environment, the chef stumbled out of the steaming hot kitchen like he'd just escaped a battle zone, a glazed, crazed look in his eyes, clasping his hands over his head. "I can't do this anymore," he groaned. "I'm done. I'll either die or kill somebody."

I guided him out the back door for some fresh air and a smoke. Somehow most of our kitchen staff smoked. "What are you talking about?" I asked, trying to console him. "The food came out great, everybody loved it and 150 people had nothing but compliments."

"Oh my God," the chef lamented, "the food was so horrible. It's like working the line at McDonald's. I feel so bad about my food."

Folly Bistro

I suddenly understood a fundamental law of every commercial kitchen: All cooks are chefs-in-waiting and all chefs are sensitive and tormented artists! Like the sculptor or painter who just created their masterpiece and is ready to commit suicide because they can't stand the thought of rejection. Or the actor or singer who just gave their best show ever but beat themselves up and lamented how lousy they were. Prima donnas, all of them, when all we needed were cooks and workers, performers and labourers. We satisfied and inspired our fans (think customers) with aromas, taste and texture, mixed in with some atmosphere, service, and visual presentation. We were in a service industry, not a gallery or concert hall.

Since the heat of the battle was past its peak, I told the chef just to go home. "We can handle it from here on," I said, and to stroke his artist's ego added, "You did a superb job this evening and your food is fabulous and unsurpassed. Thank you."

David's back visibly straightened. His chin levelled out like a big weight had been lifted from his weary shoulders.

"Thank you," he said and walked into the warm summer night, cigarette smoke trailing behind him.

When that epic night was all over, the crew tucked into their well-deserved staff meal like caged animals, devouring everything that was left over. Some mashed potatoes, a few pieces of chicken, the rest of the boeuf bourguignon, and a few baskets of frites. The kitchen looked like somebody had thrown a hand grenade at it. I opened the spigots and brought several jugs of beer to the back while Aldo and I had our drinks at the bar. I told him about the incident with the chef and filled him in on the dysfunctional lives of some of our staff. "They're all either divorced, recovering addicts or on the verge of nervous breakdowns," I pointed out.

"Yeah, but their lives are not our business. We can't control their fucked-up lives. We need to retain a level of sanity in the workplace. Don't ever ask them, 'How are you?'" Aldo said, slapping his hand palm-down on the bar. "Never ask them how they are. Just say 'good day' or 'good morning.' That's all. We don't want to know how they are and we don't want them to talk to us about their fucked-up lives, their weird thoughts, or God forgive, their feelings!"

This wasn't the first time Aldo gave me this speech, but it obviously took some time to percolate into my brain.

"We just want them to do their darn job, work, shut up, and then go back to their miserable, dysfunctional lives. We don't care if they're broke, live in the park or with their mothers. It's not our business to know. Don't encourage them!"

"All my life, I've used the phrase 'how are you' as a casual greeting, not an inquiry into anyone's personal or emotional state," I complained to Clare after I finally got home, long after midnight.

"How are you?" she said groggily and rolled over.

I lay awake, too wired to sleep, asking myself for the umpteenth time what the hell I was doing managing a lunatic asylum when all I wanted to do was run a French restaurant.

I was obviously still struggling uphill on a steep learning curve with no peak in sight. It reminded me of hiking in the Alps: As soon as you crest a hill, there is another valley and another hill right in front of you.

We had the perfect summer. Sunshine all day, every day, and all the bad weather happened elsewhere in the world: drought and excessive heat in Russia, flooding and never-ending rain in Pakistan and the Prairies. But in Vancouver, rich man's weather for all of July and August, right into September.

Whenever we had a slow day in the summer, we blamed the nice weather. In fact, we always blamed the weather. "Everybody is on the beach or at home barbecuing," was a standard explanation, or "It's too hot to eat," which should mean that during days of bad weather the restaurant should be packed. But then the excuse was "The weather is so lousy everybody stays home and watches TV and orders in pizza."

If you can't blame the weather, then it must be the tourists who all went home, the tanking economy, or maybe the phases of the moon. Never the food or the service. Never. We couldn't understand why anybody could turn down our lovely food, our outstanding service or enchanting atmosphere, and what about our bargain-basement prices and free fries?

Folly Bistro

It was a Tuesday morning and I needed to sleep in badly, since I'd gotten home late after a slow Monday night at the bistro. Once again Aldo and I had tried to solve the problem of the over-staffed and under-performing kitchen over several beers at the end of the night. If not the weather, then let's start blaming the people.

"Too many people in the kitchen. When it's slow, then somebody should go home," Aldo said.

"Yeah, I agree, but it's always the salaried people that go home, and the hourly wage earners stay."

"Cons and thieves, all of them, all cooks are fucking rip-off artists."

"Just thinking of themselves and not of the restaurant, and never of us," I said gloomily, staring into my beer.

"Never us," Aldo agreed emphatically.

"One-thirty! Jesus Christ, let's go home."

"Inshallah!" Aldo agreed.

I tried to sneak into the bedroom but in the dark tripped over my sandals in front of the bed. That woke Clare up. She put on her light and leaned on her elbow. She took one look at me and shook her heard. "Rough night?"

"Yeah, Aldo and I went over some figures. They could be better. Everybody is ripping us off."

"I thought you two agreed not to talk business at the end of the day. That's when you're supposed to sing, not talk. Peace and love, not work and money."

At 7:30 a.m. that Tuesday morning — Clare had already left for work — the phone interrupted my fitful sleep.

It was Kana. "There is water everywhere," she said.

I sat up and groaned, stabbing pains just behind my eyes. I tried to focus. "Everywhere?"

"Yes, water coming from the ceiling."

Oh shit, I thought, it must be the goddamned plumbing again. "I'll be right there, Kana."

I immediately called Sunny, our contortionist plumber, who always responded to our calls, even on Sundays. "We've got a leak somewhere in the ceiling. I'm just going there now."

"Meet you there in an hour," Sunny said.

"An hour?"

"I'm in Surrey."

"Oh shit."

I downed a couple of Tylenol with a glass of cold water and jumped on my bike.

We lived about ten walking minutes from the bistro, right by Stanley Park, Vancouver's pristine thousand-acre rainforest on the edge of the city. I often rode my bike to work, along the lagoon and through the back alleys between the multi-storied residential towers, right to the back of the restaurant. It took me all of two minutes. I was not prepared for the downpour that greeted me — it hadn't rained since July.

The instant I walked in the back door I knew this was no job for Sunny. The front of the restaurant was a lake and water was pouring out of the ceiling in three places where the tiles had collapsed. I immediately called Sunny off. I leaped up the stairway beside the restaurant and through an empty office onto the deck over the restaurant, and landed in six inches of standing water. I knew right away what the trouble was. A flat roof with tarred-on sheet roofing, the whole of it covered by a rotting cedar grate, with a drain no bigger than a bathtub that was completely plugged with acorns and leaves from the large oak tree next to the building. As soon as I cleared the drain, the water rushed down the two-inch pipe. This was a commercial building, and it had a roof like a wood shed. Our elusive landlord, Mr. Lee, never spent a dime unless somebody sued him or threatened to withhold money. I immediately called his office and promised two options to his automated voicemail: compensation for the damage in the restaurant or a phone call from our lawyer about the loss of business and his responsibility as our landlord.

I also called Aldo, who sounded as hungover as I was, but he promised to join us. Kana, who worked weekdays from 8:00 a.m. until 4:00 p.m., the only normal working hours of anybody at the bistro, had already cleared the tables and chairs out of the way and was methodically mopping the floor while I clambered around with the ladder, removing soggy ceiling tiles and placing strategic buckets and pans. This was the first rainfall in a long time and a taste of what was to come: the dreaded rainy season. We cleaned for the next three hours. Luckily, we had some spare ceiling tiles, and by 11:00 a.m. the restaurant was back to normal — we opened the doors for business as if nothing had happened.

Kana was the only clever (and sober) one of the three of us, and she took an explicit video of the whole disaster with her smartphone. She kept surprising me. Here she was, all five feet of her, in her white smock with her big hair bundled into a hairnet, quietly working and at the same time savvy as a teenager with her iPhone. When I complimented her, she gave me a big white smile. "I learned from my son."

We emailed her iPhone movie to the landlord and within two days, like magic, a crew appeared on the roof, cleaning up the debris, removing the rotten wood, and installing proper drains. A perfect example of the power of social media — which brings me to the next phase of bistro evolution.

Clare and I were having a leisurely Sunday breakfast, a luxury in those days and the only time that resembled a normal life. Clare sat back with a sigh and said, "It's so peaceful and quiet. I do enjoy our Sunday mornings," and just on cue, my phone rang. This electronic appendage, the bane of modern urban existence, never sleeps and is always vigilant, unlike myself.

Billy, our spastic prep cook, was on the line and sounded somewhat panicky; but then again, that was his nature: jerky movements, impulsive behaviour, always looking over his shoulder like he was being followed. But at the same time, alert and dependable. "I'm at the back of the restaurant and it's locked. I need to get in. Where is everybody?"

"Exactly," I said. "Where is everybody? I'll be right there."

Clare looked at me with a mixture of sadness and annoyance, but there was nothing I could do. Duty called. The clock said 11:00 a.m. and we were supposed to be open for service in half an hour. Where the hell was the chef, and for that matter, the servers?

I called Melinda, our Quebecois waitress who always ran in as if chased by a pack of wolves.

Changing of the Guards

"I'm en route, but merde, the bus is always late on Sunday."

It's you, not the darn bus! Why don't you get up earlier? Don't gimme this shit about the late bus, I wanted to scream. I was already on my bike, pedalling furiously past couples holding hands and sauntering into Stanley Park, wondering who that idiot on the bike with his hair on fire was. I avoided the main street and took the shortcut through the alley, past the Dumpsters and illegally parked cars, and arrived two minutes later, totally keyed up and in no mood for small talk.

I let in Billy, who immediately started banging around pots and utensils in the kitchen while I quickly gave the floor a sweep, which should have been done the previous night. I made a mental note to fix that, among some other things that I had on my mind — like the fact that nobody seemed to give a flying fuck about the business. I was ready to rip some heads off and break some limbs.

I looked into the kitchen and it was obvious that Billy didn't have a clue what to do. It was like he was sitting in the car but there was no driver at the wheel.

"Where the fuck is Kyle?" I asked. I called Kyle's cellphone but there was no answer. I called Kay and he picked up. I begged him to come in and help us out.

Kay had graduated from the Le Cordon Bleu Culinary Arts School in San Francisco, one of the most revered cooking schools in North America. I knew he could do the job by himself, but all he wanted to make were his pretty desserts and the flowery salads.

Finally, he agreed to help out. Luckily he lived just around the corner. At least we could serve steaks and salads. But as it turned out, the lunch crowd didn't materialize — too nice a day? And nobody noticed the difference in our kitchen.

As I found out later, the chef had given everybody the day off and had forgotten to come in himself.

"How the hell could you do this?" I confronted him the next day. "Where the hell is your head at?"

He shrugged and apologized lamely, but I could tell that his heart wasn't in it anymore. He had indicated several times in the past few weeks that he wouldn't be upset if we decided to let him go. He hated Wednesdays with a passion, and being generally unhappy, he ended up yelling at his crew, which only furthered an air of discontent. Aldo and I asked him out for a coffee at the Starbucks next door. I think he knew what was coming. We thanked him for his time and parted without any hard feelings, both mutually glad that it was over.

"I'm so happy that I don't have to make any soup today," David said on his way out the door.

Despite the ups and down, I'd miss him and especially his superb food.

Just around that time we had an unexpected visit from Rudy, our buoyant marionette master. When I saw him, I got all excited. "Any news on the patio?" I asked eagerly.

"It's better than that," Rudy replied, brushing the patio issue aside like it didn't matter any longer. "Is Aldo around?"

"I can call him. What's this about?"

"I'd rather wait for both of you, otherwise I have to tell the story twice. Meanwhile, I'll order some dinner and maybe a bottle of Château Rousselle."

Aldo walked in about an hour later, after promising to be there in ten minutes.

"Ten Aldo minutes," I explained to Rudy, who had meanwhile finished his filet mignon and three-quarters of the bottle of wine.

"Boys" — he always addressed us as "boys," like he was our scout leader — "I have some people who are interested in purchasing the bistro."

Rudy savoured our stunned silence. He smacked his lips and raised an eyebrow inquiringly while dabbing his moustache with the napkin.

Aldo and I looked at each other for a heartbeat and then blurted out in unison, "How much?"

"Not so fast, boys, not so fast. First I need to know if you're willing to sell, then my clients will want to have a thorough look at the premises and the books, and then we'll talk price. How about I bring them in on a weekday morning?"

"Okay, we'll need to pretend they're building inspectors or sent by the landlord or some such ruse. We don't want any rumours to start among the staff. We don't trust anybody with information like this, except maybe Kana."

"No worries, boys. I'm an architect and my companions will be an engineer and a draftsman, working for the landlord."

I told Clare about the surprise offer from Rudy. She was rather sceptical. "Rudy," she said, "reminds me of the wind. It blusters and blows, but you can't touch it, hold it or save it. When it's done blowing, it vanishes."

"You're wiser than a tree full of owls," I said, "but this could be good news."

Chefs or Cons

All sous-chefs — and Kyle was no exception — secretly covet the chef's job. They all want to be the big cheese and in charge; they all think they can do the job cheaper, faster and better. When we informed Kyle of David's sudden departure the previous day and asked him to take over — for now — he immediately grew a couple of inches taller, his chest puffed, and his hair seemed to stand straight up. "Absolutely, I know how to cook everything, and I have some great ideas of how to improve the menu," he said right after we offered him the position.

"There will be time for some creativity, but our most pressing concern is consistency," I said, reiterating our creed. "Our customers expect their food to be the same as the last time they were here. Keep that in mind. But you do have our full support. You also have to take charge of the ordering, scheduling and stock-keeping, as well as making a proper sanitary log because we never know when Stewy will drop by for one of his phantom visits. The kitchen needs to be cleaned at the end of the night, not on the morning after."

Kyle would have agreed to stand on his head and bark like a dog, he was so keen on the job. Mac, his sidekick, was elevated to sous-chef, and the two of them knew another one of their cronies who would take Mac's job as garde manger and prep cook. It looked like we now had a young, dynamic team of cooks with large ambitions for our humble restaurant.

The bistro was about to turn another corner and reinvent itself as new and fresh, young and vigorous, dynamic and innovative. Kyle, our newly minted chef, talked a big talk and promised miracles and magic, fireworks and nothing but a sea of ecstatic customers banging down the door to taste his fabulous creations. No modesty, no pragmatic "Let's get things under control and go from there." Oh no, sir, the jack was out of the box and full speed ahead, and damned be the petty concerns about ordering and fiscal prudence.

"Just leave it to me and I'll turn this barn into a first-class joint in no time," he proclaimed with grandiose exuberance. I suspected he was already fortified with a couple of shots from the kitchen brandy. He didn't seem like the same guy who had been sous-chef for the past couple of months, the guy who was more interested in time off than work. I just hoped the chance of being chef for an iconic French restaurant didn't cause an egocentric boil in his brain to burst.

When I told Clare about Kyle and his new-found exuberance, the fact that he was bringing in his buddies to work under him, and his ambitions to create legendary menu items envisioned inside his swollen head, it didn't bode well in her view. "It's a recipe for potential disaster. Too much testosterone, adrenaline and endorphins floating around that kitchen. You and Aldo have to keep a close eye on those boys." Clare made it sound like we were brewing a volatile cauldron of unstable soup. It could go either way: explode or surprise everyone with its wonderful flavours.

The first week seemed to prove all our fears unfounded and made me feel like a crusty old conservative with no stomach for risk or innovation, the antithesis of what I liked to think of myself as. Kyle and his buddies pulled out all the stops, worked day and night and cooked some fabulous specials which resonated with the clientele and brought in the customers by simple word of mouth. A lot of them, as it turned out, were friends of our new kitchen crew, who were given incentive bonuses like free drinks and desserts — "Compliments of the chef," as Gino told me warily.

The first Wednesday night turned into the usual chaotic frenzy, with the kitchen staff in high gear churning out the meals, Kyle on the hotline yelling and commandeering like a pirate captain, Mac hoarsely repeating the orders to Kay, who was still protecting his little space for desserts and pretty appies like a mother hen her chicks, while Billy worked the steamy dish pit like a fiendish devil. I took one look into this netherworld and concluded that only crazies or druggies, freaks or fairies could work in that kind of environment. I wasn't far off.

Gino, Roy and Melinda worked the front (Margo, our Czech beauty, refused to work Wednesdays, as did our snobby sommelier, Marcel), while Selena, Alia and Alice bussed. I worked the door and reservations, and Aldo usually stayed away from the fight nights altogether. Sanchez, our actor/barkeep, entertained the people at the bar waiting for tables, while I tried to keep the people at the door in place by offering them half a glass of house wine. The servers tried to turn the tables over as fast as possible, but that all depended on how fast the food came out of the kitchen. Everybody was yelling, laughing, and talking loudly, the French music from my iPod mixed in with the noise to create not so much a symphony as a cacophony. Amazing what a half-price steak and free pommes frites can unleash. We got through that first Wednesday with the new kitchen crew with our sanity intact but our bodies wrung out.

Kyle thought that the whole night was just great. "It was like war in there, man. I felt like I was in the midst of a battle and I couldn't feel any pain, even when I burned my arm pulling a tray of chicken out of the oven." For proof, he proudly displayed his bandaged forearm. His eyes were shining like marbles and his voice was almost as hoarse as Mac's.

I had my reservations about Kyle's mental equilibrium. "He'll be fine, he's young and strong," said Aldo, allaying my fears. All in all, we were happy with the cash infusion, which is what Wednesday nights were all about in the first place.

During the following week, I observed with trepidation as the coolers and freezers filled up with exotic foie gras and sweetmeats, black truffle mushrooms imported from France, specialty wild duck breast, bison stew and caribou steaks. It looked like we were stocking up for the royal wedding banquet, and the daily menu morphed into a feast for an emperor's coronation. Wild boar with manuka honey glaze imported from New Zealand, bison ribs basted in chocolate, caribou steak with a lovely truffle sauce, pâté de foie gras and sweetmeats in plum sauce for appetizers. The restaurant had never seen the like, and some of our eclectic customers were suitably impressed.

Our concerns about the prohibitive costs and unsustainability of such a hallowed offering of exotic foods were summarily dismissed by our new chef. A wild, exotic and aromatic wind blew through the bistro, which culminated at the end of the shifts in glorious staff meals. Steak, chicken, duck breast and boeuf bourguignon, along with fries and salad and apparently unlimited free beer for all. When Aldo walked in at the end of the day and saw the staff chowing down and swilling our beer, he asked me if this was some kind of birthday party.

I just shook my head in dismay. "Uh, the chef is offering the leftovers for staff meals."

Aldo took one look and then took me by the arm and pulled me around the corner. "This looks more like a banquet than a staff meal, " he said, chewing his lower lip.

I agreed completely. It looked like we had dropped the reins and the horses were running wild at full gallop — where to was anybody's guess.

"We need to put a stop to this," Aldo said. "It's not sustainable."

"I know, but maybe he's just trying to impress the staff. He's only been in charge a few days."

"We need to get this under control before it's too late," Aldo insisted.

"I'll try and find a moment to talk to Kyle," I promised, already dreading the task.

As on every Monday morning, I was sorting the previous week's bills in one of the alcoves near the front when I saw something flashing by in the corner of my eye. I looked up and there was Selena crossing the road in a bright red dress, her black mane flying behind her, oblivious to her effect on the early morning traffic, which resulted in squealing tires and honking horns. She blew in the front door, hardly able to contain her excitement. "I'm going to audition for a spot on the Versace team," she blurted out.

"Wow, does that mean you're leaving us?" I asked warily, already composing another Craigslist ad in my head.

"Oh no," she laughed. "I could do both."

"Selena, I doubt if any Versace model would want to work as a minimum-wage busser." It was my turn to laugh.

She gave me a long-lashed sideways look. "You're right, but I'm just auditioning."

"Good luck," I said, genuinely wishing her the best. I knew it was a long shot, but I kept that to myself, not wanting to spoil her day. As for the low-cut, tight-fitting red dress, I wasn't so sure if she should wear that to work at the bistro. Accidents would be inevitable.

"I'll change into my black funeral outfit in a minute," she laughed. "You're just like my dad." She glided toward the staff room, past the mirrors, in full narcissistic mode, causing havoc among the kitchen staff. Kyle almost dropped his soup ladle and Billy just stood there mute, jaw hanging to the floor.

Rudy had his tour that morning with the two prospective buyers, introduced as a draftsman and engineer, fooling not even Kana with their identical tight black shirts, studded belts, and fashionably unshaven mugs — one with stiff rooster hair, the other bald and sporting a large black loop in one of his ears.

"I'll get back to you boys later in the day," Rudy promised on his way out. Of course we didn't hear from him until two days later when he dropped in at 9:00 p.m., having had dinner and a few drinks elsewhere.

"Sorry boys, I got tied up and these guys had to talk to their people. You know how it is."

I didn't, but said, "Sit down, Rudy. What's the scoop?"

"It looks like this place needs a lot of work. The storage space is inadequate, the kitchen too small, the lighting old-fashioned."

"Rudy, they're buying the location, the space comes as is. If they want to change things and renovate, that's surely their prerogative," I said impatiently.

"Well, boys, here it is." He tore off a corner from the bistro paper covering the table and wrote down a figure, which he let us look at like it was the ace of trumps.

We both stared transfixed at the number and then, in perfect synchronicity, looked up at Rudy and said with one voice, "Is that all?"

Rudy crumpled up the piece of paper. "Look here now, boys. This is a fair offer and you need to let me know if you can work with it, or give me a counter-offer and I'll take it back and see what they say. That's how this works. Don't shoot the messenger."

Aldo and I excused ourselves for a minute and went out back. We chewed over the numbers. We felt that we could up the offer by 10 percent and still be in the ballpark, meaning we'd at least recoup our investments.

Rudy looked sceptical at the number we wrote down on a business card, but promised to get back to us "asap." Two weeks went by and still no answer from Rudy, who could not be reached by phone or email. Unlike Clare, I still hadn't figured out the elusive Rudy and his warped sense of time, which was worse than Aldo's. I always felt like I was the one waiting. Did I have the only working inner clock or was I seriously out of sync? Being Swiss, I was born on time, never missed a train or slept in, wore a wristwatch to bed, was always early, and yes, always waiting for the rest of the world to be on time. Was that so unreasonable?

Clare had been planning for a long time to visit the Provence region in France, ever since she read Peter Mayle's *A Year in Provence*. The fact that I owned a French restaurant was the perfect excuse to finally fulfill her wish.

"We can write the trip off as research for the bistro," she pointed out brightly. "We'll spend a few days in Paris seeing the sights and then take the train to Avignon. We'll eat at French bistros and take lots of pictures of menus and décors. No worries, we'll figure out a way to pay for it."

The night before we left for Europe, I stayed behind after the service was over and waited to close up. Aldo joined me for a drink, as well as Gino and Alia, who were the only level-headed staffers besides Kana in our small organization. We sat at the front, trying to ignore the noise coming from the back of the restaurant. We could see in the large mirror what was going on. All three of our new young cooks, as well as what appeared to be their girlfriends, and Selena and Alice, were having a rocking party. Steak and frites, large bowls of salad, pitchers of beer with the music turned way up, booming out angry hip-hop.

"They do this every night," Alia said, and Aldo looked at me disapprovingly over the top of his glasses.

"No, I haven't talked to Kyle yet," I confessed. "I thought it was just that one time. I didn't know that this was the norm every night." I felt like I was in a bad movie; all that was missing were the strippers and a couple of Harleys driving through the front door. It was a disturbing sight, but I didn't want to admonish everybody like a school principal the night before I was about to leave. I looked at Aldo, who avoided my eyes like he didn't want to own up to the fact that we'd made a colossal mistake by hiring these punks. I had no choice but to leave the whole mess in his hands for the next two weeks, and he wasn't happy about that.

"C'est la vie," I said, and Aldo replied with "Inshallah."

Our trip to France was exhilarating, distancing and refreshing — a time out for sure. When I walked out of the bistro, I had a moment of disconnect. For two weeks I didn't have to think about schedules, bills and staffing, the rain or the lack of customers or money. In fact, I felt inspired by the lovely bistros in Avignon, with their informal blackboard menus, casual atmosphere and polite servers offering simple but excellent food. Did I mention the wine? We were on the other side of the river Rhône from the Pope's vineyards, Châteauneuf-du-Pape, which gets its name from a ruined medieval castle looking down on the village of the same name. It was built in the fourteenth century for Pope Jean XXII, the second of the popes who resided in Avignon.

Our favourite bistro we chanced upon while sauntering through the cobblestoned streets inside the walled medieval city. We stepped through the arched door onto wide wooden floor planks; the walls were rough stone, the beamed ceilings high and dark. The cozy yet cave-like space was illuminated by clear, incandescent bulbs dangling on cords from the rough-hewn beams over rickety wooden tables and chairs, all different vintages and sizes; candles dripped over old wine bottles; a simple menu was written on a blackboard behind a stand-up bar with a brass foot rail much like ours. We ordered the specialty of the house, charcuterie (cold cuts, sausage and local cheeses), served on a wooden board with a basket of large slabs of brown country bread and a carafe of the vin de la maison. There was no canned music, just the chatter, clatter and laughter of the customers. So basic and yet so satisfying.

"You need to add charcuterie to your menu," Clare said, "and this wine is just so magnifique!"

Of course, we were right in the midst of some of the world's best wine country and surrounded by a people steeped in food and wine culture. Which meant that everybody could drink and eat anywhere. On a park bench, at the beach or sitting on the curb in front of the gendarmerie.

(Eventually, I did add a charcuterie plate to our menu, and it turned out to be one of our most popular dishes. Many customers came in just for charcuterie and a glass of wine, often late in the evening, after a show or a concert.)

A couple of days and a few time zones later, when I stepped back into Le Bistro, I had a fleeting feeling that it was the wrong restaurant. I didn't know anybody in the kitchen except Kana, who gave me a doleful look but said nothing. I didn't know how to deal with that. I called Aldo, who was surprised that I was already at the bistro. He promised to meet me in five Aldo minutes, which could mean anywhere from now up to a half an hour. He sounded nervous. I made myself a cup of coffee and looked at the computer records of the past two weeks. They were rather disappointing. I longed to be back in the Luberon, sipping some lovely Loire wine on a patio looking out over lavender fields in the valley and the cascading, colourful stone houses grafted onto the hilly countryside, surrounded by vineyards and fruit trees. Reality has a way of erasing any kind of fantasy, and I steeled myself for the news I was about to receive.

Half an hour later, Aldo flew in through the front door and motioned for me to follow him next door to Starbucks, out of earshot of the strangers in our kitchen.

"Two things you should know," he said, chewing his lower lip. Not a good indicator. "First off, the deal with Rudy and his punks is off."

"What? No counter-offer? Nothing?"

"Nothing. Apparently the space is too small for them and there would be too much renovating to do. It's over."

My heart sank. Deep down I had hoped that this deal would go through and relieve us of the bistro, which at the time seemed more like a burden than an asset. I knew Clare had thought all along that anything from Rudy lacked substance, like the wind, or a fart for that matter.

"I'm sure the deal would have gone sour even if we had accepted the initial offer," Aldo said, shrugging it off.

"What's the second surprise, Aldo?" I asked suspiciously. "And who are all these new people in the kitchen?"

"I didn't think it would have done any good to inform you by email of the emergency changes that I had to enact within days of your departure," he said.

"Go on," I prompted warily.

It turned out that while Clare and I were eating and drinking our way through the bistros and sumptuous street food from Paris to Avignon, through Provence and the Luberon, all hell was breaking loose at the bistro. The young gun had failed miserably and almost snapped the bistro's back.

"When I asked Kyle," Aldo continued, "to look at some numbers and menu plans, he just sneered at me like I was in his way. 'I'm the chef and you hired me to take charge and that's what we're doing. You best stay out of the way and let us handle the food and menu.' When I demanded a proper schedule and bitched about the excessive staff parties at the end of each shift, Kyle told me to fuck off. Can you believe it? 'Fuck off!' he said right to my face, with Mac and his other crony standing right behind him. I told them right there and then who the boss was and all three of them, the cocky, punk chef and his two cohorts, stood up and threatened to walk out if they didn't get 'autonomy' and 'creative freedom.' The gall! Fucking wannabe artists. I didn't hesitate one second: 'Do me a favour and get the hell out of here!'"

"You fired them?" I was aghast.

"Yep. The food ordering was out of control and Kyle's inflated ego exploded all over everything — me, the front staff, even a few wide-eyed customers were told what a bunch of losers we were. They picked up their knives and left within the hour. Firing was easy, my friend, but then we had a kitchen with no cooks. I put on an apron and made some phone calls. My old chef had a pal who was in between jobs and the two of us, with the help of Billy, Kay and Kana, managed to put food out for the next couple of days."

"You were the chef?"

"I had no choice."

Chefs or Cons

I couldn't believe it. What a time to take a holiday.

Aldo immediately advertised on Craigslist and had a dozen resumés on the table the very next day. "I hired Yussuf, new in town from Montreal, who had this incredible resumé, showed up within the hour, and jumped in with both feet that afternoon. I also hired Colin as sous-chef, a young and eager local kid with top marks from the Pacific Institute of Culinary Arts and a couple of years' experience as line cook at another French restaurant. Also, I hired his buddy Chase, an Aussie cook here on a work visa who is sharing the garde manger station with Kay and Billy, and we just kept on going. Within two days, we had a new crew, pretty much what you see now."

The whole idea of putting those twenty-something cooks in charge had turned out to be a real bad case of misjudgement, and by "bad" I mean costly. When the bills came in for our experiment in kitchen autonomy, Aldo and I had to dig deep to cover the shortfall. This was the first time I felt like we were drowning, floundering in a rudderless ship, heading for uncharted waters with only sharks, reefs and pirates for company.

I was stunned but also a bit mystified that all of this happened in my untimely absence. At the same time, I was relieved that we still had Billy, the ex-mob accountant, and Kana, our trusty Sri Lankan cleaning lady and prep cook, as well as Kay, the Taiwanese dessert artist, to give our kitchen at least a semblance of stability and continuity. Once again, within a matter of weeks, we had a brand new general in charge of the kitchen, with a young lieutenant and some old foot soldiers, hopefully ready to forge a lasting peace rather than charge into battle to conquer new territory. We were desperately in need of some stability, sensibility and good old-fashioned common sense.

Yussuf, our new chef, a displaced Egyptian-Sicilian Canadian with a perfectly egg-shaped, hairless head, commandeered a different galley than the one Aldo disbanded a couple of weeks before. Like Napoleon or Putin, Yussuf was a leader of small stature but large ego, a five-foot hulk with an appetite for power. I could feel the difference in the restaurant, which settled into a more

Folly Bistro

austere and disciplined mode. The only yelling came from Yussuf, while everyone else kept their heads down and did their jobs. We reiterated to everybody one more time our creed, that we were indeed a French bistro, not a culinary adventure into unaffordable fantasyland, and that consistency was the mother of success.

Below is the bistro's dinner menu that we expected Yussuf to cook. He did so with gusto for the first little while, until the thin, hot air in the kitchen also affected his brain in a peculiarly self-destructive way. We started to see odd spicing and combinations, like olives in the mussels, or figs in the salad.

"You're going Mediterranean on us, Yussuf," I said.

"No worries, just adding a little life to the boring dishes."

"But we're a French restaurant, Yussuf. No room for figs and dates."

Yussuf didn't know the meaning of backing down or acquiescing to another point of view. "After Christmas we'll create a new and exciting menu, you'll see. Vancouver has never seen anything like it. It will bring in the crowds from far and wide, I promise."

"Just stick to the menu, please. You know how it works. Consistency in the food, frugality in the ordering, artistry in the plating. Customers expect the same dish to taste the same, look the same and cost the same as the last time."

DINNER MENU

Les Salades et les Soupes

Salade mimosa 6
Butter lettuce and grated egg with vinaigrette

Salade mesclun 8
*Organic greens, Beaujolais-poached pears,
pecans, and Roquefort with cider vinaigrette*

Salade de chèvre au betteraves 8
*Hazelnut-crusted goat cheese and honey beets on mesclun greens
with vinaigrette de noix*

Salade frisée 8
Smoked bacon and quail's egg with Dijon vinaigrette

*

Potage du jour 6

Gratin Lyonnais 9
French onion soup with Gruyère cheese

Bisque d'homard 9
Lobster bisque with crème fraîche

Les Hors d'Oeuvre

Pâté de campagne 9
Chef's country pâté with red onion marmalade

Escargots bourguignon 9
Six in the shell

Moules provençales 9
Mussels in white wine, garlic, shallots, tomato, herbs

Crevettes au beurre a l'ail 9
Sautéed garlic prawns

Saumon fumé 9
BC smoked salmon with lemon confit on greens

Assiette de charcuterie 12 / 22
Muskox bresaola, wild game chorizo, pâté de campagne
Wild game terrine, duck rillettes, chèvre, brie

Steak tartare 15

Les Plats Principaux
Served with daily market vegetables

Steak frites 24
Steak au poivre et pommes frites

Filet mignon 29
Choice of sauce béarnaise, poivre, or champignons

Magret de canard 26
Duck breast with glazed apples and Calvados
with garlic truffle pommes purée

Poulet de Paris 19
Roast chicken with peppercorn sauce and garlic truffle pommes purée

Bourguignon d'agneau 19
Braised lamb in red wine sauce with saffron risotto

Bouillabaise Marseillaise 22
Fresh local seafood, simmered in saffron, fennel, and tomato broth

Coquilles St. Jacques 24
Classic-style scallops on the half shell, gratinée

Saumon pacifique 22
BC Salmon grilled with sauce béarnaise and saffron risotto

Mélodie forestière 18
Chef's vegetarian creation

Sides
Each 3

Légumes du jour
Ratatouille
Garlic truffle pommes purée
Risotto
Sautéed mushrooms
Additional pommes frites

Bon Appétit!

We were proud of our food, which was reflected in our customers' compliments. Our prices were reasonable and maybe too low for the kind of fare we served, which was all cooked from fresh and raw ingredients, our sauces as well as our desserts. Clare and I became spoiled by our lovely food, and we had to watch ourselves to avoid becoming food snobs.

"We'll never be able to eat anywhere else," Clare said one evening, savouring her gratin Lyonnais and mimosa salad, "unless of course you learn to cook like this."

"Are you ready for the bill, madam?" I asked. "Will it be Visa or cash? Oh, pardon me, I forgot — you're the wife of the owner. In that case, an extra glass of wine is in order." Needless to say, the tip was phenomenal.

It took little convincing to bring all our friends to the bistro, locals as well as those who passed through town, not just because they got the special friendship treatment but because our food was simply delicious. We were also situated centrally in the West End, the heart of the city, steps from Stanley Park, Coal Harbour, and the beach at English Bay, at the foot of the best shopping street in Vancouver. It helped that the bistro had been in this location for the past thirty years.

Despite some recent setbacks, I had every intention of continuing the tradition of serving fine food in a relaxing atmosphere, an oasis where everybody could suspend their mundane lives for a couple of hours. As for me, my work and all related worries and troubles seemed to be par for the course. As the saying goes, no pain, no gain.

At the beginning of November Yussuf had been absent for four days, sick, which worried me. I had hurt my knee over the weekend playing soccer, and on the day he returned to work, apparently fully restored to health, he wanted to know about my gimpy knee. As soon as I mentioned soccer, he veered off on a tangent and proclaimed with absolute certainty that the Egyptian national team was the best in the world.

"The world," I said somewhat taken aback. "What about Spain or Argentina?"

"Well maybe not the world, but definitely Africa."

"You mean better than the Ivory Coast, better than Nigeria and South Africa?"

Yussuf gave me a withering look and didn't answer. "We're playing the Dutch next and I already feel sorry for them. It's going to be a slaughter."

I just sat there trying to digest this. I actually hadn't even been aware that Egypt had a competitive squad.

"Five of my closest relatives play international soccer," Yussuf said with his usual air of superiority. "One of my cousins plays for Manchester City. His name is Assan."

I was impressed. "Wow," I said, "that's the big league."

"Yeah, he signed for 1.8 million quid and ever since then he's not answering my calls."

"Well, he's a minor deity now."

"The punk isn't picking up the fucking call from his uncle, the guy who taught him everything."

I didn't know what to say.

"You know why I was sick the past few days?"

"What happened?" I had been wondering how he could get sick for four days when I don't remember being sick on the job, ever. Even now that I'd torn my ACL, I still showed up for work.

"Well, after Wednesday night, which was super busy, I was hot and sweating, and I just came outside at the end of the rush and stood in the rain for about five minutes, cooling down."

This kind of behaviour would never occur to a northerner, I thought. Typical hot-blooded southerner.

"The next day, I was sick with fever and I stayed in bed for thirty-six hours without waking up."

"Unbelievable," I said. "Thirty-six hours? Wow, that's like a day and a half."

"Yep. When I woke up, I found out I'd missed a whole day, all twenty-four hours of it."

"Holy chromoly," I said. "And your wife just let you sleep?"

"She thought I was dead. If I wouldn't have been breathing, I would have been buried by now."

I let that one go. "Well, I hope you're feeling better. You know you've been missed. We have the Christmas parties starting and we need to do a lot of planning for the upcoming season."

"I'm 100 percent ready to rock." Without another word, he disappeared into the kitchen, yelling at his cooks to pull up their socks and work harder.

I have to admit, I kind of liked Yussuf, but he took some getting used to, and everything he said needed to be taken with a grain — no, a bucketful — of salt.

The food that started coming out of Yussuf's kitchen looked different — not so much French, more like fusion food. Flamboyant dishes as daily specials, like lamb shank on a bed of gnocchi in a ring of red cabbage infused with raisins. Outrageous dishes to match his personality. Yussuf would throw up his hands in despair whenever anybody dared to criticize his fabulous food, or even comment in a slightly disapproving way.

"I'm an executive chef and a master pastry maker," he proclaimed when I challenged him on his recent creations, desserts that weren't even on the menu.

"These pastries look like they come from a Sicilian bakery," I said. Heavy chocolate cylinders encased in a wholesome granola crust and coarse, overflowing, chunky apple tarts — not exactly the fine French patisseries we needed to be serving.

Yussuf looked at me with disdain and disgust. "Fucking snobs," I heard him murmur. He picked up his hippy pastries and vanished into the sanctuary of his kitchen.

Instead of addressing our concerns, Yussuf changed tactics and fell into an instant, deep depression, moaning about his stunted creativity and utter loneliness due to his misunderstood genius.

"Just let Kay make our three standard desserts, please," I insisted. Chocolate mousse, fluffy and creamy, not stiff and dark; crème brûlée with vanilla and a thin, delicately burned sugar crust; and the most challenging item, the lemon tart, which was still being sorted out almost two months into Yussuf's tenure. He wouldn't let Kay make it his way, although that was the proper way.

Kay felt very unhappy about Yussuf strutting his weight around the small kitchen. "He is treating me like a dog, and I cannot make delicate desserts when he yells at me. He is not a patisserie chef like I am. I feel very bad about his desserts."

Kay's sensibilities were being stretched, as was my patience. Part of the problem with Kay's pastries was that Yussuf knew his knowledge of fine desserts was inferior to Kay's, and he would have loved to fire him. I told Kay to ignore Yussuf and make his desserts like he always did, to near perfection.

One day, the chef took one look at Kay's tantalizing lemon tarts, grabbed the plate out of his hand, and smashed it on the floor. "Clean it up!" he yelled. "And never disobey me again!"

Well, that pretty well did it. Kay collected his personal belongings and left out the back door, tears streaming down his face. He had never been so humiliated, and it broke his delicate spirit.

I was at the back sorting bills when Kay hurried past me out the back door, audibly sobbing. Kana, the only trustworthy person in that kitchen, came out to the hallway, visibly upset, which was unusual for her, being so used to the Wild West kitchen environment.

"What's going on, Kana?"

"Chef smashed Kay's dessert," she said matter-of-factly. "Kay is very upset."

I immediately confronted Yussuf. "What the hell is going on?" I pointed at the smashed dish and splattered lemon tart on the floor.

"He never listens to me," Yusuf said, and with a wave of his hand dismissed the whole episode as a minor ripple in the calm sea of his kitchen. "Nothing for you to worry about. I'll handle it. Anyway, Kay is done."

"You fired him?" I asked, incredulous.

"Yeah, he is useless."

"You can't just fire people for no reason! Kay is an integral part of our restaurant and makes those desserts perfectly, better than anybody else in this kitchen, I may add."

Yussuf scowled at me. "Perfectly? He doesn't know the first thing about desserts. He is a mechanic who mixes up ingredients without feeling or soul. He is like a gazelle, hopping around all day with nowhere to go."

"And you're like a boar, charging without looking," I countered, getting rather pissed off. "Yussuf, you will apologize to Kay and will let him make his desserts. You need to work together. This is not about who is better or who is in charge, it's about the food that comes out of this kitchen. Am I making myself perfectly clear?"

Even Yussuf could sense that this time he had overreached, but instead of admitting any wrongdoing he immediately turned his narrative around. "Absolutely. I can work with anybody. I am a man of the world. It's just a misunderstanding. Kay is too sensitive. He's so gay."

"Yussuf, you know that you can't bring that up. We're all different and therefore equal. You do understand that, don't you?" Boars and gazelles, indeed.

I got hold of Kay and assured him that the chef had promised to leave him alone and that I stood behind him 100 percent and we needed him badly.

I informed Aldo of this latest incident and he just shook his head in resignation. "They're all crazy, these chefs. They're all goddamned prima donnas. Nothing we can do about that. Let's hope they can get along. We need Kay to make those darn desserts. Come to think of it, I'm starting to hate French food."

Yussuf's food was deliciously spiced and anything but boring. He found plenty of admirers among our patrons. His sauces were not as fine or as delicate as David's, but coarser, darker and more savoury. His presentation was a combination of sculpted and classic, old and new cuisine. It resonated with the new customers, and we received many compliments as well as complaints from those surprised by the change. The poulet de Paris suddenly appeared with a hunter sauce instead of a peppercorn sauce, and the magret de canard morphed into duck à l'orange instead of apples and Calvados. Also, the frites that Kana prepped seemed to be different. When I asked about it, she demurely admitted that the chef wanted the potatoes unpeeled.

When I confronted Yussuf, he dismissed me like I didn't know what I was talking about. "The frites are much more flavourful and we save time and money. You let me worry about the food, you worry about the advertising and the payroll."

I felt chastised, but it looked like we were stuck with Yussuf for now, for better or worse. He did thrive during busy times, especially the crazy Wednesdays, excelling in his element. Some people function better when the world around them goes chaotic. They come alive in the eye of the storm. Yussuf was one of these creatures.

One day, as soon as I walked in the back door, Yussuf confronted me, dramatically throwing up his hands and clasping his egg head. Obviously a major calamity had occurred. Either the Egyptian soccer team had lost to some minor club or the kitchen had burned down.

"Billy called in sick. He's not going to make it today. I need him," Yussuf moaned.

"What's the matter with him? He was fine yesterday."

"It's his high blood pressure."

"Blood pressure? I had no idea. Isn't there medication for that?"

"Actually it's not his blood pressure, although his absence is affecting mine."

"What do you mean?"

"Well, it's his new girlfriend. She attacked Billy with a knife."

"With a knife?" I asked, incredulous.

"Billy defended himself, she called the cops, and of course it was him they took away. He's not allowed to go near her now and has to find places to sleep every night."

"What the hell is wrong with all of you?" I asked, throwing up my hands. "Everybody is in some kind of fantastic drama. Does anybody here have a normal life?"

Yussuf just looked at me with those charcoal eyes of his and retreated into the kitchen.

I liked Billy. He worked as if driven by invisible demons, charging between the storage room and the kitchen as if the place was on fire, chopping and washing the dishes with jerky movements, always in a hurry as if time was about to run out. He had never missed a shift before and was always early, seemingly happy to be there. That was before he fell for the knife-wielding girlfriend.

Billy came in the next day looking haggard, with his eyes darting back and forth.

"Are you all right?" I asked.

"I'll be fine," he said evasively.

"I heard about the incident," I said.

"What incident?"

"Well, the knife attack and the police."

"What knife attack?" Billy asked, taken aback.

Now it was my turn to be surprised, but I should have known better. "Yussuf told me that you were attacked with a knife by your girlfriend and the police showed up."

"Yussuf?" Billy said, exasperated. "We had a fight and I told her to leave. There were no knives and no police. I had to sort it out yesterday. It's over and done."

I left it at that, not wanting to pry into his personal life. Aldo's words echoed through my mind: Don't ask them how they are, don't get involved.

I should have known. Yussuf had the ability to blow everything out of proportion, but he didn't see it as lies and exaggerations; he saw it as necessary and valid embellishments on the truth. When I told him that there were no knives and no police in Billy's story, he put his hands on his hips and said, "What world do you live in? You think they just had a little civil discussion and then she left? It was a mean fucking fight, I bet, and then he tossed her out, throwing all her stuff out the window, yelling and cursing until the neighbours called the police. You bet. I can just see it. Believe me, I know how this happens."

"You must talking about yourself, not Billy," I said, and left it at that, turning my back on Yussuf.

Christmas was just days away and we needed a well-functioning kitchen. Yussuf promised to do his best. "I'll even work Christmas Day if you want me to."

"It's the only day of the year we're closed," I said, "but I need everybody to do their very best, and please, no missing shifts."

Even though he was a habitual liar and con artist, Yussuf was a tireless self-promoter. Not a day would go by that he didn't relate some outstanding event or incredible, underappreciated achievement of his. Whenever anybody told a story, he had a better and bigger one, and whenever somebody related a personal accomplishment, Yussuf trumpeted about his own triumphs.

"I served prime ministers and celebrities, had restaurants from Montreal to Vancouver, was the lead singer in a famous rock band," (that was a tough one to visualize) "lost hundreds of thousands of dollars in under-appreciated fantastic endeavours, and also fathered a daughter with the most famous French actress."

"Who was that?" I wanted to know.

"Oh. I can't tell you. But if I did, you would recognize her instantly. I talk to her almost daily."

Bloody amazing, I thought. What a con.

One day he brought his beautiful Estonian wife to the restaurant and introduced her to Clare and me. "This is Maarika, and she's a doctor."

That piqued Clare's interest. "What kind of doctor are you?" she asked the very pretty, tall and blonde Maarika.

But before she could answer, Yussuf jumped in. "She is a specialist," he said, and with a wave of his hand tried to dismiss the subject.

"I'm a reiki healer and foot masseuse," Maarika said with a lovely, toothy smile.

I had told Clare about Yussuf, and now she could admire him in full, self-propelled action. At a total loss for words, Clare took a large swig of wine.

Maarika, Mrs. Yussuf, had brought their cute three-year-old daughter along. Considering that Yussuf was a few winks shy of fifty and, with his large, bald, egg head on a fire-hydrant body, not the most attractive-looking bloke, he must have been the luckiest man alive, with his gorgeous wife and their princess daughter with her lovely cupid curls.

"Hair just like her dad," I joked.

They both stared at me, and I didn't know for a dreadful moment if I had made a faux pas, but then they both broke out laughing and Yussuf gave me a generous buddy slap on the back. A little bit too hard, I felt.

Sex and the Kitchen

Cooks are always falling in lust with one another or with the girls in the front staff. Maybe it's the close, sweaty environment of the kitchen, the physical proximity to each other, or maybe the general lack of social lives and skills that give rise to the dubious, temporary dalliances, a constant distraction in any kitchen, it seems.

At the very beginning, just after the Olympics, we briefly employed a second cook, Caleb, who hailed from Fiji and stood all of five feet tall with a flat, large punched-in nose, a lopsided, watery mouth, and two protruding buck teeth. In other words, he was by far the ugliest man I have ever had the pleasure of knowing. He had large hands, completely out of proportion to the rest of his scrawny body. He didn't walk and move like other people, but slithered and slunk along walls, always with a sideways glance, more like a thief afraid of getting busted than a cook who had to pay attention to his surroundings. But he worked tirelessly and without complaining and did what he was told, washing the dishes, mopping the floors, cutting vegetables, or taking out the garbage.

Somehow he settled his unsavoury longings on Jenny, a young temporary dishwasher about a foot taller than Caleb. That apparently didn't stop them. I caught them once in the back by the coolers struggling against each other, with Caleb's head burrowing inside Jenny's black cook's jacket. I had no idea what attracted her to him, but she would wait for him after work and the two of them would sneak off together. Beauty kept hanging out with the beast against all odds in our own restaurant kitchen, except that Caleb would never turn into a prince, of that I was certain.

Their dalliance lasted a couple of weeks, until suddenly a distinct wall of frost could be observed between them. Jenny made big circles around Caleb and took great pains to avoid any contact with him. Caleb, on the other hand, was obsessed with her, and his shifty eyes would be digging into her back and following her wherever she moved. It became very disruptive for the other staff members and somewhat ridiculous. At the end of her shift, Jenny would disappear the instant she dropped her apron, while Caleb had to hang around and scrub the kitchen floor with clenched teeth, his furtive eyes darting back and forth, his mind obviously somewhere else.

It was a Monday morning when Caleb called in sick and said in a muffled voice that he wouldn't be around for a while. Naturally I wanted to know what was up. Apparently he was at St. Paul's in the emergency ward. I promised to bring him his latest pay cheque and some of the clothes he had left in the staff room.

I found Caleb lying in bed with an IV tube in his arm and his chest all wrapped up in heavy bandages.

"What on earth happened? A car accident?"

"Not really," he admitted. "I did something stupid. I won't do it again, I promise."

I waited for an explanation.

"She didn't love me anymore and I wanted to die."

"Love? You and Jenny? Are you crazy, Caleb? You were drinking again! You know you're not allowed to drink at work." Despite his sorry state, I was furious.

"I couldn't help myself. I gave her a fair choice, boss. Either she loved me or I would kill myself right then. She just turned and walked away. I don't know what came over me, but I grabbed an empty wine bottle, smashed it against the side of the building and stabbed myself. She didn't even see me or pay any attention."

"You impaled yourself with a wine bottle? You're crazy!" I was incredulous. I couldn't have somebody that crazy and volatile working in our kitchen. No bloody way.

"I guess that means I'm fired, right?" Caleb asked without any remorse.

"Yes, I'm afraid so, Caleb. I hope you get well, and maybe you should get some counselling."

I hoped never to see or hear from him again, but fate had other plans.

All the boys in the kitchen were secretly in love with both bussers — Selena, our navel-gazing aspiring Versace model, and Margo, the Czech Sophia Loren of the bistro. Neither girl could walk by the kitchen without several pairs of eyes following them, hands suspended in midair, stir-sticks coming to a sudden stop.

Naturally both girls were well aware of their unsettling effect on the boys and took full advantage of their allure, getting better staff meals than everybody else.

When I surprised Alice and Kyle, our new sous-chef, coming out together from the tiny staff room, flushed, dishevelled and obviously compromised, it came as no surprise to me. At least the two of them fit each other, not like Caleb and Jenny.

It was no secret that Kay was desperately in love with Chase, our new Aussie cook. Chase — six feet tall with large puppy eyes and blonde curls draping over his forehead, such that he had to constantly sweep them back with his hand — was a quiet, even-tempered young man. Nothing fazed him, not the Wednesday nights and not Kay's overzealous attention to his every need and want.

"I can teach you desserts if you want," Kay offered Chase.

"Yeah, sure, Kay, that's nice," Chase said, pitching Kay into a love-torn tizzy.

"I can stay late and show you," Kay cooed.

"Thanks, Kay, but not tonight, I've got a date."

Kay manifestly atrophied internally and his knees visibly buckled. It was a pathetic sight, but nobody could tell Kay that Chase was anything but gay.

Most sex in the kitchen is not blatant and physical but instead revolves around fantasies and desires — full of innuendo, teases and jokes. Worst of all was our hot-blooded chef, Yussuf himself, who despite his apparent domestic bliss displayed a natural roving eye for all things female. He exhibited his yearnings openly, completely at ease with his desires and in no way embarrassed by his lecherous behaviour. For the holiday season we had just hired a middle-aged French assistant, Yvette, for the front staff, and immediately Yussuf took an unhealthy shine to her.

One day I noticed the girls — Alice, Selena, Alia, Melinda and Margo — all giggling uncontrollably, clustered around something on the table at the back of the restaurant. I walked over to see what was so hilarious. They all flitted about like a flock of surprised birds. "What's that?" I asked, pointing to the fancy wrapping Yvette pressed to her chest.

"Nothing," they all said, unable to control their giddiness.

"Let's see 'nothing,' now that I'm curious."

Yvette coyly placed the glittery package on the table and revealed a bright red set of frilly, sexy lingerie.

"Wow," I said, trying hard to be nonchalant.

"A Christmas present to Yvette from Yussuf," Alia blurted out, and they all started giggling again, loudest of all Yvette herself.

Outrageous, I thought, unable to wrap my head around this kind of behaviour.

One night Yussuf came out of the kitchen shaking his sweaty head. "I'm totally in love," he proclaimed "and I can't concentrate."

"You're a lucky man, Yussuf," I said. "Your wife is a princess."

He looked at me as if I'd had a stroke. "The blonde on table three. Are you blind? She is a goddess."

"Yussuf, you're a happily married man, I thought."

"I am, but monogamy is for swans and penguins; it's not natural for men. I can work up an appetite, as long as I eat at home," he said, winking at me as if I was a co-conspirator.

Party Time

It's a well-known cliché that the customer is always right. Any reasonable request or complaint will be accommodated and we bend over backwards to please any and all patrons. This has nothing to do with being right or wrong. If the customer wants the salmon cooked to cinders, calling it well-done, then we do that. No argument. Or so I thought, until Yussuf threw the salmon through the pass-through, screaming that this was as well-done as possible, any more and it would be reduced to charcoal.

Roy, our Scottish server with thirty-five years of experience, looked on astonished. "I've never seen that before. Great stuff." His ruddy face lit up like a Jack-o'-lantern. He was obviously undaunted by Yussuf's antics. "I'll have that salmon Cajun style, please," he shouted back at Yussuf, who was in an owly mood that night. He might have heard that he was the butt of his own ludicrous Santa imitation by gifting frilly undies to a middle-aged waitress. What a class act.

Roy was our in-house joker, and no matter what the mood or the weather, he usually had a Scottish quip at the ready. Some of them were definite groaners, but they always lit up the moment. Instead of lowering himself to Yussuf's level, he rose above it with his joke of the day: "You know the difference between Mick Jagger and a Scotsman? Mick sings, 'Hey, you, get off of my cloud,' while the Scotsman yells, 'Hey, McCloud, get off of my yew!'"

For the rest of that evening we all stayed as far away from Yussuf as possible, fearing an instantaneous combustion and explosion of pyramidal proportions at any moment.

The episode of the flying fish was soon all but forgotten and, according to the chef, never happened. "I was merely trying to show Roy the fish when it slipped through my fingers."

I personally witnessed the fish fly horizontally at great speed through the pass-through, missing Roy by inches. I suppose it was just a moment of weakness, a loss of self-control during a stressful evening serve. By itself, it was nothing unusual during the dreaded Wednesday fight night, except that Yussuf tended to raise anything dramatic to another dimension. With Christmas just a couple of weeks away, the pre-Christmas Wednesdays evolved into a regular stampede which we barely contained and which stressed everybody out to the maximum. Not even Roy found time for a joke, nor did Selena have a chance to check herself in the mirror, and Alice, well, she had to come down to earth for a few hours and actually work.

Not only the cooks had to heed customers' wishes and demands — it went for everybody. When somebody booked a birthday party for eight people and wanted to bring their own cake, then that was fine with us — or it should be. I had just gotten off the phone with that very customer, who had cancelled his party because Marcel, our arrogant in-house snob, with his French nose up in the air, had explained to the perplexed customer that such a demand would cost $300 per head and was not in the interest of our fine establishment.

"Really?" I said to the affronted customer. "He said that?"

"Yes, and his attitude was anything but inviting."

When I confronted Marcel, who was very sensitive about his Frenchness even though he was from Quebec, he explained in his nasally accent that the customer had made unreasonable demands and was in no way cooperative. I pointed out that the customer's request was indeed reasonable and the cooperation had to come from us. Marcel tilted his head back and focused his eyes along his aquiline nose into the far distance, past me, and just said, "As you wish, sir. I will do my best next time."

We all liked Marcel despite his snobbish mannerisms. He had an infectious laugh, and I suspected his whole French persona was a cloak, a protective skin. He suited our establishment and he knew his wines, in more ways than one, as it turned out. I initially thought that he lent our establishment some authenticity, but maybe not the socially correct kind anymore. He was stuck in the same bygone era as Ken, our initial maître d' — an age when the server belonged to a distinctly lower class than the wealthy patron, an age when service derived from subservience and discretion and distance were expected. Today's social relationship between customer and server is much more casual, and nobody pretends to be on different social platforms, even though money still commands a modicum of respect, mostly aimed at garnering a large tip.

"Marcel is another dinosaur," I complained to Aldo, who agreed.

"He's a snob who's not making us any money. In fact, he's costing us. He likes his wine a bit too much, I think."

Marcel only worked a couple of evening shifts — Mondays and Tuesdays — and often these were our slow evenings. When Alia complained in her shy way to me about Marcel being drunk, arguing with the customers and mixing up his orders and bills, we had to address the problem. I let Aldo be the bad cop. I was much better at smoothing the tempers after everybody was properly flogged and disciplined.

Marcel acknowledged that indeed he'd had a spot too much that afternoon. "I had to attend a wine tasting," he explained a bit too loudly, his usually over-pronounced French accent even more so.

"You're supposed to spit out at the tastings, not swallow," Aldo said.

Marcel admitted that, yes, maybe he swallowed a few too many samples.

Since we were getting close to Christmas, we could ill afford to lose any of our staff and we needed Marcel to get through the season. This was the time of year when we actually did make some money, thanks to the office parties and people taking each other out for dinner.

Marcel fell off the wagon within a week. He staggered around, mixing up his orders, pouring glasses of house wine to overflowing and yelling at Alia, who was close to tears when she called me.

Again, one of our few precious dinners at home was interrupted by the insistent marimba ring of my phone. I gave Clare an exasperated look and she just put a hand on my arm. "Answer it, dear. It's your restaurant."

It was a drizzly, dark evening, best spent indoors. I jumped on my bike and rode through the festively adorned West End neighbourhood, balconies and windows displaying strings of lights, and the odd blow-up Santa or reindeer leaning over the railing several stories up. Vancouver manifests the jolly season with public and private light displays, from lit-up hotels and construction cranes framing the glittering city skyline, to the thousands of illuminated apartments and houses. The colourful displays made this dark time of year a lot more fun.

I arrived at the back of the bistro, wet from my short ride and none too happy, despite the fact that we were busy and everybody was in a festive mood, including our head waiter of the evening. Of course it wasn't Marcel's fault that his friends wanted him to taste their wines in the afternoon before his shifts. After all, he was the sommelier at Le Bistro and indulging his passion was part of his professional hazard. I politely told Marcel to go home, which he did without much protest, and Alia and I finished serving, with Selena, looking glamorous with a string of blinking lights around her swan-like neck, pitching in as our assistant and dazzling the customers who didn't mind waiting as long as she brought fresh water and more free bread and frites.

Drinking is the constant latent temptation in any restaurant, where all the wine and liquor is just a glass away. It's very easy to become a successful alcoholic in no time at all. After a busy night, when everybody has gone and only the dishwasher and the servers are left, the spigots open and the bottles pop. Or how about a little nip of that new Scotch we just got in? It's the reward at the end of a busy shift or the emotional lift after a slow evening. The price is right and the night is always young, since the next day's shift doesn't start until 5:00 p.m. That's why Marcel got away with his problem — it was recognized as a professional hazard, tolerated as long as you didn't make a fool of the customer or yourself.

We decided to stay open for Christmas Eve after Yussuf told us that he would be happy to work. But as the day approached, he tried to weasel out of his commitment. I pointed out the thirty reservations we already had on the books.

"It's my daughter. She is flying in from Montreal. It's a surprise."

"That's great, Yussuf. You can spend Christmas Day with her. We definitely need you here tonight. Bring your family in for dinner."

Folly Bistro

He liked that idea and promptly brought his pretty wife Maarika, his lovely three-year-old daughter, and his other daughter, who was about the same age as his present wife. Alia overheard them talking: Yussuf's wife, the foot-masseuse doctor, was telling the older daughter, whose mother was the famous French mystery actress, that Yussuf had owned this restaurant since August. And because this was Christmas Eve after all, they would order a bottle of Moët & Chandon first and follow it up with a bottle of Saint-Émilion. Yussuf had assured Gino, who was in charge of the front, that he would take care of the bill with Aldo and me. Which was news to us. Yussuf had never mentioned the bill, which was upwards of $300. He really was the most honest con I have ever met. He was such a natural, seeing absolutely nothing wrong with his constant manipulation of the facts. I suppose he considered it his rightful Christmas present, and when I asked him why he was telling customers and suppliers that he, Yussuf, was the owner of the restaurant, he just said, with utmost honest conviction, "Everybody loves it when the chef is the owner. I'm doing you a favour, my friend."

After Christmas we put together an exclusive New Year's Eve party menu and celebrated in style. We had a completely booked-out restaurant and were fully staffed in the front: Gino, with a black bow tie; Margo, gorgeous in a silver tiara; Yvette, in a classy white shirt and narrow black tie; Roy running the bar in a sparkly green waistcoat, looking like an oversized leprechaun; and Selena, Alia and Alice, bussing.

Yussuf loved the energy and outdid himself, excelling flamboyantly at being the big chef at the little French bistro in the West End. I let him revel in his glory, even though he still had no handle on the food costs, no inventory, no sanitation plan and his people skills were those of an overseer on a slave galley. We'll have to talk soon, I thought, but not today.

New Year's Eve turned out to be the best night of the year, both in terms of income and everybody's enjoyment . The servers loved the lavish tips and the free drinks at the end of the night, and the cooks felt that they had indeed been part of a masterpiece created by you-know-who — the Egyptian-Sicilian chef de cuisine.

But there is always one spoiler in the barrel. This time it turned out to be Yvette, Yussuf's misguided lust interest and receiver of the frilly panties, who for the holiday season we had promoted to a server, since Melinda was in Montreal with her boyfriend.

Yvette served my friend John, the photographer, and his family, and when she handed John the bill, I thought I noticed a look of surprise on his face. Later, I checked the bill to make sure she hadn't charged him for the champagne or the wine, which was on the house. What she'd done instead was add the gratuity onto our friend's bill and never managed to tell him. Sure enough, there it was right before the sales tax: gratuity at 18 percent. John hadn't seen this and had tipped her on top.

When I confronted Yvette, she pleaded ignorance and oversight and called it an honest mistake. I called it naked greed and a blatant rip-off. She knew she'd fucked up this time. The question remained: How many other times had she gotten away with this before? I wished her a happy New Year — somewhere else, not with us anymore. She slunk out the back door, and when Yussuf asked with a sly grin where Yvette was, I told him she had places to go and people to see and wouldn't be coming back. The old lecher was visibly disappointed but carried on celebrating with the rest of us into the wee hours of the new dawn.

Here is Yussuf's masterpiece, the New Year's Eve five-course celebration dinner.

Folly Bistro

HAPPY NEW YEAR!

Amuse-bouche

Palate teaser

First Course

Five oysters on the half shell
or
Charcuterie plate, duck pâté, assorted meats & cheeses

Second Course

Classic lobster bisque
or
Mimosa salad

Main Course

Served with seasonal vegetables and pommes frites

Roasted rack of lamb
with tomato, goat cheese, and mint tapenade
or
Filet mignon & prawns Pernod
Choice of Béarnaise, peppercorn, or mushroom sauce
or
Magret de canard
Duck breast with glazed apples and Calvados
with garlic truffle pommes purée
or
Alaskan black cod
Roasted fillet with olive, cherry tomato tapenade,
citrus coulis, and wild mushroom risotto

Sorbet
Palate cleanser

Dessert
Chocolate mousse or crème brûlée

or

Poire belle Hélène

Bon Appétit!

4

The Prince, the King and a Slave

To commemorate our one-year anniversary, I wanted to finally use all those fondue caquelons and réchauds that we'd purchased from the Swiss pavilion after the Olympics were all over. We got such a good deal for the twenty or so sets — I think we paid a mere $300 for the lot — and we needed to put them to use. I suggested to Yussuf the idea of hosting a fondue night at the bistro, maybe on Sundays or Thursdays, traditionally slow nights, in order to bring in some extra customers and cash.

"No problem," he said with his usual bravado. "I'm the Fondue King. Let me know when and it shall be so."

I should have known better. The other day he called himself the Prince of Pizza, none better from coast to coast, from Montreal to Vancouver, from New York to San Diego. "If you ever taste a better pizza than mine, you have to have yourself checked out by a doctor because there is something wrong with you."

That night, he made his world-famous pizza for the staff dinner. Mediocre, I thought. The doughy crust was more like a floppy flatbread, something you'd see in the Middle East. I wisely refrained from commenting and instead gobbled up the soggy, spicy cheese and tomato pie.

"This could make a good staff dinner," I said and was rewarded with a withering look of disdain from His Highness. If his fondue was anything like his pizza, we were going to be in trouble. I suggested a tasting, maybe an early lunch for Aldo, me, Gino and whoever else wanted to partake.

"No problem. You will see what Yussuf has up his sleeve."

The Fondue King. It was going to be a cheesy coronation, I feared.

I told Aldo, who was sceptical and rightly so. He also didn't really care for Yussuf's world-famous pizza, but hey, Aldo agreed, give the guy a chance. He was the best self-promoter by far, and maybe he would surprise us.

Gino, being the only real Italian (by way of Montreal), didn't think much of Yussuf's cooking skills in the first place and was definitely not impressed with the "world's best pizza," so he was equally unconvinced about Yussuf's fondue expertise. "You must be kidding. Fondue King, my ass. More like King of Bullshit."

Since I have a bit of a fondue background, having grown up in the land of cheese, I tried to suggest a couple to Yussuf. I was swiftly rebuked.

"Leave it to me. Emmenthal and Gruyère are too expensive, and what was that other one? Applezoll? Never heard of it."

When I came back around 4:00 p.m., I could see the spread from the back door, and the smell of chilies and cheese wafted throughout the whole restaurant. The table was laden with every kind of raw vegetable you could think of: carrots, celery sticks, broccoli, mushrooms, green onions, etc., and for bread Yussuf surprised us with some dark crumbly pumpernickel cut in thin, long slices. How to get those on the end of a fork and in and out of the melted cheese remained a mystery and a challenge at best. This was the most unusual fondue I'd ever come across.

Two caquelons with melted cheese sauce awaited the stunned and very silent tasters around the bizarre table. I gingerly dipped a carrot stick in what was a rather liquid fondue that dripped all over the place before I got it into my mouth. The surprise was supreme. The closest thing I could relate it to was Alfredo sauce. Not one to immediately judge, I tried the second, reddish-looking concoction, and immediately regretted dipping my celery stick into it. This was firebrand sauce of the most potent calibre, made of cheddar and habanero chilies.

We all dipped and searched for words to describe the disaster in a polite fashion while the King of Fondue stood over us, arms folded over his broad chest, expecting nothing short of an outright endorsement of his fabulous creation. Words for once failed me, and luckily the phone rang so I could take my leave. Aldo also had a sudden family matter to tend to, and we left Gino and Alia in charge of the leftover bushels of uneaten vegetables and the gooey, cheesy sauces that were slowly congealing into a thick paste.

Gino cited dietary reasons to get out of the mess, while Alia had to get the pungent smells aired out of the restaurant in time for the evening service. Yussuf, aloof to the whole disaster, thinking we were all philistines, went back into his kitchen and started yelling at his crew that they'd better get off their lazy asses and clean up before anybody copied his Egyptian Fondue Alexandria. We never mentioned fondue again around Yussuf, who also opted to ignore the whole fiasco and move on.

It was the January blues, which was also the time the December bills came home to roost, and those lofty sales suddenly didn't look so good anymore. The food bills were high and the liquor and labour costs were extreme. Everybody received their holiday pay at the end of the year, and on top of that, some other yearly bills came in, like the workers' compensation payments, the insurance, the security system and all the licenses: health, liquor, business. We were up against the wall with a gun pointed at our wallets by the taxman. Payroll taxes and sales taxes were due. The party was officially over.

Since we'd taken over the restaurant, two levels of government — the city and the province — had thrown three curveballs at us. They put a lot of restaurants out of the game and buckled others to their knees, where they either begged the government for relief or prayed for a miracle, both equally futile. These three new rules made the "cooked food delivery and service" business, which is what restaurants are, a tough and almost impossible endeavour.

First strike: HST. When we took over the bistro the year before, it was the age before harmonized sales tax (HST), the hated 12 percent consumer tax the government imposed on its unsuspecting citizens and businesses with the stroke of a pen, after promising during the election campaign that they would never do such a thing. The HST was a combination of the previous provincial sales tax and the goods and services tax (GST). Before the HST came into effect, only the 5 percent GST was charged on restaurant meals. Now the consumer paid 7 percent more — totalling up to 12 percent on all restaurant consumption, including alcohol.

First off, we can only deduct what we pay out in services, alcohol purchases, and rent. On food that is classified as essential, we do not pay any HST, but we do charge the 12 percent on top of all the food and drink we sell. In other words, 12 percent of our daily, weekly and monthly total sales belongs to the government, and we're just collecting it for them. Maybe we should bill the government for our part as tax collectors, bankers and administrators. It truly sucks. The more successful we are, the better off they are. But if we sink, we sink alone.

Before the implementation of the dreaded HST, restaurants were also entitled to a 10 percent discount on alcohol purchases. The government took that away as well.

We and all the other restaurateurs I talked to used the daily 12 percent extra in their tills as cash flow until the time, every three months, when the dreaded, massive tax bill was due. Then we all scrambled, borrowed, and diverted from Peter to Paul — i.e., credit cards to cash — just to pay the piper. This hurts from two sides. The customers don't like paying the tax (and as a consequence go out less) and we hate collecting it and paying more to the government.

The public outcry at the time was immense, and a petition to rescind the hated tax circulated. I was sure they'd change it before the next election.

Second strike: 0.05 blood alcohol. The second knuckleball came at us in the shape of a draconian knee-jerk law that lowered the allowable blood alcohol content to 0.05, from the previous, equally arbitrary 0.08. The law itself was ludicrous enough, because 0.05 is just some number and doesn't imply inebriation or drunkenness. Some zealots in the provincial government handed the police unprecedented powers to check, harass, judge and punish the unsuspecting public, and instead created real hardship and personal disasters with their banana-republic enforcement of a stupid rule.

Roadblocks appeared everywhere and drivers were pulled aside in record numbers. There were so many cops swarming the city, it made Vancouver look like a police state. Not only could they now force you to blow into a machine, they could confiscate your car and driver's license and then make life miserable for your foreseeable future if it read over 0.05. The people who get snagged in this net do not cause the carnage on the roads; it's the ones who keep drinking and driving, speeding and ignoring all kinds of laws, and probably don't have a license in the first place.

The busted citizens have no recourse short of taking the government to court. Not too many can afford that. What the Liberal government had done since the law came into effect was confiscate 2,500 licenses and cars from ordinary citizens who'd had some wine with dinner. Now the public's fear of getting caught was so great that hardly anybody drank anymore, which left us scrambling for cash. The liquor bill used to be half the food bill, and more in a French restaurant, where the wines tend to be a bit pricier. Now it constituted one-third, with 12 percent of everything going to the government to pay for all those cops who never did get laid off after the Olympics.

I overheard a radio commentator from Victoria who had started his early day by gargling with mouthwash. He happened to be snagged by a roadblock and blew over 0.05, resulting in the confiscation of his license and car. The poor bloke couldn't believe what had just happened, and he vented his anger publicly on the air. His case just highlights the ludicrous, righteous prohibition mentality and the abuse of power by the cops and the lawmakers.

Third strike: bike lanes. Strike number three came in the form of an equally ludicrous pseudo-environmental policy by the city legislators, and the gung-ho new mayor in particular. He wanted to turn Vancouver into a bicycle city like Amsterdam. They closed entire car lanes on major arteries, painted them green and dedicated them as bicycle lanes. They took away parking, access, and left-hand turn lanes all over the city, narrowed bridges and intersections, erected concrete barriers, and cancelled natural routes in front of businesses and restaurants. All in the name of being "green." This legislation had been enacted without consultation of the affected business community and residents.

Also, these restrictions on traffic had not been offset by more frequent and accessible public transport. I have driven along Seymour a hundred times and hardly ever do I see a bicycle in the dedicated lane (and never in the winter), which now results in congestion and lack of parking. The worst change was the entrance from Beach Avenue onto the Burrard Bridge. Notoriously congested as a two-lane entrance, it is now gridlocked as one lane and a green bicycle lane. This one-sided policy has had its intended effect. Fewer people want to drive into the city and therefore fewer customers frequent downtown businesses and restaurants. Who is paying for this experiment in social engineering? You and I, once again.

Add to all these hurdles the implosion of the US housing market due to brinkmanship investment vehicles like unsecured bundled mortgages, unfettered gambling by the big banks, insurance companies, and unregulated financial markets. We were lucky to be in business at all during the resulting worldwide recession, which is a euphemism for depression. But we were not about to knuckle under and cry like babies. No way! We were there to stay and make a mark. We had a good restaurant in the best location in the city, and we would get through this valley of tax and debt to climb once again the cliffs of glory toward solvency and self-respect. Amen.

Without Tourism Vancouver's annual Dine Out promotion, we would never have made it through the post-Christmas blues. All participating restaurants offer a special three-course menu at a set price that, in most cases, is a great deal. It fills the seats every night and overlaps the fifteen-day celebration of the Chinese New Year. That explained the predominantly Chinese clientele during Dine Out, keeping us busy for two weeks.

As on most Monday mornings, Aldo and I went over the accounts from the preceding week. We matched the daily sales against the cash and the credit card printouts. Three percent of the gross sales went to the kitchen, and it became my job to divide that money among each member of the kitchen staff. I used to hand over the whole amount to the chef, who then divided it (fairly, I'd hoped) among the members of his crew. Simple, right? The grumbling started shortly after Christmas.

"Aren't there any kitchen tips?" Colin wanted to know.

"Of course, we handed them to the chef," I said.

A couple of weeks passed by until Colin asked me again about the kitchen tips. I started to smell a rat. I confronted Yussuf on the Monday morning, holding back the kitchen tips from the previous week.

"They don't deserve any rewards," he barked, acting all insulted and browbeaten. "They don't work hard enough — no point spoiling those lazy fucks and rewarding them."

"What are you talking about, Yussuf? For weeks I've been handing over all the kitchen tips for you to split among the staff. You're telling me all that money vanished straight into your pockets?"

"The kitchen tips are for the kitchen and I am the kitchen," Yussuf said indignantly, with not even a sliver of remorse. "You don't understand. Without me there is nothing, no food, no discipline, no restaurant!"

"From now on, I disperse the tips, Yussuf. Do you understand that? We cannot cheat the staff out of their due rewards, and the servers wouldn't like it if they knew that their contribution goes into your pocket. You should know that a happy crew is a more efficient crew than a cheated one, which is no good for you or the restaurant."

"You are questioning my authority?"

"No, I'm questioning your honesty."

Yussuf just walked away without a comment. It wasn't in him to ever admit to any wrongdoing or fault. He was always right and never erred or failed. It was in his blood.

When I saw Aldo later in the day, I couldn't hold my anger back any longer. Yussuf was really starting to get to me. "Yussuf screams and yells at his staff as if they were rabid dogs. He throws their food onto the floor and then tells them to clean it up and make it again. He rules the kitchen with a jailhouse philosophy and keeps everyone subdued and suppressed, afraid to complain in fear of punishment. He's a despot. We can't go on with this guy, Aldo. He's cheating his own staff, he is a liar and a thief, and who knows what else he gets away with? Maybe it's time to look for another chef," I said, feeling quite pissed off at the scoundrel's latest scam.

"Sort of like how the whole of the Middle East is ruled," Aldo said.

He had a point, but it didn't make it right. We were just seeing the widespread uprising against the despotic rulers all along the African Mediterranean. "The Arab Spring" was the commonly used misnomer. Yussuf exemplified the same kind of dictatorial mentality in his kitchen as did Mubarak or Gaddafi in their respective domains.

Of course, he would never see it that way. Yussuf was an expert liar, an honest and proud thief and con artist, and he didn't think there was anything wrong with that. In his own mind he was doing nothing unusual, and being the chef in charge of the kitchen entitled him to free food, kitchen tips, and God knows what else. I knew he regularly took food home, as well as some of our tools which he thought would be better off with him, and he treated the restaurant as if it were his own, telling merchants and clients exactly that.

"I told you before, clients like it better if they're dealing directly with the owner. Don't worry about it, it works out in your favour," he told me without any shame.

"But you don't own the restaurant, and you open accounts with merchants who then call me for the money. You can't do that. I need to know what I owe."

"Relax, it's all under control. And by the way, I'm the most sought-after celebrity chef in town and I have offers almost daily," he said unabashedly. He was nothing short of delusional.

Every week I handed out advances, most of them to Yussuf and on a regular basis to Billy, who for some reason was always behind on bills. I found out that Yussuf also borrowed money from his crew, which left them short of cash, forcing them in turn to come to me for advances. Of course Yussuf never paid anybody back.

Sometime after Christmas, I noticed a new creature in the kitchen: a scrawny, furtive man who could have been from India or the Middle East. He seemed to be always in Yussuf's way, for the chef kept yelling at him, mostly in a foreign language. Once, out of the corner of my eye, I thought I saw Yussuf slap him on the back of the head, but that might have been my imagination.

"Who is that?" I asked Kana one morning.

"His name is Luey and he is a friend of Yussuf's." I noticed she hesitated on the "friend" part.

"Well, what does Luey do, Kana? Is he working here?"

"He helps Yussuf, fetches things for him, sometimes washes dishes."

I waited for my chance and caught Luey when he tried to weasel by me, head pulled in like a turtle.

"Hi Luey," I said, trying to be casual. "I'm the owner here and I haven't met you yet."

Luey's eyes darted around and his head swivelled back and forth while he licked his lips with the pointy tip of his tongue. He seemed extremely nervous. He also smelled like a mixture of stale booze, old socks and mouldy cheese. He was dressed in ragged clothes at least two sizes too big. He looked like a street person. "Hello, please to meet you. I'm friend of Yussuf, only helping," he said in a hoarse voice with a thick accent.

"Okay, I must get your SIN number and address. How much did Yussuf tell you your wages would be?"

"No need to pay me — you pay Yussuf," Luey said, noticeably distressed.

I shook my head, not knowing what to do. "Don't worry, I'll talk to Yussuf," I said.

"Please don't say bad things about me to Master Yussuf," Luey pleaded and scurried out the back door.

Master Yussuf?

I confronted Yussuf when he strode in the door, fashionably

late for his shift, complaining about the traffic and that people didn't move out of the way when he honked his horn.

"Yussuf, we need to talk. Who is this Luey guy, and what's going on? We can't have illegal immigrants working here. I hope you know that."

Yussuf looked at me, then looked around, searching for Luey. "He left a few minutes ago," I said.

"Luey is a distant relative and I am taking care of him, teaching him how to work in a kitchen. You can pay him minimum wage. No need to pay taxes, just give me his cheque and I will handle him."

"Yussuf, we can't do that and you know it. You act like he's your personal slave, or what? Besides that, he looks and smells like he just crawled out of a Dumpster."

"His family owes me money and he is working it off, doing the honourable thing," Yussuf said haughtily. "You should be happy to get cheap labour."

"This isn't happening, Yussuf. You can't bring in some personal serf who is probably illegal, most likely drunk, and for all I can see, mentally unstable and definitely unhygienic. I will not have him back here."

Yussuf turned his prominent nose up in disgust and disappeared into the sanctuary of his kitchen without another word. I only saw Luey a couple more times, lingering out back, waiting for his master to finish his shift for all I knew. The whole sordid episode was incomprehensible to me. There seemed to be no end to Yussuf's shenanigans.

Most Honest Thief and Chocolates

Most restaurants, including ours, are always for sale. If it's making money, nobody wants to sell — meaning the price goes up — and if it's losing money, nobody wants to buy — meaning any price is a good price. Lots of jokes about owning and running restaurants are like the jokes about boats: your two happiest days are the day you buy your boat and the day you sell it. Ditto a restaurant.

Aldo, who is much better connected in the restaurant world than I, put the word on the street, so to speak. It didn't take long for the rumours to take hold and get people whispering. "The best way to get a rumour started," Aldo said, "is to say, 'Please don't tell anybody, this is strictly confidential.'"

"I thought the best way was to start it yourself."

Within a couple of days, everybody from the dishwasher to the head waiter had heard or knew that the bistro was for sale. I asked Gino what the gossip was.

"Oh, well, apparently Yussuf is buying the bistro."

"Yussuf, our chef?" I asked, taken aback.

"Yeah, just ask Kana. She'll tell you."

Since this was Saturday, I had to wait until Monday to ask Kana what it was all about, but meanwhile I told Gino in no uncertain terms that that scenario was absolutely not the case. "Yussuf just asked me for another $200 advance. With what do you think he's going to buy the restaurant?"

Before I confronted Yussuf, who would just deny or contradict, I wanted to wait until I talked to Kana. She was the only one who would tell me the naked truth.

I came in early and she was already at work cleaning the floors, but instead of her usual sunny self she seemed down and distracted.

"What's the matter?" I asked, trying to sound nonchalant.

Kana didn't stop sweeping. Looking at the floor, she said, "Yussuf told me he would have to lay me off when he takes over because he would hire his own staff and his wife would run the front of the restaurant."

This was unbelievable. "No, no, no, Kana," I cried emphatically, "it's not at all true. Nobody is getting laid off and Yussuf is certainly not buying the restaurant."

She stopped sweeping and looked at me, very much relieved, and then told me that he had put everybody on notice in his kitchen.

It was pure madness and delusion. Yussuf had shamelessly told everybody for months that he was the owner of Le Bistro ("I get better deals from the suppliers, more respect from the customers, blah, blah"), and now he was about to buy it. As it turned out, his fallacy had a lot to do with our old nemesis, Ken, the ex-maître d' who'd walked away from us back in May. What a scheming bastard.

Aldo substantiated the gossip and told me that Ken had in fact called him and made a vague offer to buy the bistro.

"Did the name Yussuf come up in conversation?"

"No, why should it?"

"Because our Egyptian chef is telling the whole world that he is buying the bistro."

"Ah, maybe Ken, the old bastard, is leading him on, promising a partnership or some such thing."

We both found it bizarre that Ken of all people would want to buy the restaurant. Either way, Aldo agreed to talk and meet, since Ken had already announced that he, along with some partners, would have lunch at Le Bistro. I elected to observe the monkey business from a safe distance — riding my bike around the park — and let Aldo handle the face-to-face interactions.

When I got back, Gino filled me in on the aftermath of what looked like a plumbing problem in the bathroom.

"You wouldn't believe it," he said, absently wiping the bar counter. "Ken outdid himself, playing the Grand Pooh-bah. He started with double martinis for everybody, progressed to white wine and then to a bottle of red all by himself, and for lunch he gorged on steak tartare followed by a rare steak 'n' frites. Then he demanded that I pour them all liberal shots of XX cognacs."

"Did they tour the premises? Did they talk about the restaurant? How much was the bill?"

"They never even looked past their glasses of booze. The bill came to over $400. When I was about to present the bill, Ken suddenly stumbled off to the bathroom, where he proceeded to throw up all over the toilet and the surrounding walls. When he staggered back to his table, he grandiosely waved the bill away. 'Aldo will take care of it,' he said."

That was why Kana, armed with rubber gloves, mop and detergent, was busy attacking the bathroom when I walked in. When I said how sorry I was, she didn't utter a word of complaint, and with the dignity of an army doctor mopping up the battlefield, only said, "Ken is not a nice man."

When Aldo heard about the sordid episode, he immediately called Ken and threatened that we would expose Ken's cheapness to the rich friends he had invited to the lunch. Ken feared nothing more than to be made a fool of in front of the very people at whose feet he grovelled. He was such a sycophant and groupie, it was disgusting. Ken reluctantly paid up, and no word was ever mentioned about buying the bistro again. Yussuf's delusional ambitions faded into the shadowy recesses of his own addled mind, and he consequently dubbed Ken an asshole and imposter who he would never have anything to do with. How allegiances can change in the blink of an eye.

Payday was every two weeks, on the first and the fifteenth of every month. Twice a month I was signing cheques until my fingers bled. No wonder we weren't making any money. I didn't begrudge the people their dough — they earned it. After I handed out the cheques, the invariable lineup started, with the discrepancies, the missed hours, the wrong totals, mistakes from all around, including me. Then it would all settle down again for two weeks, when the whole ritual would repeat itself. Where was my pay cheque or Aldo's? In the cosmic realm. Our rewards were purely spiritual, and a profitable future in the material world had to be just around the corner. All I knew was that we were surely and steadily going deeper into the red with every month. How were we to get out of this downward spiral?

I tried not to dwell on the fact that we were slowly going broke. I always repeated the same mantra in my head: We're just 10 percent short of making it, just a lousy 10 percent. Surely achievable. Any day now, our fortunes will turn around. I heard the joke about how to end up with a million-dollar restaurant: Start with two million. I feared I was going to break out in hives or develop a nervous facial twitch because of our financial woes. Never mind my extra ten pounds with all that free booze and fries, or my hair turning grey or my bloodshot eyes from lack of sleep and worry.

Once in a while every kitchen runs out of an item on the menu. It happens. The kitchen informs the servers, and they in turn pass this info on to the customers. One, two, three, easy as that. But this didn't apply while our kitchen was under the wary, wandering mind of our notorious Egyptian-Sicilian chef.

We served a lovely old-world dish, coquilles St. Jacques: six scallops in a mornay sauce with Gruyère gratin, surrounded by a ring of garlic mashed potatoes and then baked. A classic dish and very popular with our older patrons — except when the dish was not what it was supposed to be.

An irate customer called over Marcel, our own in-house snob, and pointed an accusing finger at his coquilles St. Jacques. "What is that?" he asked, rather peeved.

Marcel bent over and his eyes beheld, oh horror, what appeared to be six pieces of white fish.

"These aren't scallops, are they?" the customer whined.

"Indeed, you are correct, monsieur," Marcel replied. "Let me ask the chef."

Marcel whisked the dish off the table and marched it into the kitchen, from where some aggravated shouting and yelling in French and Arabic could be heard.

"All part of our lively kitchen," we assured the worried customer.

Marcel appeared a couple of minutes later, his face the colour of raw meat, his back arched like a matador who had just danced around a bull. "Our chef informs me that, sadly, we have run out of scallops, and he has assured me that the halibut is equally as good. Of course, we will not charge you for the dish and offer our apologies."

That episode only cost us a few dollars, and the customers did eat the (now free) dish, feeling mighty proud to have observed the blatant switch.

Of course Yussuf defended himself with a shrug of his shoulders. "What you want me to do? We were out of scallops."

That just piqued my suspicions. "How many of those coquilles St. Halibut did you serve?"

"I can't remember, and who cares?"

"I care!" I shouted and stormed out of the kitchen before I did something stupid that I would regret.

For Yussuf, every day and every thing was a full-blown drama, and at that time he seemed more short-tempered than usual. He admitted that he was spending most of his nights in front of the TV, following the turmoil unfolding in Egypt.

"I feel so useless. I should be home helping my country," he said, and for once I sympathized with him.

For lunch that day, the Duke and three guests showed up, which made the lunch a success because their bill always included at least one good bottle of wine and steak tartare all around.

"What's with the olive-and-fig garnish?" Monsieur Ducat wanted to know, pointing at the black olives and mission figs surrounding the steak tartare. It used to be capers and some red onion.

"It's our Egyptian touch," I explained, trying to appear undaunted when inside I was seething. "Our chef's head is in Cairo these days."

"Interesting," the Duke said, and slid the olives and figs off to the side.

Just after lunch, Yussuf came running in the back door, from a smoke break, I assumed. He was very agitated.

"What now?" I asked warily.

"I just got robbed. My laptop, my brand new iPhone, an envelope with $15,000 in cash, my briefcase. All gone."

"Gone from where?"

"My car. Broken into, in broad daylight."

We both ran back outside and, sure enough, there was nothing in his car. No laptop, no big brown envelope, no iPhone, nothing.

Also no visible marks on the doors and no broken windows.

"How did they get in?"

"They must have been pros, probably had a jimmy or popped the lock open with a tennis ball. I can't believe it."

"I hope you have insurance. What $15,000?" I was somewhat mystified by this very clean robbery. Not a mark or a scratch or a witness, even though there were always people coming and going, parking or walking by.

"The money belongs to my brother-in-law. He owns an apartment building." As if that explained anything.

"You want me to call the cops?" I asked.

Yussuf looked at me horrified. "The cops? What good would that do? No, we certainly do not want to involve the cops. We have a restaurant to run."

Of course I had to write him an advance cheque.

I came in the back door, and there was Yussuf busily clicking away on a laptop, just like the one that was stolen the day before.

"Oh, that's my old computer. Luckily I had it sitting at home. Also, look, my iPhone was on the floor of the car. I must have dropped it."

"What about the fifteen grand?"

"Gone for good. They got that. It was supposed to be for my brother-in-law, rental income from his apartments that I collect for a small fee."

"Don't believe one word of it," Aldo said when I told him the story. "He just wants more money out of us."

We still offered halibut, a very expensive West Coast fish, on the Dine Out menu. I asked Yussuf if he had his halibut price and orders under control.

"Don't worry," he said, his standard answer to all my inquiries.

I was worried when I saw him lug in a large black fifty-pound fish the next morning. It still had the head and fins and didn't seem to be gutted. And it sure didn't look like a halibut. "What's that?" I asked.

"Oh, that? It's a fantastic deal from a friend of mine."

"Okay, what is it? It doesn't look like a halibut."

"It's better than halibut. It's a sablefish, an Alaskan black cod."

"So what is it doing here? I don't see black cod on the Dine Out or the Valentine's menu."

Just at that moment, the phone rang and I had to deal with some other issues. I momentarily forgot about the cod, until a couple of days later when Roy came back with a rejected plate from a customer who'd complained that the halibut was rather oily. Halibut is usually dry, meaty and flaky.

"What happened to this halibut?" Roy asked. "Maybe it was caught in an oil slick," he added with a wink and a nod toward the kitchen.

I knew instantly what had occurred. The wily bastard. I marched into the kitchen and demanded an answer. "I want to see the halibut you're serving."

"We're out of halibut and I had to give the customer something," Yussuf replied with a casual shrug of his shoulders. "Don't worry, nobody will know."

"Are you kidding? All I need is a food critic who will notice the difference, and we're done for. Just now a customer is questioning the fish. You can't do that! You need to tell the servers when you're out of something. They can inform the customers that we have no halibut but we do have fresh sablefish. We cannot just lie and cheat!"

Yussuf stood on the other side of the pass-through from Roy, who had just asked for a piece of "oil-slick halibut." Yussuf made some unusual guttural, rumbling noises, like a volcano about to erupt, and in the next instant a large black piece of raw fish came flying straight at Roy, missed him by a hair, and slithered onto the floor.

"A fish is a fish is a fish!" Yussuf yelled with both his hands in the air, throwing more pieces of fish around the kitchen.

Roy and I were transfixed by this bizarre expression of excessive rage. I turned the music up and casually sauntered toward the kitchen so as not to alert any customers, steeling myself for the confrontation with the Mad Hatter. But the crafty bastard had already slipped out the back door.

Folly Bistro

When I came home that night, after racing my bike through the rain-slick, dark back alleys, all the time thinking about what do about our delinquent chef, I couldn't go to sleep and sat up watching some meaningless TV.

Clare appeared in her nightgown. "What's the trouble, love? It's that crazy chef of yours, isn't it?"

"Yeah. I don't know what to do with him, he's driving me bananas. Today he switched the fish without telling anybody and then he threw a raw piece of it at Roy. I saw it. I stood right beside him. We might as well call the bistro The Flying Fish. This is the second time he's thrown fish at Roy."

"You'll have to let him go, maybe after Valentine's Day. Otherwise you're going to have a nervous breakdown. Come to bed and get some rest."

I fought Yussuf on a daily basis. He kept adding olives, figs and dates to various dishes: olives in the mussels and the salads, figs in the beouf bourguignon, dates with the charcuterie. Very unorthodox and confusing for both the servers and the customers, and definitely not French. Did Yussuf get a deal on olives? Did someone, somewhere, demand olives in everything? He dismissed my concerns and treated me as somebody who didn't have any imagination, not like him, fearless creator and artiste extraordinaire.

Clare was right — Yussuf was driving me crazy, slowly but surely, and he seemed to enjoy the daily challenge of achieving just that. I could hardly sleep anymore and would wake up bathed in cold sweat, banishing feverish visions of the grinning chef taunting me with large fish heads and pots full of yellow curried stews while cartoonish mice jumped from counter to counter.

Valentine's Day was just a few days away and we had over fifty reservations booked. We needed the chef in his best form. We all knew that, especially Yussuf, who enjoyed nothing more than to be the centre of attention.

Then came the chocolate invasion, just in time for Valentine's Day. Having grown up near the Lindt chocolate factory, I had an instant case of déjà-vu when I smelled the familiar scent even before I stepped through the back door. I felt my knees buckle and my eyes pop when I saw Yussuf proudly surveying trays of chocolate cubes, chocolate forms, chocolate balls — hundreds of them, spread out over all the back tables.

"What is this?" I asked with an air of desperation.

"What?" Yussuf asked. "You should know. It's chocolate, my man."

"Yes, I can see that." I swallowed hard.

Chocolate everywhere. And the smell of it, warm, bubbling chocolate on the stove, in pots and bowls, and our chocolate-covered chef looking very pleased with himself and this inexplicable display of confections.

I looked for Kay, our dessert master, but he was nowhere to be seen.

"I sent him home," Yussuf said. "This is my show and we will blow the crowds away, smother them in chocolate," he grinned.

"What are these chocolates — treats for the chef?"

Yussuf shook his large bald-egg head, put his hands on his hips, and proclaimed with an air of a king addressing the ignorant masses, "It's Valentine's Day, for crying out loud. The day of love, sex and chocolate!"

Valentine's, the most important day for all restaurants, was only a couple of days away, but I failed to see the correlation with Yussuf's chocolate orgy.

"I'm about to make pralines, truffles and chocolate treats for everybody. It will be the crowning, spectacular finish to our fantastic menu."

This was news to me. I realized we put treats on the menu for everybody, but I envisioned a couple of boxes of pralines from Costco, not this bacchanalian extravaganza the chef was creating.

"What about the cost?"

"Nothing," he said. "Cheap. I got such a good price on it all."

I didn't believe one word, and when I called Aldo to come and see the chef's latest stunt, Aldo just took one look, tried a couple of pralines and simply said, "That does it. He's going to put us in the poorhouse."

Folly Bistro

Enough was enough. Aldo and I had made up our minds a couple of weeks before, and this latest spectacle sealed the lid on Yussuf's coffin.

Valentine's Day: besides New Year's Eve, by far the biggest day in any restaurant. We were packed, and the kitchen as well as the front staff performed exemplarily. The bistro never looked so good as on a day like this when everybody was in a good mood, the servers because they made great tips, the kitchen because that's what they excelled in, and the owners because the till for once was full. The food came out through the pass-through with flair and aplomb, and Yussuf was in his element, functioning best in the eye of the storm.

True to his promise, he had filled the entire length of the bar with trays and trays of dripping, drooping chocolate treats. They weren't pralines, as he called them, but nuts and strawberries dipped in chocolate, and pre-formed chocolate thimbles filled with liquid chocolate and garnished with raisins, nuts and candied fruit. Hundreds of them were spread across the bar, to the delight of the customers and the staff, slowly melting, pooling and dripping in the warm restaurant atmosphere. After everybody had left, more than half of this extraordinary display of free treats was sadly left behind and slowly congealed all over the bar and dripped onto the floor. When I looked around for Yussuf to ask him what to do with this spectacular mess, he was long gone, vanished like a thief in the night. We stored what we could in the fridges and let the delighted staff fill their boots with chocolates.

When Yussuf sauntered in through the back door, fashionably late and in a good mood, we handed him his last cheque, including a one-month severance package and a record of unemployment stating "shortage of work." His facial expression went through a series of rapid response movements. First it was outrage, then dismay, quickly changing to surprise, and after looking at his sizable cheque, a shrug of his shoulders, dismissal and resignation. All of these emotional changes took less than a minute. He stood up, shook our hands, and packed his knives and tools, as well as some things that I thought were ours — like the electric hand mixer and the expensive vanilla beans. He left trying to save face.

"No need to explain, I fully understand. Now I am free to help my country."

"They need a new chief, not a new chef," I said, thinking my joke quite funny. Yussuf did not. He gave me a scornful look, turned on his heel, and was gone. There went chef number three, and we already had our next chef, Big Bad Bob, waiting behind the curtain, so to speak.

When the bills came in from the chocolate supplier, it was over $400, but this was after Yussuf had left us for a one-way flight to Cairo to save his troubled country.

The ghost of Yussuf haunted the bistro long after he was gone to assist his people in their uprising against Mubarak. We kept finding trays and containers full of chocolate and fillings, figs, dates, and exotic nuts. We also discovered a whole bag of large frozen oysters. Even I know you can't freeze oysters; they expand and pop the shell, dying in the process. Another hundred bucks down the proverbial drain.

Despite it all, I still liked Yussuf. He was the most honourable con artist and honest thief I had ever had the pleasure of meeting, and he was certainly the most entertaining.

Here is Yussuf's pièce de résistance and swan song at Le Bistro. Note the chocolate strawberry treats for everyone.

Folly Bistro

Valentine's 5 Course Celebration Dinner $69

Amuse Bouche & Kir Royal

♥

Alaskan King Crab Soup

or

6 Oysters on the Half Shell
wine reduction vinaigrette

or

Salmon Tartar
crème fraîche, avocado

or

Artichoke Heart Croquette
with Goat Cheese

♥

Palate Cleanser - Berry Sorbet à la Maison

♥

Canard à l'Orange et Cointreau

or

Filet Mignon
Barolo Reduction

or

Sable Fish Fillet
roasted fillet of Alaskan Black Cod, fish broth,
Julienne vegetables & pickled citrus

or

Roasted Alaskan King Crab
Chipotle Saffron Risotto

♥

Crème Brulée

or

Truffles & Chocolate Coated Strawberry

or

Frosty Lemon & Lime Zapagion

♥

Chocolate Strawberry Treats for Everyone

The Reign of Big Bad Bob

Big Bad Bob had been a chef for all his working life and had worked for Aldo in his Italian restaurant. We hired him because he was available, had classic training, and came relatively cheap as far as French chefs go. As his name implies, he was a big man, well over six feet and 300 pounds, built like a fridge, with hands like shovels, a big round head with a grey, receding hairline, and a fat grey moustache that reminded me of a walrus.

Coupled with a loud, booming voice to match his large body, he was an imposing presence and had our young girls running for cover. I had my first encounter of the unpleasant kind with Big Bad Bob not even a week into his employment. His mandate was to re-establish our classic French menu after it had morphed into Middle Eastern fusion food under Yussuf's tenure. The directive was this: Match the actual food to the written menu. Make it the same every day. When the customers ordered mussels, they didn't want olives in a spicy tomato sauce and they didn't appreciate surprises like figs and raisins in the salads. The beouf bourguignon, furthermore, could not be Irish stew; but that was exactly what BBB created. Instead of the classic recipe containing pearl onions, bacon and beef, Bob substituted the pearl onions for white, coarsely chopped onions, added carrots, and left the bacon out altogether.

When the second customer returned the dish, complaining that this was not the beouf bourguignon he expected to be served in a French restaurant, I wanted to know from Big Bob what the issue was. He stared at me through his steamed-up glasses and leaned dangerously close. That was the moment when I found out that Bob prefers confrontation to any other form of settling a disagreement or dispute.

"This is the way I make the classic French stew, that's how it's made in Paris, and that's how it's made here from now on in," he snarled. "Adding the carrots after the stew is cooked saves meat and therefore money and also tastes better. Do you have a problem with that?"

"Indeed I do," I replied, trying my best boss stance, legs apart, hands on hips, chin up. "Maybe during the war it was made like this, but we need to make this dish as we always have — the way it was before Yussuf turned it into Egyptian goulash. And now you've made it into Irish stew without the Guinness," I said, trying hard to not be intimidated by the looming hulk of a pissed-off Big Bad Bob.

"Why don't you just make it yourself?" he hissed, thrusting the large stir stick and the apron at me like a lance and a shield. I backed out of the kitchen, emphasizing that he was indeed the chef but we needed to please the customers first and foremost and only then could we consider personal preferences.

I called in Aldo for backup, and he in no uncertain terms told BBB that the beouf bourguignon recipe was to be cooked as it always had been, with pearl onions and bacon. End of discussion.

"Why doesn't he listen to me?" I asked Aldo, who is smaller than me and younger but is somehow able to put people in their place.

"Because you're too nice, as usual, and let people walk all over you. You're not a referee, you're the boss. Don't try to convince them that you're right, just tell them how it is. And besides, I know Bob from before and he owes me."

On some rainy winter nights in November or February there were more people working in the kitchen than eating in the restaurant. It was rather depressing to see Kay or Chase whipping up bowls of chocolate mousse or Colin making twenty litres of onion soup while Gino watched the hockey game on TV and yours truly, the manager, was trying out the new keg of beer. No matter how many times I looked at the daily sales on the computer, no matter how many excuses I could dream up, the fact remained that on these days we were not only not making any money, we were losing it.

That's when the ideas started sprouting.

"We should have a pretty girl out front dressed only in the menu board," Roy suggested, which didn't go over well with Margo or Melinda. Selena, on the other hand, thought it a fine idea.

"Why not a giant inflatable basket of fries on the roof?" somebody chuckled.

Or how about changing the lighting, the paint, the floor, the menu, the awning, the name, the tablecloths, and on and on.

Change would bring in people just like magic, goes the naive belief. The later the hour, the better and grander the ideas, the more fantastic the schemes and dreams. Then the phone rang. Everyone jumped up. It's a reservation for a late birthday party! No, it was just a cancellation. There was nothing more challenging than keeping a positive outlook when there were no customers in the bistro and the kitchen was loaded with food and cooks.

It was bound to happen. Marcel, our token French waiter and snobby sommelier, had received two warnings before Christmas for showing up tipsy and had been observed many times since taking a fortifying nip behind the counter.

It was a Monday night and at 6:30 there were only two deuces — two tables of two. A good time for me to slip away and maybe spend an evening at home with my Clare. We usually just decided on a silly movie to take my mind off the restaurant.

After I got home, I received the inevitable phone call from Alia, who whispered into the phone like the bistro was some sort of a crime scene. "You have to go to the bistro."

"What's going on?" I whispered back like an idiot. "And why are you whispering?"

"The baby is asleep," Alia told me. "Marcel is drunk."

I put the phone down and stared at the TV screen without seeing it.

"What's wrong now, honey? Is it something that Aldo can handle? Is anybody hurt or dying?"

"Marcel," was all I said.

Clare squeezed my hand and said, "I'll tell you all about the movie when you get back. Go easy on the poor man."

I jumped on my bike and despite the steady drizzle pedalled through the dark and wet West End. I arrived two minutes later and Alia just nodded her head in the direction of the bar, where Marcel was arguing loudly with Colin through the pass-through. I could tell from Marcel's loud voice and deteriorating accent that all was not as it should be. There were still only three tables, but one middle-aged, well-dressed couple on table four seemed quite agitated. I took it upon myself to investigate.

"Is everything all right?" I asked, trying to sound undaunted.

"No, it certainly is not. We had to correct our order three times because your waiter either forgot or misunderstood. And now we've been waiting for dessert for over fifteen minutes. It's not like it's overly busy, is it?"

"I'm very sorry. I'll look into this right away."

I took Marcel by the arm and led him off to the side. "What's up with table four? Where are the desserts?"

"Nothing is wrong," Marcel shouted. "It's the cooks and the kitchen who screw everything up, and I will not tolerate it any longer."

I patted Marcel consolingly on the back and asked him to please quiet down. "No need to shout."

"I'm not shouting!" he bellowed. "This is a French restaurant and only French people should work in here."

At that point, the couple from table four got up and headed for the door. I quickly followed them, apologizing profusely. "Do you think there's something wrong with our waiter?" I asked the lady, who turned around in disgust.

"He's either drunk or off his meds. We will never be back. This was supposed to be our anniversary and he properly ruined it. He brought the wrong wine, the wrong food and no dessert."

I was able to waive the bill and save a bit of face, but the damage was done. The woman turned on her heel and her husband hauled her out the door.

Meanwhile, Marcel was shouting at the two guys in the kitchen, who valiantly tried to ignore the drunk server. I'd had about enough. Not only had he cost me money now — those people would tell their friends and they would tell theirs — but he had also ruined my evening at home.

"Marcel, your behaviour is unacceptable. What would you do in my shoes?"

He leaned back and waved a pointed finger in the air. "I would have to fire me," he declared proudly, and, building on his lucid observation, he shouted, "I have no choice but to fire myself. And tell your Italian partner to go back to Italy!" (referring to Aldo, who had never been to Italy). Marcel left out the back door, swaying from side to side, his nose high up in the air, waving his accusing finger at all who were not properly French. And that's how Marcel fired himself.

Just at that moment, the front door opened and about a dozen people walked in. A table of five, one of four and a deuce. Suddenly I had over a dozen people in the restaurant and not one waiter — only Alia, who was very capable but had never served any tables.

"Alia, it's you and me," I said. "You take the table of five, I'll take the deuces on tables three and four." I picked up Marcel's discarded apron and became a waiter for the night.

It turned out to be a busy evening, and with Alia's help and the two cooks, Colin and the Aussie, as well as Billy in the dish pit, we managed to serve twenty-five covers before the night was over. To my delight, I made over $100 in tips.

"And how far did Marcel make it that night?" Aldo asked me when I called him after it was all over. Apparently, he'd made it just two doors down to the Japanese sushi bar, where he passed out after a couple of glasses of wine.

When I told Clare what had happened, she had to laugh. "Your evening sounds a lot more entertaining than the silly flick I tried to watch."

We needed to try something different — any gimmick, any deal, anything that would bring in more customers during those dark and dreary winter days. And just like magic, in walked a magician for lunch. He came in with his wife and looked about my age, with Buddy Holly glasses and slicked-back black hair. He asked for the owner and I walked over to his table, expecting a complaint or a special request. Instead, he palmed his business card out of thin air and handed it to me.

"Hi, my name is Mandrake." When I looked at the business card it turned into the jack of diamonds.

"You probably have heard of my dad by the same name. He even had a comic book named after him."

Indeed I had heard of Mandrake the Magician, and now I was intrigued.

He wanted to know if there was a chance for him to entertain the dinner crowd. "You know, go from table to table, do some card tricks, maybe some small illusions, like this." He pulled a red piece of fabric out of each ear and then pulled alternately on them, like the cloth was going right through his head. He offered to do a show for the price of a dinner for him and his wife and a small fee.

Why not? I thought. We shook hands and he turned the jack of diamonds in my hand into the ace of spades. We needed some kind of magic to bring in more customers — maybe this was it. Mandrake left behind some posters, which we displayed, and I also sent out a mass email.

When Aldo heard about my latest scheme, he looked at me like I was going to need some serious treatment. "What's a magician got to do with French food?"

"Nothing, but who doesn't love magic, tricks and the mystery of illusions? Why not try to mix up a bit of magic with a coquilles St. Jacques or a filet mignon? I think it's worth a try."

"When are you bringing in the dancing girls?" Aldo asked, shaking his head.

We needed to replace Marcel, our drinking sommelier, but I was loath to advertise for a waiter on Craigslist, fearing an avalanche of responses. Instead, I suggested that we offer the job to Alia, who had been with us almost since the beginning and had done really well a couple of nights before as a server. She was conscientious, dependable and, although quite shy, very attractive.

"You want me to be a waitress?" she asked, taken aback and excited at the same time.

"Yes, Alia, just for the time slots that Marcel had and maybe a couple of lunches."

I had no doubt that she would do a fine job. She knew the menu and the workings of the bistro, and when she realized how much money she could make, there was no turning back. In her place, we hired a new buss girl, Mandy from Manila, a young, petite and spunky girl who just happened to walk in the door with a resumé and a confident attitude. Mandy wanted to be a waitress. I promised that she could be our lunch waitress in the upcoming summer, but she started waiting tables long before that. Every time someone called in sick, which happens regularly in the restaurant business, she just took over the shifts. Mandy had lots of ambition, which could be seen as naked greed.

As long as she didn't outright steal anybody's shifts, I reasoned, it would be okay. Mandy also had another valuable asset: She turned out to be a computer whiz, and thanks to her expertise and nimble fingers on the keyboard, we finally, after over a year in business, got a handle on our email lists and were able to send out proper mass announcements and promotions and manage our online presence. I thought Mandy was a rare find. Once again, we had a full crew, ready to serve the masses.

We picked a Sunday, since Sundays are notoriously slow evenings. Put a little magic in the weekend, be a child again, maybe learn a new card trick. I was excited. "Like a little kid going to the circus," Clare said. Mandrake was going to work the tables, engaging the customers and amazing them with the odd sleight of hand — nothing as stunning as removing bras, watches and socks from customers, but still entertainment.

As Aldo predicted, the turnout was rather miserable and the only people who were attracted to Mr. Magic and his tricks were the staff and Clare, who loved a good card trick, as well as Aldo, who wanted Mandrake to show him how it was done. The few unsuspecting customers who were approached by Mandrake were rather mystified by the interruption of their anniversary or birthday dinner and were not there to be dazzled by coins pulled out of their ears or playing cards showing up in their wallets. I had to admit, the evening turned out to be a total flop. But hey, it had been worth a try.

As his nickname implied, Big Bad Bob was big and mean, and closer to fifty than forty. He had a nasty temper, loved confrontation, and settled arguments by imposing his size, weight and fury on the opposing party in such a way that most people just backed off. Any confrontation with BBB had the real potential of physical violence, or at the very least verbal abuse. Why did we hire Bob? Aldo knew him to be a formidable chef, French trained and with all the tricks and know-how of someone who had owned a restaurant and been cooking in most of the city's kitchens throughout his thirty-year career.

BBB promised stability and consistency, quality and a firm hand in a kitchen that seemed to be always teetering on the brink of mutiny, disintegration or explosion. We needed a real general to put back some discipline and order into our dysfunctional kitchen. Yussuf had exemplified a culture of entitlement, lackadaisical stock-keeping, and arbitrary ordering from a number of shady suppliers, as well as favouritism and no respect for his crew or their skills. We had good people in the kitchen: Colin, Billy, Kana, Kay, Chase, and Maria from Mexico, our new weekend dishwasher, all of whom were now Big Bad Bob's crew.

Within days of his hiring, we could see a difference in the food quality. The peppercorn sauce was back to its creamy, peppery wholesomeness, away from the curry-flavoured, black, spicy sauce Yussuf had introduced. Also the chicken looked like the poulet de Paris again — crisp on the outside, juicy on the inside, sliced and sculpted with the leg bone sticking out and with just the right amount of sauce, not swimming in a black puddle, as was the Egyptian way. A sense of calm settled over the kitchen, or maybe it was just naked fear. The small, hot room became a serious work environment, maybe a bit too stern and serious. I didn't hear anybody laughing anymore.

The other reason Aldo liked BBB was he came with a completely dysfunctional home life, so bad that he spent every day at work, no matter if it was his day off. He built shelves, fixed doors and puttered around the place in a methodical, busy manner. Who wouldn't like a guy like that around?

Then the unthinkable happened. Bob fell head-over-heals in love with the Russian waitress from the Italian restaurant two doors down the street. Mirka was a skinny twenty-three-year-old with a body like a boy's, a winning smile, and long, thin hands. I always thought those hands should play a piano, but when I asked her, she just laughed and shook her pretty head.

"This is not going to end well," I prophesied. Aldo and I solemnly agreed. "What is he thinking, or better yet, what is the matter with her?"

Aldo just shook his head in disbelief. "Nobody is thinking here. Maybe they're just friends."

"Yeah, right."

The consequences were as predictable as they were dismaying. Not only did our besotted chef now spend all his free time and a lot of ours chasing after Mirka, he now also forgot to order certain items. It became increasingly clear to me that his mind was not on the job. Big Bad Bob epitomized the textbook stereotype of a fifty-year-old man who hadn't been laid in, let's say, a long time. The miracle of new-found youth and virility had befallen our chef for all the world to see. Not only was he thinking with the wrong head, his big head was about to spin off his shoulders. He felt invincible like superman and strong like King Kong, and acted about as smart as a tractor. He could do no wrong.

I became seriously worried when I looked at his new schedule and noticed that he had only slotted himself in for three full days. On those days he would come in between 10:00 and 11:00 a.m., not like before he'd met Mirka, when his massive F350 Ford would pull in around 9:00 a.m. He now waltzed in late and sat at a table, calling and chatting up suppliers, morphing into an executive chef, spending more time on his phone than in the kitchen. He was also handing over tasks like stock-keeping and the sanitation plan to Colin, our young and very capable sous-chef.

BBB would go into the kitchen, poke his finger into the sauce, sniff at the soup, check the contents in the coolers, and then sit back down at his table, speed-dialling Mirka. "Hi sweetie, I'm just calling to see how you are. Honey, I miss hearing your voice. Yes, I can be off early today. Sure, I'll give you a ride," and because I was standing right in front of him, waiting for him to hang up, "I gotta go, but I'll call you right back. Don't go anywhere," and then to me, "Yeah, what is it now?"

"Well, I'm just wondering about the schedule. It doesn't look right," I said.

"Don't you worry about my schedule. Don't you have things to do? I worry about the kitchen, you worry about bringing in the customers and the payroll." He summarily dismissed me with a wave of his massive arm. It seemed like déjà-vu, back to Yussuf's beginnings. He had rejected me on similar terms. I seemed to get no respect from these lunatic chefs, and it was driving me crazy.

Big Bad Bob's infatuation was nauseating, both in a disturbingly imaginary way and also with regards to our kitchen floundering once again on the shoals of madness and disintegration, this time with captain Mad Bob at the helm.

We were surely cursed. Whenever we thought we had it figured out, it turned into something completely different than we intended. That was the slow time of the year, and we could not afford another expensive, unproductive and distracted chef. The bistro deserved better, and it just underlined the importance of being in control of all the tasks, jobs and duties within the whole restaurant structure. The chef knew that we needed him or someone like him to cook the darn French food. That apparently was the unassailable truth — or was it? I wasn't so sure anymore, since all the work seemed to be done by Colin and Chase, the Aussie cook who always seemed happy and never complained.

"It's the business, mate," he said when I asked why he never seemed to flip out like everybody else. "Kitchens are the same the world over."

Cooks were not doctors or scientists, not magicians or miracle workers. What the hell did we need another expensive, delusional, self-aggrandizing and love-struck super chef for? And then he called Kana a "darkie" and Kay a "poofter." He called Chase "Kanga" and renamed Billy "the Chink." Who knows what he called me. Surprise, surprise. Big Bad Bob revealed himself to be a bigoted, racist Nazi redneck prick on top of everything else.

Every chef we'd hired so far had failed as a leader. Without trust, there is no respect; with neither trust nor respect, the motor stalls and becomes an anchor, the supposed leader turns into an abusive dictator and rules by threats and punishment instead of by example as a role model and a teacher. It's elementary and universal, whether in politics, health care, education or in a kitchen. Instead of nurturing their team with compliments and guidance, every chef yelled at them, and in place of an enthusiastic crew we were left with an unhappy, demoralized kitchen staff working in fear of the chef and always looking for another job.

A Small Mistake and the Rites of Spring

It was a Friday afternoon and Clare and I were about to leave town for a weekend away from the bistro and the city. Usually it's me who's waiting for her, but today it was Clare who was ready to go while I was still talking on the phone to Gino, making sure everything was under control, as well as paying some overdue bills on the computer. We had a great weekend planned at Harrison Hot Springs, the famous resort just two hours east of Vancouver on beautiful Harrison Lake. We had booked a room overlooking the lake and had dinner reserved at the authentic Japanese restaurant. I knew Clare was really looking forward to getting away from the hospital as well as the bistro.

"Let's pretend you don't have a restaurant and I don't have a job for a couple of days. We need some distance, some time out," she said.

"Just one more thing, love. Trying to pay this Telus bill."

"Can't that wait?" she asked.

"Here we go. Click, click, and out."

At exactly that moment, I did just about the stupidest thing I've ever done in my life. At the time it was just a routine online bill payment, something I had done many other times, directly from our bistro bank account. The Telus bill was one of those monthly recurring expenses. Compulsively, I insisted on paying the phone bill before heading out the door. I should have listened to Clare instead. There was no rush.

I typed in $116.52, or so I thought, and made three clicks: continue, confirm, pay. Then I ran out the door, following my impatient wife. We spent a fabulous weekend relaxing, floating in the hot pools, sleeping in, watching a couple of movies, and dining out. We got back home late on the Sunday night, refreshed, rejuvenated and happy. For two days we didn't think or talk bistro or work. That was the deal.

That Monday morning — as on most other mornings — the first thing I checked was our bank account, which to my consternation was within a few dollars of being empty. What the hell! Where was all our money? I was sure we had over ten grand left. I had the payroll coming up and needed this money, and usually after the weekend we were flush. There must have been a mistake, a malfunction, maybe cyber theft. You heard about all these identity thieves who can burrow into your life and bank account. I scrolled down feverishly, checking the outgoing amounts with a rising sense of panic and calamity, and there it was: an online bill payment in the amount of $11,652 to none other than Telus. My eyes bulged, my throat constricted and my brain short-circuited, repeating over and over, *decimal point, decimal point,* and then, *idiot, idiot, oh, I'm such a fucking loser.*

I immediately called the bank, only to be told that, sorry, it was too late to reverse the payment, since more than forty-eight hours had elapsed. "Call Telus directly and they should be able to reverse the payment." I could tell the bank teller felt genuinely sorry for me.

For anyone who has ever called Telus, the routine is familiar. First, there is the electronic menu, then the recording which states that they "are experiencing a larger than normal call volume and a representative will be with you shortly. Your call may be recorded for security and training purposes, blah, blah, blah . . ."

I clung to the phone, listening to torturous, tinny elevator music, soft hits from the seventies. All I wanted to do was explode. Most of all, I chastised my own stupidity and negligence. I had nobody else to blame but myself for all that had gone wrong with the bistro — my failure to stand my ground, my inadequacies as a leader and inability to get a handle on the restaurant business. Who was I trying to fool? I had no qualifications to run a French restaurant, no experience, and no education that gave me any credentials, and here I was trying to swim against the prevailing current of cheap and fast food.

I knew I was disillusioned, but I didn't want to disappoint Clare, who had stood by me unfailingly. I didn't want to disappoint Aldo, who counted on me, and I definitely didn't want to fail our customers, who expected the best. In other words, I was depressed and discouraged and felt like such a fool, such a sucker. And now this embarrassing fuck-up, "faux pas" in French. Neither the excruciatingly painful elevator music nor the fact that it was my money after all and I would get it back made me feel any better. All these emotions flooded my mind while I was being suspended in time, listening to the whole of Elton John's "Benny and the Jets" and most of Paul Anka's "Time of Your Life." At last, somebody with an Asian accent picked up the phone and I had to switch gears and return to the pressing and immediate present. I obligingly answered a lot of personal questions, while all I wanted was to talk about the missing $11,000.

As is the case nine times out of ten, the person on the other end spoke lousy English and everything had to be repeated at a third-grade level.

"I made a mistake and paid too much money. Can you please send it back?"

"Sir, I will transfer you to the billing department." Click. More music, and then another operator who went through the same spiel about my phone number and identification, and then, "What can I do for you today?"

Again I explained my situation, only to be told that because it involved a large amount, it would take some time to verify the facts. I wanted to scream but knew it wouldn't result in any positive action.

"Please call back in two business days."

"Two days? Can't you see that I overpaid by $11,000?"

"Yes, sir, I understand. Please call back in two days. Is there anything else I can do for you today?" I wanted to crawl through the phone and strangle them.

I called back two days later just to be led through the same weary ordeal until I got to tell my story. This time I had somebody on the line who actually understood my predicament and promised to investigate and get back to me. I actually got the call back and they told me that yes, indeed, the mistake had been acknowledged and a refund would be issued in the form of a cheque but that it would take from two to three weeks. I forget what I said but it wasn't pretty.

"No, sir, there is nothing you or I can do. Can I help you with anything else today?"

A Small Mistake and the Rites of Spring

Springtime.

Time for budding flowers, for nesting birds, time for love and misplaced affections. Alice, our spacey busser, seemed to be more distracted than usual. She put the forks on the side where the knives should go and forgot to prepare the butter dishes for the bread or check that enough napkins were pre-folded, all jobs she was supposed to be able to do in her sleep.

"What's the matter, Alice?" I asked. "You seem to be distracted." Like accusing the Pope of being Catholic.

"It's nothing."

"Oh, come on, Alice, you can tell me. I won't bite your head off."

"You're gonna hate me," she said.

"Of course not. Alice, what is it?"

"It's Caleb. He's been writing me letters almost every day."

"Caleb from Fiji? Caleb the impaler?" I couldn't believe it. "What on earth do you see in him? You know what he did, don't you, when he was after Jenny? You remember that?"

"Yeah, but he says he's different now and doesn't drink anymore, and he keeps writing to me."

"Alice, you can't believe him. Don't answer him. Please don't do that, don't encourage him. He's not worth it. The guy is an absolute nutter and you don't want anything to do with him, believe me."

"I knew you'd be mad," Alice said, eyes downcast, as she fidgeted absentmindedly with the napkin rings in her hands.

"Where is he and what's he doing?"

"I think he's living and working at the convention centre in Kamloops."

"Convention centre? Kamloops? Do you have any of his letters?"

She fetched her purse and pulled out one of a dozen or so identical envelopes.

I looked at the return address and almost choked. "Alice, can you read that? It says 'correction centre,' not 'convention centre.' That's jail, Alice. He's writing to you from jail!" I stabbed my finger at the stamped address in the upper left-hand corner of the envelope. "Did you know he was in jail?"

"Not really. He told me that it's not true what people are saying about him," she said miserably.

"Alice, people like Caleb are not innocent. He has been busted and convicted by a court and a judge. He has been found guilty of whatever charges he was accused of."

"I don't know what to do."

"Alice, write and tell him that you don't want anything else to do with him, that you have a new boyfriend, or that you're moving — anything to get him to stop bothering you. Tell him to leave you alone. End it. Alice, forget about Caleb. He's just using you. You really need to keep your mind at work when you're here. We need you here, please."

She nodded in agreement, holding back her tears. The poor kid had been completely under Caleb's spell. I explained the dilemma to Alia and asked her to have a chat with Alice, woman to woman, and hopefully set her head straight.

I borrowed $10,000 from my personal line of credit to fill the void left by my Telus fiasco and called them back. By now I knew the routine, and again I explained the whole scenario to another anonymous operator.

"Yes, I can see that a refund will be processed. No, I cannot tell you exactly when. Yes, this is the billing department. Sir, I understand. Is there anything else we can help you with today?"

Every day I checked the mail for the cheque, but to no avail. By now everybody in the bistro knew my stupid story, and every day somebody asked, "Any luck today?" Then, judging by my reaction, "No, I guess not."

We sat down for our weekly Monday morning executive meeting between Aldo, the chef and me to talk about schedules, menu changes, improvements and other concerns. I brought up the point that on the slow days it would really help us out if the chef, who was on salary, would stay and close up instead of an hourly wage earner like Colin or Chase.

Big Bad Bob took a beat and then leaned his large head forward with unblinking eyes, halfway across the table, while I backed up, pressing into the bench seat. He laid one big meaty paw on the table while the other hand balled into a fist, the index finger stabbing through the air at me and then at his hand on the table, demanding with a menacing undertone to his big booming voice, "Does this look black to you?"

I looked at his hand, trying to digest what I had just heard. He went one step further, just to make sure I got the point: "Do I look like a nigger to you?"

Now I was truly speechless, looking helplessly over at Aldo. "He looks quite brown," I said, trying to make a lame joke, pointing at Aldo.

"Well, I guess that makes him half of one," Bad Bob snarled through his quivering grey moustache, eyes ablaze behind the thick lenses, while he leaned back dangerously in the small bistro chair, his beefy arms folded defiantly across his barrel chest.

Stunned, I tried to change the subject to something more mundane, like what kind of special we were planning for the upcoming week. The conversations fizzled out soon after. The chef withdrew into his kitchen and I walked Aldo out the back door.

"Did he just call you the N-word?"

"I think he did," Aldo said, shrugging his shoulders. "Don't worry, I'm used to it. Every time I go through an airport it takes me hours to get cleared. It's called racial profiling and they all do it."

I had no idea, and the whole thing was making me ill. "We can't tolerate that kind of talk, Aldo, and I know he also talks pidgin English to Kay and Billy and calls them chinks, and I know he called Kana a darkie. We need to get rid of him. He's a fucking Nazi, never mind his distracting infatuation with his Russian love interest."

"But we need him," Aldo objected. "His food is good and he really stabilized the kitchen. But I know what you mean. Let's wait, and hopefully he'll settle down."

I had my doubts. Leopards don't change their spots overnight, as the saying goes.

The evening service was slow and as usual BBB took off early and left Colin and Chase in charge, along with the new dishwasher, Maria from Veracruz, who at five feet tall could hardly reach inside the dish pit, which didn't stop her. She worked hard, her face and hands red like raw meat from the constant steam. She never complained. I caught BBB just as he was about to take off in his big truck and pointed out to him that this was exactly the sort of situation in which I would like him to stay and send Colin or Chase home. He gave me a spiteful look and gunned his diesel truck.

"You're a racist asshole!" I yelled as he was pulling out. I'm sure he heard me, but I didn't care. He really had me going in circles. Why did I have to put up with these people? I would never have associated with these kinds of individuals were it not for the bistro. I'd never had to face anything like this before. It was a real dilemma and a personal quandary.

I woke up in the middle of the night and couldn't go back to sleep. Something was deeply troubling me, fundamentally out of sync, and I felt a discord deep down inside. I knew it had to do with our chef and the nasty remarks he'd made the previous day. I disliked BBB intensely. He gave me the creeps. I felt trapped inside a round room, looking for a corner to hide in.

I told Clare the whole sordid story first thing in the morning over coffee. "I don't know what to do. I can't even sleep, it's got me all fucked up."

Clare called it "moral distress," a known syndrome afflicting nurses in palliative care situations, defined as distress caused by situations in which the ethically appropriate course of action is known but cannot be taken, for example, withholding treatment at the wish of the afflicted or the spouse. She diagnosed my dilemma exactly, but I didn't seem to have much of a choice about it. All I knew was that I couldn't waste my time enabling a fascist redneck like Big Bad Bob, whose main argument was "I was born here, buddy!"

Addressing moral distress requires changes in order to preserve your dignity and authenticity; in other words, it calls for decisive action, which means that we had to come up with a plan rather than reactionary, emotionally driven knee jerks. Another meeting was in order. This situation was starting to chip away at my personal relationship with Aldo, and that was a price neither one of us was willing to pay. We'd come this far and survived a difficult journey through rough waters, steered clear of shoals, plugged leaks, changed crews, captains, and even headed entirely off into uncharted waters as a high-end, low-priced French bistro, which was now once more on the verge of disintegrating.

I wanted Big Bad Bob gone, while Aldo argued that we needed him because we were coming into the busy season and his expertise, experience and skills superseded any personality shortcomings. A tough argument to swallow, but unlike me, Aldo was shrewd and much more business-minded. I always seemed to be caught up with everybody's personal stories, which, according to Aldo, should be left at the door.

"We need to make it clear to Bob that he has to park the racist, bigoted Nazi persona with his monster truck outside the premises," I insisted.

To lecture BBB would not have changed a thing. We already knew he was the smartest man in the room, in the bistro, if not the world — according to him. Pointless to lecture the smartest guy, since he already knew everything. We needed a strategy that would move us forward, solve the present stalemate, and benefit the bistro as a whole.

After much debate between Aldo and me, as well as Clare's insistence that we needed to do something before I had a nervous breakdown, we decided for starters to offer Colin a salaried, full-time sous-chef position. This would put BBB on his toes, since now he would know that a transition would be easy: a loaded gun in the shape of Colin, cocked and ready to shoot, waiting in the wings. We didn't say anything to the smartest man in the world but instead decided to wait patiently, knowing that in due time he would fall on his own sword.

In addition, I also apologized to BBB, eating a large helping of humble pie, for having called him a racist asshole. He accepted magnanimously and seemed relieved that the train was back on track and not a wreck on the side of road, leaving him looking for another job. Aldo was right. We were in no position to change chefs at this time; the kitchen was in dire need of some focused stability. We needed to concentrate on the food and the coming summer season — but I also knew that BBB and I were not going to get old together.

Folly Bistro

Some time in April, Sysco, one of our main suppliers, presented a seminar by a genuine French chef from Paris and a marketing guru from New York. If nothing else, it was a free lunch. Aldo, BBB, and I attended, and to my surprise we came away with some great ideas and new insights.

"There are three stages of eating," Maurice said with an obvious French accent. He waited a beat, looking at us past his formidable French nose, and continued, "You can eat until you're satisfied, stuffed, or until you hate yourself." He chuckled and added, "Like the French, the Italians or the Americans." We all laughed. He continued: "Where does your restaurant fit in? Quality or quantity? On the other hand, who cares if your food is French or Greek or Italian, as long as it sells. Give the people what they want. Make something cheap look and taste expensive, like chicken livers or even burgers." This from the authentic French chef.

The American marketing guru in a sky-blue golf shirt, with what looked like a gold Rolex on his hairy wrist, nodded his angular, close-cropped head approvingly and introduced himself. "I'm Rupert and I specialize in menu presentation and design." He looked at us expectantly, then launched into his spiel.

"Most people scan a page from the top right corner across and down. In other words, don't hide your most popular items at the bottom right of the page. Also, don't highlight the prices. Hide them among the item description, in a smaller font, even. The price needs to be discreet and secondary, not the primary focus."

We looked at corporate restaurant menus from the Cactus Club and Earls, and at first glance I couldn't even find the price. It was buried in the middle of the text describing the dish. My eyes just skipped over it. We also talked about the advantage of prices with cents, as in $8.95, as opposed to round numbers like $9. There were two schools of thought, but most modern views came down on the solid numbers without the pennies, which was always my preference.

Aldo, however, extolled the merit of adding pennies. "Nine ninety-five looks and feels better than $10. Also you can raise it like at the gas pumps to $9.99. Four pennies for every order add up to hundreds of dollars over the year."

A Small Mistake and the Rites of Spring

We eventually opted to keep the modern version — no pennies. But we decided to rework our menu for content and also for looks. We came away from the seminar with folders full of ads, menu examples and interesting facts and figures. It felt like school, but thanks to the lovely tasting menu, was an altogether positive outing.

I was all pumped to introduce and implement some of the points we took away from the seminar. We needed to draw in some more of the young crowd. Maybe our classic French menu held no recognition factor with the Y generation. They had no clue what coquilles St. Jacques or even pommes frites meant. We needed to add something that everybody recognized.

"What are the two most popular foods in North America?" I asked Aldo over a basket of frites at the bar.

"Hamburgers and pizza," Aldo said.

"In fact, there are only five foods North Americans between the ages of fifteen and thirty-five recognize," Big Bob said. "Hamburgers, pizza, pasta, steak and chicken."

"Okay then, we already have chicken and steak, we can't do pizza, so let's offer a burger — how about a lamb burger?" I suggested.

The chef was on board right away, while Aldo had to think about it.

"A fish burger and a lamb burger. Let's make them special and put a big, bold sandwich board on the sidewalk. What's there to lose?"

"It's not very French," Aldo said.

"Who cares? The bank doesn't ask what kind of food we make the money from."

"He has a point, Aldo," the chef said. "Let's do it."

"Let's call it lamb-borghini," I suggested.

"Let's not push it," Aldo said.

We also added Caesar salad and a classic lobster mac 'n' cheese, and deleted some of the dishes only French people over seventy would recognize. Instead we added lamb, salmon, and chicken burgers. Within days, the results were obvious: Half of our lunch orders were burgers and the customers loved them. Not one person complained about the missing coquilles St. Jacques or croque monsieur.

Another two weeks had gone by since my last call to Telus. No cheque, no news, nothing. I was starting to feel like I might never get my money back, that this whole Kafkaesque farce was going to end in me driving my truck through the front entrance of the Telus building in Burnaby. That might get me some attention. I really needed answers, and this time I wasn't going to be put off to another department or another day. Now this was personal. As soon as somebody answered, after the usual twenty minutes of elevator music, and after I had answered all the preliminary identity questions, I asked the operator where he was. "Asia, Africa, the Middle East?"

"I'm not allowed to tell you, sir."

"Come on, humour me. Is it warm there?" Yes. "Is it in North America?" No. "South America?" No. "Central?" Yes. "Mexico?" No. "Nicaragua?" No. "Guatemala?" Bingo. "There is a Telus call centre in Guatemala City?"

"Yes, sir, there is."

"What's your name?"

His name was Charley. We were going places now.

"Charley from Guatemala City, please help me out here. I've been waiting six weeks and still have not received anything from Telus. I'm starting to worry that this nightmare will never end and I will never get my money back."

Charley promised to investigate and call me back. He did call me back and told me that a cheque had been issued two weeks before and it was probably stuck in the mail.

"Maybe in Guatemala, but not here in Vancouver." Mail doesn't get stuck for over two weeks. Unheard of. This was a Friday. I panicked and asked Charley if he could stop payment on this cheque and have a new one issued.

"I can do that, but it will take two to four business days."

"Okay, please initiate the process. And Charley, can you call me back in a couple of days and keep me posted? You can't do that? But you can, Charley, you're the only person who has ever called me back."

On Monday the cheque arrived. The envelope's address window was obscured by the red cancellation stamp. It was also circled and several arrows pointed toward the partially obscured address of the bistro. I could see what had happened. The envelope had been upside down in the Telus stamp machine. The postie couldn't read the address and returned it to Telus, who put it back in the mail until another postie took the time to figure out the address and deliver it — probably two weeks of back and forth.

I ran the cheque over to the bank and wanted the teller to confirm that it would clear right away.

"Sorry, sir, this cheque is drawn on the Bank of Montreal — you need to go and check with them." I did just that, only to be told that that particular account was too large and not accessible by a branch in Vancouver.

"It's your cheque, it's drawn on an account with your bank, and you can't confirm that it will clear?" I said, exasperated.

"No, sir, I mean yes, sir, we can't confirm. It will take up to forty-eight hours to clear."

Again I called Telus and desperately pleaded with them to not cancel the cheque that I had just deposited. I'm sure the operator thought I was nuts.

"Is there anything else I can help you with today?"

I had to wait until Tuesday, and to my great relief the cheque did clear and finally I got my money back. What's the moral of this story? Don't underestimate the power of the decimal point.

If not magic tricks, then surely live music would bring them in. Who doesn't love a live entertainer? What kind of music would suit a French restaurant? A mandolin player? How about a squeezebox artist? Maybe a classical guitarist?

As our luck would have it, the perfect candidate walked in the door just after lunch.

"Hi, I'm Jojo. You might have heard of me. I just happened to walk by and thought to myself what a perfect place this joint would be to entertain some classy folks."

"Wow," I said, thinking that this was surely serendipitous. "We were just talking about having some live music in the bistro. What's your, uh . . . forte? I mean, your specialty."

"Man, I've been playing the circuit all my life," Jojo said. "From rock bands to solo gigs, from jazz to funk. These days, I mainly do experimental stylistic interpretations of famous songs, but hey, I can play anything, man. I'd love to play this place — it's small, intimate, exactly what I'm looking for. I'll bring in all my friends and fans. We'll fill the place and have a great time."

"How about next Sunday?" I offered on the spur of the moment.

"Done deal. How about a bowl of soup for a starving artist?" Jojo asked.

"Hey, Colin, can you make the man an onion soup, please?" I even topped it up with a pint on the house.

Nothing could possibly go wrong. Aldo, of course, was ever the sceptic. "Another magic evening at the bistro?" he said sarcastically.

"You wait and see. Maybe this is going to be a weekly special." I had high, albeit possibly desperate, hopes.

"Even if it's just going to be a one-night stand," I reasoned, more with myself than with Clare, who was equally dubious. "His buddies will more than compensate for the $100. I promised Jojo a dinner and a couple of drinks."

I had a quick poster printed with a promo photo Jojo had left behind. "An Evening with Jojo, Virtuoso Journeyman Guitar Player at the Bistro." His postcard-sized picture showed him as a young troubadour with a blue guitar, looking like a cross between Dylan and Donovan and probably from the same vintage.

When Jojo first walked through the door on Sunday, already half an hour late, he looked like he'd just got up from a park bench. Unshaven and smelling faintly of mildew, glasses askew, hair tucked under an Irish cap, fingernails black. He claimed to be in a tough spot, down on his luck temporarily, nothing to worry about. He looked at least thirty years older than his poster, and like himself, his blue guitar had faded to a dull dark grey. Right away he asked for something to eat. He inhaled a bowl of lobster bisque and two baskets of bread and butter along with a glass of our cheapest house wine. I started to get more than a little suspicious when he asked for a second glass of wine.

"Maybe later," I said. "Let's get you set up."

I had a prominent spot near the window in mind, but when I saw his battery-powered and beat-up little amp, I relegated him toward the back of the restaurant, out of the way, so to speak, close to the washrooms. I left him alone until one of his friends arrived, not to dine but to sit next to Jojo, hoping for a free glass of wine from the house. No bloody way. First I needed to hear some music. Jojo twanged a few strings on his battered old guitar, and then started chatting up a couple of young women who were customers and definitely not part of Jojo's entourage.

The restaurant filled up reasonably well for a Sunday night, but none of it had anything to do with our virtuoso entertainer. In fact, his uncouth personality, which matched his guitar playing, if you could call it that, had the opposite effect. People frowned, perplexed, when they saw and heard Jojo plucking his strings on his ill-tuned guitar. No recognizable songs or melodies, no coherent music, just random strumming and plucking with no structure or technique. It was an embarrassing disaster.

Desperate, I asked him to take a break, which meant more wine and more food. After the third glass of wine, I cut him off.

"Where are all your fans, Jojo?"

"Good question, man. They all promised to show up. I don't understand it myself. How do you like the show so far?" he had the guts to ask.

"It's very experimental stuff you're playing here," I said lamely, wanting to tell the truth — that he totally sucked, that he was an imposter, a con, and a loser.

"Yeah, man, I got away from conventional music, out on my own, reaching for higher ground. Know what I mean, man?" I had a vague idea that it had something to do with his self-delusion, helped by an unhealthy amount of illegal drugs.

Meanwhile the guys in the kitchen had a good front-row view of Jojo and killed themselves laughing, yelling out taunts like "Play 'Stairway to Heaven'! How about 'Do It My Way,' or how about 'Born a Loser'!" Jojo complained about the catcalls and taunts coming from the kitchen.

"Maybe it's best if you wind up your performance, and no, no more wine." I shuffled Jojo and his buddy unceremoniously out the back door, along with their crappy equipment.

Just then, Aldo came in to check out the action. "Well, how was the musical evening? Looks like the show is over?"

"No comment" was all I said.

Jojo pretty well wound up our Sunday night entertainment series, and I realized that we needed to get back to basics. Work on the food and service, maybe do some advertising, and create some new dishes that would bring in the masses.

For the third year in a row, the Vancouver Canucks were playing Chicago in the first rounds of the playoffs, and once again they battled right to the end: game seven and OT. Almost like it was scripted to squeeze the most amount of commercials, stadium rental and TV time. But any conspiracy theory that involves more than three people will never stand the test of scrutiny. Someone will always talk, feel bad, try to con the other two or confess from the sheer weight of guilt. Nobody except the goalies could throw the game, and Luongo just didn't seem the type. He made too much money as it was without having to cheat.

These hockey nights were a boon for the sports bars, the arena employees and the CBC, but crippling for restaurants like us. Aldo and I were Canucks fans who wanted them to lose so people would abandon their TVs and pizzas or take-out, and go for dinner at one of the over 2,000 restaurants in town.

We buckled under the pressure and installed a TV, hoping to attract some business. Instead, the TV became hugely popular with the staff, who then had their own sports bar. A few people watched from outside through the window.

The Canucks were on a tear and up three straight games, and we were all talking a sweep of the Blackhawks. Some restaurants created new dishes, like a burger called Blackhawk Down Burger, and the whole city celebrated like we had already won the cup. Then the Hawks trashed the Canucks three games in a row and suddenly we were into game seven of the series. Nail-biting time in Vancouver, and there restaurants were deserted in favour of living room couches across the city. The TV was on full blast, with the whole kitchen and serving staff stacked up at the bar watching the game while I sat in the back with the calculator figuring out how we were going to pay the HST, which was an amount equal to or greater than the cost of a small compact car — money we were supposed to have saved and stashed for the government. Eventually, I joined the crew in front of the screen, and when the game went into OT, I too had butterflies in my stomach and secretly hoped for a win. They did, with a great goal by Burrows.

The euphoria quickly gave way to a reality check. Now what? For all we knew they could go all the way, which could mean another twenty-one (three times seven) game nights at the bistro. Maybe we would just do 50 percent on game nights or donate 25 percent of the food to Canucks Place, the team's children's charity. Or create a lottery, or raffle off a trip to Paris.

It was one week until Mother's Day, which was (after New Year's and Valentine's) the biggest day of the year for restaurants and flower shops. We desperately needed these commercial days to lift the daily average, which was in the doldrums during the glum shoulder months.

Clare and I tried the newly launched Sunday brunch: eggs Benny Pacific served with smoked salmon, a fruit bowl and pommes frites, all for $12.

"Does anybody know what a great deal this is?" she asked, right to the point as always.

"I hope so. We have the sandwich board on the sidewalk, we took out an ad for Mother's Day which mentioned the brunch, and apart from hiring a clown or a bikini girl with a megaphone, we rely on the walk-by traffic and word of mouth," I said, wondering how else to promote this super deal.

We left out the back door and surprised Chase, the Aussie, and Alice standing face to face, inches apart, with their hands linked. Oh my, I thought, it looks like she got over Caleb the Impaler rather quickly.

"How come these young people can't find anyone outside of their immediate work environment?" I asked Aldo. These dalliances seemed rather incestuous to me. Colin and Selena, Caleb and Jenny, Yussuf and Yvette and now Chase and Alice. Who would be next? I knew Gino had his eyes on Margo, but then so did everybody. Roy, the Scottish joker, was the only one who was happily married, and his loves were sports cars. He always shouted with pleasure whenever one roared by the bistro. Kana was married, and her husband, who was exactly the same size and body type as her, worked as a second cook in an Italian restaurant. Billy was too scattered to have any kind of relationship, and Alia had a Latvian boyfriend. Mandy, pretty as a spring flower, had a few boys on the run. Melinda kept breaking up and getting back together with her Quebec boyfriend, while Kay apparently had an older partner, but mostly loved his mom. And we all knew about Big Bad Bob's infatuation with Mirka, the Russian princess. Restaurant folk are like a small, isolated tribe, a subculture in the midst of civilization that exists all around us but somehow passes us by like a vast river around an island.

Monday lunch was a lonely experience at the bistro. I did the accounts for the past week and handed out the kitchen tips (3 percent of the gross sales), and after paying out the tips owing to the servers, I had nothing left to put in the bank — never mind my cut or Aldo's. We were just the owners. There was a minimum-wage law for the staff, but that didn't apply to us.

At that moment Monsieur Ducat, the Duke, the wine merchant, and his big German partner, Rupert, along with two other well-dressed businessmen, walked in for lunch. All it takes is one good table to lift everybody's spirits, as well as the daily average. As much as I detested snobs, rich snobs were always welcome. I loved and hated them. The tall, thin Duke, with his pencil moustache and longish grey hair, and the thick-chested, boisterous Rupert were two very snobby customers. They were exactly the opposite in appearance, like Laurel and Hardy, but both equally conceited.

The Duke regularly ordered steak tartare all around, along with a $100 bottle of wine. When he brought along friends or business partners, like on that lucky day, the bill doubled. Rupert always acted as if he owned the place, gesticulating exuberantly with his large hands, snapping his fingers for service, never looking at or engaging with the servers, while the Duke always complained about the food or the temperature of the wine or the fact that they had to wait too long. We suffered these elitists, gritted our teeth, and bowed and curtsied like we were in a medieval play.

A Small Mistake and the Rites of Spring

The servers did it for the tips, I did it for the money, and the Duke and Rupert did it because they could.

The phone rang at 9:00 a.m., when I was just going over the bills from the night before. I was hoping for an early reservation. Instead, the caller identified himself as Jean. "Jean," he repeated, "not John," and he wanted a meeting with the owners about the possible sale of the restaurant. Just like that, out of the blue. I didn't know what to say, but agreed to meet next door at Starbucks at 3:00 p.m. for a casual chat-and-info meet.

I excitedly called Aldo, who was rather sceptical but agreed to join in.

"We're not really getting rich here, and who knows, maybe this Jean guy is for real," I said.

I was half an hour early for the meeting, rehearsing my reluctant sales pitch, feeling like I was being invited to a poker game with no idea of the rules. Jean turned out to be an easy mark: with his proper French beret and Maurice Chevalier pencil moustache, he was the quintessential French guy. I wondered if he drove a Citroën. Jean carried himself with an overly confident demeanour, like a proper businessman: friendly but distant, polite but at the same time a bit condescending. He was French, after all. "From Paris," he said with emphasis on the last syllable and the correct intonation. "I've been watching you two for the past year, and from what I can tell, your bistro needs a few more customers in the door," he said in perfect Canadian English. I supposed he could switch the accent on or off, depending on the situation.

I furtively scanned the place for Aldo, who was late as usual. Aldo was born late, has been late since day one, and he readily admitted to it. When he says five minutes, he means up to half an hour; when he says an hour, it could be half the day. His tardiness increases at an exponential rate.

"We're doing okay, better as time goes by, but yeah, more bums in the seats would always be welcome," I said. "And why are you interested in the bistro?"

Just then, Aldo blew in through the front door and joined us, out of breath like he had been running, apologizing for his tardiness. "Ah, John, it's you," Aldo said, to my surprise. The two knew each other.

"Aldo, you're still the same," Jean said, ignoring the fact that Aldo called him "John." I wasn't sure if he was referring to Aldo's being late or complimenting him on his appearance. I was just glad that now we were two against one. I let Aldo carry the conversation, which quickly came to the point. Jean was not one for small talk. As it turned out, he used to work at the bistro as a waiter; in fact, it was his first job when he came to Canada some thirty years before. Besides his nostalgic motivation, he also had some ideas he felt should be implemented in order to make the bistro once again the flagship French restaurant it used to be. We didn't mention any dollar amounts, but Jean asked for financial statements and we promised to keep in touch.

Mother's Day. We had publicized a sumptuous dinner special, decorated the bistro with roses, carnations and a splendid bouquet from our favourite flower shop next door. We were pumped and ready, but as usual it all turned out to be different than we'd expected. We were completely overrun at lunchtime with walk-ins of entire families, and struggled to get the food out. I became the de facto bartender and served up every ounce of champagne and fizzy water. An emergency shopping trip to the liquor store and Costco loomed for the afternoon.

Gino called in extra help for the front, Mandy was elevated to server, and Big Bob was yelling at everybody in the kitchen, which resembled a boot camp. I ran around cleaning tables and seating customers. The rush was over by 2:00 p.m., and then I went shopping while the kitchen staff worked fiendishly to prep for the evening. At 5:00 p.m., we were ready and fully stocked once again. And then . . . not very much happened. We had about thirty reservations and they all showed up, but hardly any walk-ins and no late reservations. Apparently, all mothers were treated for lunch, and for dinner they were back home cooking, which meant that our Mother's Day dinner didn't live up to expectations. We ended up sending servers and cooks home early. Such are the breaks. Still, all in all, a good day.

A Small Mistake and the Rites of Spring

The sun finally broke through the clouds and once again summer made its first hesitant appearance. We left the front door open, hoping prospective customers would be enticed by the inviting gesture.

"What we really need is the goddamn patio!" lamented Aldo, and he was right.

"Where is Rudy with his permits that he promised almost a year ago?" I asked, but Aldo just looked at me, shaking his head.

"We're on our own this time. Rudy, you know how he is, full of talk and bluster and then we don't see him for months."

After lunch I walked up and down Denman Street and couldn't believe how many restaurants just put tables and chairs out onto the sidewalk — no railing, no enclosure, and apparently no permit. Alright then, I thought, we'll do the same.

Aldo insisted that we go to City Hall to check out the legality of this decision. "No problem," we were told, "just don't serve any alcohol and fill out this 'small patio' permit. That will be $140."

"That's it?" I said, surprised. "And we waited over a year just to find out we can put tables and chairs out on the sidewalk?"

And voilà, le patio appeared. Within minutes of dressing the tables outside, we had customers sit down at them. Within two days we had paid for the three tables we bought, and this simple addition became the best form of advertisement.

Since there was no alcohol involved, we put Mandy in charge of the outdoor tables, which was nothing short of a bonus for our feisty young waitress, considering what had just happened a few days previously.

When Mandy first walked into the bistro a couple of months before, I promised her a possible serving job for the summer. Within a couple of weeks, she already knew everything about the restaurant and just needed to learn about the wines: how to pour and sell, how to serve and open a bottle properly. She figured that out in no time, and we had ourselves a smart and sassy new server. Patrons liked her easygoing manners, and since she was cute and friendly she could easily upsell desserts, even if the customer couldn't eat another bite.

Then one morning, Margo, our Sophia Loren from Prague, mumbled something about Mandy not even being old enough to drink, and there she was a full-time server. I stopped in mid-stride. "What was that? Not old enough to drink?"

"Well, yeah," Margo said. "She's only eighteen."

Oh my god! She can't drink, but here she is selling and serving liquor. I had even made her try the different wines so that she could describe them. I was stunned. It had never occurred to anybody to check her age. How stupid was that?

I immediately called Aldo. He was equally taken aback.

"We could be shut down at a moment's notice if a liquor inspector walked in and saw her opening bottles of wine and shaking martinis — no warning, just a notice at the door and a revoked license and that would be the end of Le Bistro."

On her next shift, I cut Mandy off at the door and made her sit down. I got right to the point.

"Mandy, how old are you?" The question was rhetorical because I kept right on going. "You're not nineteen, you're not legal to drink, but here you are serving liquor to the public. Are you aware that we could just be closed down at a moment's notice and that everybody in here, not just me and Aldo, could lose our jobs and livelihoods?"

"But I have the Serving It Right certificate," she said defiantly, looking at the floor.

"Well, Mandy, you must have lied about your age, because you can't serve liquor until you're nineteen. You know that. You can't drink it and you can't serve it! That's it. It's nothing personal, Mandy."

"You're firing me?" She still didn't want to get it.

"No, Mandy, I'm demoting you back to busser until you're nineteen."

I couldn't just fire her, although I had good reason to. We needed her computer skills, and nothing escaped her alert eyes; she was confident and astute for her young age. She lived with her parents, who she probably helped to support, and she was always on time, which was already more than I could have said about most anybody else. Also, it was our fault that we hadn't checked her age. So it seemed fair to offer her the weekend brunch server shifts and now the patio tables.

A Small Mistake and the Rites of Spring

"As long as you don't serve alcohol, you're fine."

Mandy unhappily accepted her demotion, having no choice, knowing to her chagrin that she would make a lot less money as a busser. Once she'd had a taste of the tips she made as a server, it was a hard step back to minimum wage and menial labour.

I came in the back door, loaded down with boxes of supplies from Costco and the liquor store. Another rowdy Wednesday night loomed just hours away.

"We had a visit from Laura, the liquor inspector today," Alia said sheepishly, never breaking stride while polishing wine glasses. Alia was a true multitasker. She could talk, answer the phone and check on orders, all at once. She was also our smoothest and most perceptive employee, on a two-year work visa from Latvia. A struggling country, according to Alia, inhabited only by old, feeble and uneducated people because everybody else had left or was about to leave.

"Oh yeah? What did she want?"

"She asked to have a beer out on the patio," Alia said.

"Oh shit. What happened?"

"I pointed out that we're not allowed to serve alcohol outside. Laura laughed and said that was the proper response."

"Did she say anything else?" I asked, hugely relieved.

"No, but she had a burger and fries for lunch and loved it."

I was glad that Alia had been in charge. I probably would have served her the beer outside just in order to make a sale, thereby sealing our fate. I shuddered to think what would have happened if Mandy the teenager had served up a brew to the 200-pound liquor inspector. Instead of a burger, she would have eaten Mandy for lunch and me for dessert.

All bartenders tend to be showboaters. They entertain, tell jokes, listen to tales of woe, and generally engage with their drinking customers. Sanchez, being an aspiring actor, saw the space behind the bar as a stage. With his outgoing, positive personality, always smiling and laughing, his Latin good looks and his skills as a drink connoisseur, he made people feel good and forget their daily worries for a few moments. We couldn't do our crazy Wednesdays without him.

That day during the height of the rush, with the restaurant packed and over a dozen people lined up at the door, Sanchez started swooning and talking incoherently out of one side of his mouth. The other side of his face went slack. He started drooling and rolling his eyes. Gino took him by the arm and led him to the rear of the bistro and sat him down. His condition was rapidly deteriorating; his right leg began twitching uncontrollably. Gino called 911. Within minutes, chaos erupted. The ambulance, the fire truck and a police cruiser arrived at the front of the restaurant with all lights flashing and sirens blaring. It looked like a scene from a bad cop movie. Instead of coming discreetly into the back door, the paramedics, cops and firemen came storming through the front door, suspending all restaurant activity. Sanchez looked like he was in bad shape. They put him on a stretcher and carried him out the front door, past all the customers and in front of the whole kitchen and front staff, who lined up as if at a sports event.

Moments later, the parade of lights and sirens moved away and everything reverted back to normal, as if nothing happened. Cooks were yelling at each other and the servers were yelling at the cooks, bussers carried armloads of half-eaten plates into the dish pit, and the customers were busy enjoying themselves. I turned up the music to a dim roar above the ambient cacophony and took over the bar in lieu of Sanchez.

In the midst of this chaos, Maria, the five-foot-tall Mexican dishwasher who always flirted with the boys in the kitchen, decided to clean the dishwasher, probably because it was plugged. She grabbed a milk crate for a stool in order to get a further reach. She leaned forward, the milk crate slipped on the greasy floor, and Maria dived headfirst into the filthy dish pit. She came back up splashing and screaming in Spanish, while Chase and Billy grabbed her by whatever they could get ahold of and hauled her back to the floor.

Maria was by now hysterical and in no shape to continue working. But apart from her messed-up hair, full of flotsam and food scraps, and the soaking, greasy, T-shirt clinging to her, she was all right — all shook up, but nothing broken or hurt, except her pride and dignity. We stuffed her unceremoniously into a cab and sent her home, while Billy and Chase finished doing the dishes. This happened within minutes of Sanchez being carried away on a stretcher.

After we closed, I tried to call the hospital, but since none of us were relatives of Sanchez, who hailed from El Salvador, I couldn't find out any info on the poor guy's condition, if he'd had a stroke or a seizure. I knew for sure that he would no longer be able to work. Nobody could replace Sanchez, but we needed somebody behind the bar on busy days, especially on Wednesdays.

"Isn't that Claude Julien, Boston's head coach?" asked Roy, our Scottish server and celebrity-spotter. He could hardly contain his excitement. He was referring to table seventeen, where four guys were having a quiet dinner.

"You're right, that's him," said Gino, equally mesmerized. "What should we do?"

"We can't very well go over there and wish them good luck tomorrow. We do want the Canucks to win Lord Stanley's cup, don't we?"

"We can't pretend we don't know who he is, not when half the restaurant seems to recognize him. He's been a regular daily face on TV for the past couple of weeks. I'm just going to tell them a hockey joke," Roy said.

Roy walked over to the table, carrying a tray with four shots of complimentary Frangelico, an Italian liqueur. "Gents, this is on the house. What's the difference between a hockey game and a prizefight?" Roy waited a beat before delivering the punchline. "In a hockey game, the fights are real."

They all laughed at Roy's joke and thanked him for the drinks. Out came the iPhone, and then Roy was posing with the entire Boston Bruins coaching staff.

"What a ham," Gino said to Alia, who had no idea what all the fuss was about.

Roy was flushed with pride and excitement, grinning from ear to ear. When the four Boston guys were leaving, all Roy said was, "Enjoy the game tomorrow, and bring the whole team back here."

Folly Bistro

The Canucks beat Nashville and then San Jose to face the Boston Bruins in their first Stanley Cup final since 1994, which ended with a heartbreak loss for the Canucks to Mark Messier and the New York Rangers. This time around, the whole city was convinced that the Sedin twins and Luongo would bring the cup to Vancouver, despite three massive trouncings by the Bruins in Boston and three squeaker wins at home.

Game seven turned out to be the most anticlimactic game of the year. A fully deserved no-contest win by the Bruins left the Canucks deflated. They just didn't show up for the final game. The Boston Bruins won the Stanley Cup at General Motors place (commonly known as the Garage) in Vancouver.

We served 130 covers that night, despite the hockey game. It was fight night, after all. Instead of post-game coverage and interviews, pictures of a madcap riot out front of the stadium floated across the screen, and a sense of unreality settled over the restaurant.

What transpired in the streets of Vancouver in the aftermath of the humiliating 4-0 loss erased sixteen years of effort to rebuild the city's reputation after the last Stanley Cup riot. Vancouver has always projected the image of a fun and welcoming city to live in and visit, where thousands of people could gather peacefully and have a good time, as we showed the whole world during the Olympics.

Contrary to this perception, the dramatic TV images showed riot police trying to scatter the crowd with batons and tear gas while plumes of nasty black smoke from burning cars rose over the city core. These images could easily have been from Athens, Cairo, Yemen or Libya, where street riots and burning cars were common dinnertime news entertainment. But in those places, the revolts stemmed from real conflicts and tragedies, consequences of real terror and tyranny; they reflect genuine fights for rights and causes, not riots over the loss of a sports game played by millionaires in a modern, free city — one that has been proclaimed the best place in the world to live.

A pall had fallen over the crowd at the bistro, which slowly dispersed, not boisterous as usual but subdued and kind of depressed, both from the disappointing loss to the Bruins and the sad aftermath. All of us still at the restaurant, some late customers and staff alike, sat mesmerized at the bar, watching those disturbing images flicker across the screen, events that seemed to belong to another world but were happening just up the street from where we were sitting.

The smoke cleared and the crowds finally dispersed in the early dawn. The damage and destruction to the looted stores, the burned-out vehicles and the debris left behind had transformed the modern urban landscape of glass, concrete and steel around the stadium into a littered battle zone, closed to early-morning traffic.

The riot bruised the city's reputation and soul, if there were such a thing. The destruction and looting perpetrated by a few dozen punks, high on booze and dope, kicking and thrashing their way through the post-game crowd, was replayed on TVs all over the world. The thousands of fans who had peacefully gathered outside the stadium to watch the game on huge screens got caught up in the ensuing mayhem. Many panicked trying to get out of the downtown core, but many stayed and passively watched, fascinated by the chaos.

As it turned out, the violence was no spontaneous reaction to the loss of a hockey game; no sir, these losers came armed with baseball bats and hockey sticks by SkyTrain and buses from the outlying communities, looking for trouble and intent on instigating mayhem and ruin, causing our shiny city to lose face for the whole world to see.

On the morning after, Georgia and Howe were littered with glass and debris. A wreck of a burned-out car was left in front of the post office, the pungent smell of burning rubber mixed with tear gas lingering over the inner city, along with the collective shame of a stunned and shocked population, overwhelmed by the mess of it all. How did this happen? Where were the cops with their trillion-dollar security budget? Could nobody stop these spoiled, ignorant, *Grand Theft Auto* punks, high and flushed with testosterone and booze from wreaking such havoc among the 100,000-plus peaceful spectators?

Then, from early morning and all through the day, a spontaneous outpouring of shame and grief took shape in thousands of written sentiments and comments on the temporary plywood that covered all the broken windows of The Bay's store on Georgia and Granville. Thousands vented their emotions with words, poems and prayers, creating a testament, giving voice to their hurt about having their city, their civic pride and their goodwill and good intentions so shockingly trampled and sullied.

The politicians, including the premier, promised swift and vigilant persecution of the perpetrators, but the mark of shame would take a long time to erase and changed future public gatherings in the downtown core. An era had come to a disgraceful end and we all felt like we'd lost something important.

5

Crisis Management

It was the first day of summer, the sun was high in the sky, and tourists and locals were out early, walking or riding bicycles, heading toward the seawall around Stanley Park — surely the most pristine and beautiful ten-kilometre trail any city has to offer. I stood out front of the bistro, watching all the eager sun-seekers renting bikes of every size and colour at one of the half-dozen rental shops across the street, all of whom did a swift business on sunny days.

I was hoping that some of these bikers would work up an appetite to be satisfied at Le Bistro. The air smelled fresh, the temperature was perfect, and I had the fleeting feeling that this was going to be a glorious day.

For starters, our recently demoted busser Mandy walked in half an hour late for her shift with her right arm in a sling.

"What happened?" I asked, my elated feelings quickly dissipating.

"I was blocking a kick from my brother. We're both training for kickboxing."

"Oh, I didn't know that."

"The doctor said it's a hairline fracture."

"I'm sorry, that's terrible, but you can't work like that."

"Sure I can work. See? I can carry plates with the other hand and can do everything else with one hand."

"No, Mandy. You can't work here with an arm in a sling. First of all, it doesn't look right and is probably illegal, and secondly, you need to rest the arm and cannot work until the doctor says it's healed and okay."

Mandy looked dejectedly at the floor, her tough and feisty stance dissolving into that of a lost little girl. Either she was a great actress, or she was genuinely in trouble.

Then she pulled a fat envelope from her pink purse and showed it to me proudly.

"What's all that?" I asked, taken aback.

"I cashed in all my cheques today," Mandy proclaimed, smiling. "That's why I'm late." Looking at the wad of cash in her hand, she was clearly already feeling better. "It's the only way I can save any money. For my trip back to Manila."

I was horrified. "How many cheques did you cash?"

"All of them. About eight, I think."

Two months' worth of pay cheques amounted to over a couple of thousand dollars, I figured. I was seriously pissed off. "Mandy, I'm not your darned bank and you can't do that. Now I'm going to be hit with an extra couple grand that I wasn't expecting."

Mandy looked at me utterly baffled. It never occurred to her that she'd done something silly. Either these young kids were stupid, or they were very good at acting stupid. Either way, the result was the same.

"When are you planning to go to Manila?" I asked, exasperated, feeling a headache creeping up behind my eyes.

"At the end of the month. I'm sure I already told you," she said.

I had totally forgotten that she was leaving. But it didn't matter anymore. She'd broken her arm and was already out. I paid Mandy her owed wages up to date, including her holiday pay. Contrary to her earlier mood, she left quite happy. I now felt like shit.

"You'll never see her again," Aldo prophesied when I told him the whole story later in the day.

Now it would be me taking over bussing and serving shifts, I thought miserably. I took two Tylenols.

Then our temporary cook, Jake, didn't show up for work. Again. The second time within the past several days. We'd hired Jake a couple of weeks before because he made such a great initial impression. Smart, eager and flexible. "Going back to study in the fall," he told us. The perfect candidate for a summer job.

Nobody could get ahold of him, not even his own dad, whose number Colin somehow found. By now we all suspected he was on drugs. Billy confirmed our suspicions when he told us that Jake had a constant craving for sugar and was stuffing his face full of desserts all day long. "I even saw him pouring ketchup down his throat straight from the bottle."

Turns out that he also owed money to everybody in the kitchen, including me, due to an initial advance.

The third calamity of the day arrived when the former minister of finance and her well-known husband walked in for lunch. Neither Melinda nor Aldo had a clue who they were, and all was well until they tried to pay their bill.

That day, of all days, we were having trouble with our card reader. Melinda proceeded to verify her credit card by phone, which resulted in a tedious and awkward wait for the ex-minister and her hubby.

When I realized what was happening, I took charge and apologized profusely, mumbling something about unreliable modern technology and silly machines, feeling once more like Basil Fawlty. I gently shoved Melinda, who was still on hold, aside and returned the credit card with a dismissive wave as if the whole ordeal of paying for lunch was an unpleasant necessity. The ex-minister was very gracious about it all, and I ushered them both out the door without further delay, wishing them a pleasant day and hoping that they would come back.

When I explained to Melinda and Aldo, who had watched the whole scene from the back, who the customers were, they both accused me for not informing them.

"I didn't want them treated differently from other patrons, so they could retain their anonymity and incognito status," I explained, feeling cornered.

"But I look like idiot," Melinda said. "Is not fair for me."

But I am the real idiot, I thought to myself, having demeaned Melinda and probably scared away some very good patrons, and I still had to deal with the malfunctioning card reader.

"I need a drink," I said.

First thing that morning, Big Bob informed us that he was also off on a two-week holiday.

"I told you a long time ago that the first two weeks of July will be my holiday," he said without one iota of concern about anything but his own royal persona.

"Did he tell you he was going on holiday?" I asked Aldo, who puffed out his cheeks and admitted that, yes, he had actually told him, but way back when we'd hired him.

"He's going camping," Aldo added, "with Mirka."

"Camping? With Mirka?" Some disturbing images floated through my head.

"Well, I wouldn't call it camping. He's towing a thirty-foot fifth-wheel camper into some RV park in the Interior," Aldo said, nervously pulling at his trimmed moustache and biting his lower lip.

"Ah, shit, I hope he gets eaten alive by mosquitoes," I said.

"Or blows himself up with the barbecue," Aldo added.

In his stead, Bob put Colin in charge for the next nineteen days straight, much to the dismay of Colin, who had only been informed of the situation at the last minute. "That's not what I signed on for! My girlfriend will kill me."

I happened to agree with his girlfriend. Nobody can work nineteen days straight in our hot, crowded kitchen in the summer without snapping or collapsing. Chase and Kay offered to man the Mondays for Colin, which was not an ideal solution. We needed to talk to our self-important redneck chef. I really wanted to tell him that he should take the rest of his life off, but apparently we were not in a position to do that yet. I offered to fire myself instead, but Aldo wouldn't let me. Not only was I not paid, I couldn't get fired, either. Once again, our kitchen was stretched to the limit.

On the upside, we bought a lovely, undemanding, always smiling and unflappable plaster-of-Paris statuette of a French waiter. All of four feet high, with a top hat and a silver tray in one hand and the other folded properly behind his back, he stood on a small pedestal at the front entrance, greeting the customers.

"He'll be your most loyal and valuable employee," Clare said. "He'll never complain, won't ask for a raise, doesn't need any staff meals, isn't an alcoholic, doesn't have girlfriend issues and never goes on holiday."

We called him Chevy, short for Monsieur Chevalier. All the kids loved Chevy and every day they would stop their parents and engage with him, chatting to him, touching him, obviously taken in by the debonair little man with the top hat and the pencil moustache. One small boy was literally crying when his parents hauled him away, almost toppling poor Chevy off his pedestal. Others were charmed into the front door, I had no doubt, thanks to our little man.

Billy ran into Jake at the SkyTrain station on his way to work. "Oh boy, Jake was filthy, smelled like a skunk, and was totally out of it. I gave him ten bucks."

Something was definitely not right with our very temporary cook. Even before he went missing, I thought he looked rather ghoulish, with his large, glassy eyes, and so tired that he fell asleep one day sitting down while the restaurant was at its peak supper hour. I'd dismissed it as the usual party-party-no-sleep syndrome of his age group. As far as the bistro was concerned, that was the end of Jake. Another one down, another one to replace.

The consequence of all these people going AWOL, having accidents and seizures, going on holiday, or getting strung out on drugs was that we then needed a new bartender, a new busser, another dishwasher, and another temporary cook. And on my wish list: a new chef. Just when summer was starting, and the bistro was finally getting busy.

"Having a restaurant is like having another kid," I said to Clare, around 2:00 a.m., tossing and turning, unable to sleep, with a head full of worry. Instead of an answer, she rolled over, obviously not in the mood for a lament or a discussion.

Just like a kid, I grumbled to myself, always unpredictable, constantly in need of money, unable to solve their own problems and always, always driving me — the de facto parent — crazy.

Summer should have officially arrived, but the weather wasn't cooperating. Cold, wet and cloudy days with the occasional flash of sunshine pushing through does not a summer make.

Folly Bistro

The tourists were here, though. The cruise ships had docked, and the Germans, Dutch and Asian travellers could be seen gliding through the city on the hop-on, hop-off tour buses, or gathered in photo-snapping groups around the totem poles in Stanley Park. Occasionally, they wandered into Le Bistro, telling from the puny amounts of US dollars that came in. Maybe it had to do with the high Canadian dollar, but most likely it was reflective of their deflated mortgage bubble and the resulting economic hangover — considering that Walmart, not the car industry, was now the biggest employer in the US yet was paying only minimum wages.

The first Wednesday without BBB in charge we served 150 covers and the kitchen resembled a galley on a sixteenth-century slave ship. Hot, greasy steam poured out of the stainless-steel room, where the temperature reached 135 °F (or 57 °C), just short of 140 °F, when the fire suppression system was supposed to go off (which would have smothered the kitchen in foam and shut the whole operation down). The kind of heat that makes your blood boil. A slave galley for sure, or a medieval tanning pit.

Our new dishwasher, another Maria, this time from Italy, probably thought she'd landed in hell's kitchen. She quit halfway through the shift, crossing herself on the way out.

The conditions were unacceptable. The whole crew was ready to mutiny. It was a case of déjà-vu from the year before. Our small kitchen just couldn't handle that kind of volume, especially in the summer. Even Aldo was forced to finally come to this conclusion when he stuck his head in. Then the ventilation fan packed it in. The place was about to explode. That's when I gave the order: all systems down, front door closed, and everybody out of the kitchen, out the back door. Close down the ovens and the salamander — an overhead high-temperature grill.

Everybody stumbled into the cool evening air like miners escaping a major blow-out. Colin, the sous-chef, was glassy-eyed and near delirious, while everybody else gulped the fresh air like a bunch of newborns. Customers left in protest, because now the greasy steam was issuing into the restaurant, since the vent shafts were plugged full of liquid grease and the roof fan had quit in protest.

Everybody finished what food they could and we gave away free beer and pop all around, placating the patrons as best we could, explaining that the kitchen had an emergency situation due to a mechanical breakdown.

The next morning we replaced the fan motor and had the filthy vent stack cleaned. The grease was four inches thick, which even surprised the cleaners, who had seen it all.

"Worse than a Chinese restaurant," the Chinese cleaner commented with a toothy grin.

Summertime Blues

Jean called. He wanted another meeting about the bistro. The three of us sat down once more that afternoon at Starbucks next door. Aldo talked, I nodded and figured that if we wanted to get out of the bistro then Jean was our only option. He was the only fish on the hook, but he was going to be a tricky catch at best. All business and no bullshit, and Jean already knew everything there was to know about the bistro: the past, the present and apparently the future.

"You boys aren't making any money, that much is clear from your muddled financial statements. On the plus side, you're still open and for all the world appear to be a successful restaurant. Am I right or not?" he asked but didn't really expect an answer. "What about the lease? How is the landlord?"

How about an offer? I wanted to ask, but held back. Don't act panicky. Play it cool; give the fish some line and then snap, sink the hook, and reel him in. Sounds easy, except Jean was one slippery fish. He promised to get back to us once he had a chat with Mr. Lee, our landlord.

"The Pacific Northwest is under a sustained low-pressure system with temperatures in the low teens and periods of rain and showers over the next few days," Claire Martin, the CBC's weather anchor said, and then added gleefully, "We should just forget about this summer and look forward to next year."

Thanks a lot, Claire. Not that it was her fault. She was just pointing out what everybody felt about this weather. Only Roy, our jovial Scotsman, kept his sense of humour. "What do you call six weeks of rain in Scotland? Summer!"

The lousy weather should have been good for the restaurant. It should have driven people inside, but that theory was just that: a theory, and a flawed one at that. There were events all over the city, with live concerts in the park, Shakespeare on the beach, ethnic festivals, and events almost every night, and all of those venues sold food, including all the street vendors up and down the beach. Even right across the street there was a donair stand. In fact, I had one myself one day. Pretty good for six bucks. The competition was stiff, the customers were choosy, and we counted once again on our stalwart local patrons, of which there were still a few.

Like Paddy, the seventy-five-year-old Irish obsessive-compulsive who still came in once or twice a week for an early lunch at 11:30. He sat at the same table, seven, and ordered his usual bottle of rosé, mimosa salad and bread — no butter — a rare steak 'n' frites, and the TV on the golf channel. We also still saw old Harry and Herby, but mostly on Wednesdays. They were cheap, just like the Wangs, Roy's least-favourite rich and stingy patrons. Once in a while, we'd serve Doc and Jewel, which always made for a good night. They drank expensive wines, ate steak tartare before their meals and always left lavish tips. A couple of times each month, we counted on the thin French Duke and big Rupert to make an appearance at lunchtime. Their bill always made up for half a dozen bargain seekers who didn't drink, always asked for extra bread and didn't tip.

Marvin still came in regularly with his spry and youthful eighty-five-year-old mom, Collette. When they weren't celebrating somebody's birthday — like Einstein's or Jack Kennedy's — they were in early and on their way to the opera or a play. They were avid opera buffs and theatregoers and could enthuse about a play or singer just like teenage fans. They also travelled a lot and brought back stories about the fantastic museums or concerts from their latest trips. We also could count on them to give us an honest opinion about our food. "I was getting worried when Yussuf, the Egyptian chef, was in charge," Marvin confided, "but now the peppercorn sauce is back to what it should be."

Calvin the lawyer and his mom were predictable and welcome clients. She loved her overcooked salmon, he his pink steak. She reminisced about the good old days being on the embassy staff in communist Moscow; Calvin talked about his latest ski trip or told me how cheap and fantastic the restaurants were in Florida, where they spent a couple of months every winter. I once pointed out to him that we had a better health care and social system in Canada and that not everybody with money has to live in a walled compound with private security.

Calvin smiled and said, "I know all that, but the food is still cheaper and so is the wine, by the way."

Most times I suppressed my instincts and avoided offering my opinion, smiling and keeping my thoughts to myself, following Aldo's advice: "Don't tell them what you think, tell them what they want to hear. We're here to sell food and drink, not make friends or, worse yet, piss them off."

I hate to kowtow, but I found out that it was part of the restaurant cliché that the customer is always right, even if they're assholes and just plain wrong. We catered to the rich snobs and wealthy know-it-alls, took their money, and kept our opinions to ourselves. It was one of the hardest parts of running a restaurant, and instead of confronting the customers, I bitched at home to Clare, who usually managed to put it all in perspective.

"If it helps you to complain to me about your clients and wonky staff, just be happy you don't have to deal with the sick and dying. As long there is nobody on life support, you don't have any problems or worries, just a situation."

What could I say? I couldn't compare my woes to a nurse's, one who dealt with real issues — not some snobby rich guy turning up his nose at the overcooked chicken or whining that his steak was medium instead of rare.

We picked up a couple of new regulars. One was Jean-Luc, a French Canadian and professional translator who worked for the CBC and translated political dialogue from French to English. He ate at the bistro at least twice a week, always sat at the bar and never took up a whole table for himself, even when there was ample room. He ordered and ate fast, gulped down his pint, and was gone the minute he'd swallowed his last bite. The servers liked him because he was a generous tipper.

Owen, a 300-pound, wheezing, jocular insurance broker was hard to overlook. He always sat at the end of the bar, where he sipped his dry martinis, one after the other, with no apparent ill effect. His round, ruddy face and small, veined nose were always flushed, and his wire-rimmed glasses could never seem to find a purchase, since he always pushed them up with his forefinger at least once every thirty seconds, mostly to get a better look at one of the girls. He was totally enamoured with Selena and Margo, neither of whom minded and happily pocketed his generous tips.

Owen had a friendly countenance with a booming voice and a deep bellowing laugh. When I jokingly told him he looked like Friar Tuck, he hollered and slapped me on the back. "Not far from the truth, my friend. I was three weeks away from being an ordained Catholic priest."

"What happened? Must have been women trouble," I guessed.

"No, that was before I had trouble with women, long before my four wives, who are the only reason I'm still busting my ass working. No, it was because it was the mildest winter in Saskatoon; that's where the seminary was. Blame the weather," he chuckled. "But actually, I am the only one to blame, along with another aspiring priest, who had a chemistry background. We had quite a bit of spare time, which we were supposed to spend in prayer and meditation, but instead we aspired to another kind of spirit, 90 percent proof. We stored full bottles near the outdoor ice rink in the snowbank, never suspecting that a week of mild weather would melt the snow. When one of the janitors walked by the ice rink, he made an unusual find. It wasn't hard to figure out who the culprits were, and when I was called up to the rector's office, I knew that the Lord had another calling in mind for me besides the pulpit."

"Wow. Were you sorry you didn't become a priest?"

"Not me, but it broke my mom's heart. She was set on having a priest in the family — that would have pretty well guaranteed a prime seat in heaven. Oh well. As the rector told me that day, there is more than one way to serve the Lord."

"You never struck me as the religious type, what with your roving eye for the girls."

"I didn't say I was religious; I just meant that I served the Lord in different ways, by spreading my love as far and wide as I could." He winked at me, slapped his hand on the bar and asked for another martini, extra dry.

Wednesdays in the summer were twice as crazy as those in the winter. Then we also got tourists. Where we usually served 80 to 100 covers in the colder months, in the summer we served up to 140 covers, half of them filet mignons, which is the most tender and expensive cut of beef. Since the cows are much bigger these days, the tenderloin is also bigger. In order to make the filet mignons perfect, the chef had to stretch and roll them in a special sock to reduce the diameter of the steaks.

We had everybody on deck in the front. Aldo was tending the bar, filling in for Sanchez, who wasn't in good shape, according to Gino, who had visited him a couple of times. I did the door and manned the phone. Gino, Roy, Melinda and Margo served, while Selena, Alice and Alia tried to keep up with cleaning, setting the tables and supplying water and bread to all the customers.

Temperatures of up to 130 °C (and temperaments up to 500 °C!) were the usual environment in our hellish galley. Usually two guys slaved on the hot side, with all six burners and the oven going at once. While one cook plated, adding sauces and garnishes, the other flipped and marked steaks, and yanked chicken, duck breast and casseroles out of the broiling oven while making sure that nothing fried in the salamander, which burned constantly at a full roar just at face level.

The orders were coming in steadily and the two garde mangers were whipping up salads, appies and the odd dessert, while our third Maria, this time from Mexico, was fighting it out in the dish pit. Overtop all the noise, everybody was yelling, demanding or confirming orders, and in the midst of all this chaos the bussers brought in the empty dishes and stacked them onto the overflowing counter for Maria, who cursed in Spanish and raised her hands and eyes toward the ceiling, pleading for divine intervention: "Dios mío, ayúdame!" — as if God lived above the bistro's kitchen.

It was total bedlam. And to top it off, our Aussie cook, Chase, was glaringly missing in action, which left Big Bad Bob, just back from his two-week camping holiday, handling the hot side by himself.

All 300 pounds of him dripped like a sponge, and his face had the pallor of chalk. At one point, he swayed and almost keeled over. He just made it out the back door for some fresh air, hyperventilating like he was drowning. At that point, we once again closed the front door for an hour and turned about two dozen customers away just to give the kitchen and everybody else some breathing room.

After everybody had left and the girls had cleaned up the wreckage, we all sat down to a staff meal, wolfing down whatever was left over. At last, Aldo, Gino and I collapsed at the bar in front of well-deserved pints. We had served 145 covers — a record — but it was abundantly evident, even to Aldo, that these Wednesday nights were a monster out of the cage, devouring the restaurant and everybody in it. It was time to put the monster back in the cage — and lose the cage altogether.

"We should just cancel these crazy Wednesdays. We don't make any money anyway, when nobody drinks and everybody just eats filet mignon and duck," I said.

Aldo woefully shook his head from side to side, but finally he came around to the same conclusion I had come to a year earlier. "Let's take the banner down and it's over. Just like that," he said.

At that point, Chase, our AWOL Aussie cook, showed up to take Alice home. I wanted to know what the hell had happened and why he wasn't there that night. Chase never got excited and he felt bad about it but said, "The chef told me it was fine to take the day off. I was having a tattoo done." For proof, he held out his bandaged arm.

"On a Wednesday!" I cried. "Never before did you get Wednesday off. You know how crazy it is here?"

Chase just shrugged and said, "The chef knew about it."

Of course, BBB was long gone. It turned out that the chef was feeling all charged up after two weeks in the camper with Mirka, and did indeed give Chase the night off. An almost fatal miscalculation for BBB himself, who I'd thought was going to keel over with a heart attack on top of the burning stove.

Between the chef just back from holiday, Chase with his bandaged and tattooed arm, and everybody assuming that everybody else was in charge, the whole crew looked like idiots.

Funny thing though — they all wanted to get paid and nobody ever shouldered any blame. It was always Aldo's fault or mine. It was time for an orientation meeting, and since we were all present except the chef, I took the opportunity to give my speech from behind the bar while everybody assembled in front.

"Here's how it goes," I said, taking a sip of beer. "Aldo and I are the government, the chef is the general in the kitchen and you," — pointing to Gino — "are the general up front. We —

the government — set policy, manage the bureaucracy and pay everybody. The two generals, on the other hand, are responsible for the operation of this here ship, which seems to be floundering at sea once again, missing our desired destination — a full house, every day. Both generals also carry out the wishes and orders of the government. Does everybody understand the way this is supposed to work?"

"You're not really an elected government, more like a monarchy. Are you king and Aldo the queen?" a cheeky Selena asked, to everybody's delight.

"It's more like the king and I," I replied, raising a toast to Aldo.

Everybody laughed and nobody challenged or questioned my stump speech.

"Okay, everybody gets a pint on the house, and thank you all. And by the way, we're cancelling the crazy Wednesdays." And since everybody looked stunned, I said, "You heard me. No more 50 Percent Discount Wednesdays after next week!"

Everybody cheered like they'd just won the lottery. "No more crazy Wednesdays! No more fight night!"

I left around midnight and quietly opened the door at home.

Clare heard me and sleepily asked, "Crazy night, was it?"

"Yes, the craziest yet, but after next week it's over. From then on, Wednesdays will be just like any other day."

"Good luck," she yawned and rolled over.

I couldn't sleep, and watched a couple of episodes of *Fawlty Towers*, which felt uncannily familiar.

Aldo and I were studying the latest bank statements. Apparently we had made no money in June (no surprise there), owed more on Visa than we had in the bank, and had to come up with a fortune for the dreaded HST payment, due at the end of the month.

"This can't go on," Aldo sighed. "We need to make some major changes."

We'd travelled this road many times before. Changes are great, ideas and visions are inspiring, but a plan and a concept built on facts, as well as a way to finance the plan, were what was needed. We had no plan, just a jumble of ideas that ranged from painting the ceiling to ripping out the front windows to building the ever-elusive side patio. Would any of those changes bring more customers through the door? That was the million-dollar question. We both knew that the only things that brought in customers were

1) consistency in the food and service, which we now had;
2) location, location, location — none better than ours;
3) price point — we couldn't go any lower.

Add to all these woes the dismal state of the current economy, the uncooperative weather, the whimsical nature of any disaster or sports event that kept people from going out for lunch or dinner, and it all added up to one simple fact: it was really out of our hands, and no amount of paint or different-coloured napkins would bring in one extra customer.

The ideas always became more elaborate and further away from reality as the night wore on and the drinks kept flowing. We always had the best ideas first thing in the morning but the most fun and elaborate solutions at the end of the night, most of which evaporated into thin air by the next day.

"We need to put in some money," Aldo finally said, voicing the unthinkable. "Ten thousand each would get us out of hock for now, and we could move on without worrying every day about the end of the month.

"Ten grand! I suppose we have no choice."

"It's your restaurant and your responsibility. I have some savings to which you're welcome," Clare offered.

"No way. We're not touching money that took you years to save. We have a line of credit. I'll let the bank give us some cash."

"It's called borrowing, as in accumulating debt."

"It's called creative financing. We'll pay it back at the end of the summer."

Aldo and I had agreed on the one change, which would not bring in more customers but fewer, when we decided to do away with half-price Wednesdays. Yes, we were addicted to the cash infusion, but was it worth the fight? Not after the total mayhem and near mutiny week after week.

Folly Bistro

We sent out a mass email, cancelled ads, changed our web page and painted over the banner on the awning. We erased every mention and trace of the 50 Percent Discount Wednesday and acted as if it had never existed. After the initial euphoria, the kitchen staff reacted with the usual mixed response: Would this cost us hours of work? Was anybody going to be let go? Would they now be getting fewer tips? Not one question or comment about if this was better for the bistro or morale. Nope, it was all about them, their wallets and their own myopic world. Fight night at the bistro was over, except for one more. We had to honour the existing reservations, which already guaranteed a full house. We braced ourselves for the last of the wild and crazy Wednesdays, about to transition into legend.

"Let's go out with fireworks! Let's make this one count!"

Summer arrived suddenly with a vengeance, the sun burning through the layers of persistently rainy clouds that had covered the land like a lid all the way through June and half of July. Nobody had seen worse weather, ever, except maybe the year before or the one before that — weather memory is short — but at least it was weather people talked about and not famine, war or disease like in large parts of this world.

A funny thing happens every summer when the sun is hot: The beaches beckon and music festivals and outdoor concerts spring up all over the city. Waiters and cooks call in sick and miss shifts. What kind of virus is this? It was the same the year before. The worst offenders didn't even call in; they just didn't show up, which always left the rest of the staff scrambling. The group afflicted most by this weather-induced malady had, nine times out of ten, not yet reached the mature age of thirty. As age progresses, the world outside one's body temple slowly takes on more importance and starts to include others, like co-workers, parents and less fortunate fellow humans and environments. The teenage bubble bursts sometime in the twenties for most girls, while boys take a bit longer. Suddenly the world is a lot bigger and also more inclusive than the immediate space around one's own head.

Alex, our most recent, charming young server, could sell anything to the ladies, make the men choose a better wine, and talk anybody into dessert. Alex could do no wrong, except for one fatal flaw: He had no sense of time and was notoriously tardy, or even worse, an outright no-show, which left his co-workers and the restaurant handicapped. I issued one warning, a second warning and threats of money fines. I gave him passionate lectures about responsibility to others, to the business, the importance of all the spokes being necessary to make the wheel. He smiled elusively with his charming grin, but none of my speeches made a lasting impression. One day, once again, he just didn't show up. Which meant I had to serve the lunch crowd myself.

"The next time is your last time," I said to him, knowing full well that within a couple of weeks we'd be posting Alex's job on Craigslist. Too bad, because I liked him, and he was a good waiter. There were always those who quit after two or three weeks, who were overwhelmed while still in training. We paid them just like everybody else, paid their taxes, and got nothing in return. It's the nature of the beast, as the saying goes.

Restaurants are perceived as being on the bottom end of the working world; any idiot can set and clear a table or wash dishes. Yes, but only strong characters can stick it out for the long run. We had a few of these exceptional individuals working for us, but for every Alia or Margo or Gino or Roy, who were professionals, we had to put up with a few Alexes, Jakes or Marcels.

Either the word had gone out that this would be the last legendary Wednesday at the French bistro, or it had to do with the improvement in the weather or some other cosmic intervention which flushed people out. At 5:30 p.m., a lineup snaked out the door just like at Vij's, Vancouver's most popular Indian restaurant. In order to hold people in place, I employed my old trick and offered a glass of red or white wine. With glass in hand, customers waited patiently, chatting to others behind them, making new friends while waiting to be seated. It resembled a kind of carnival atmosphere. Maybe holding all of those people was a mistake, but I didn't want anybody to get away, not this time, and damn the consequences.

Folly Bistro

We served over 150 covers, unheard of in any French restaurant of our size and with the kind of menu we offered. That night, once again, almost broke the kitchen in half. Only the mantra that this was indeed the very last time kept them fighting it out in the hot, greasy, cacophonous inferno. When the last customer left, we closed the doors, opened the taps of beer and celebrated like it was New Year's Eve. The sweaty, exhausted kitchen staff had just come through hell, and they drank like camels coming out of the desert. An era had come to an end and a new day would dawn, with a leaner, more streamlined and hopefully saner business model.

The kitchen, the restaurant, the coolers, and the storage areas were all still in a state of turmoil after the previous night's mayhem, and although we all tried to restore order at the end of the long night, we did the very minimum, all being too beat up and tired to do a diligent job, as well as having partied on until the wee hours. As Murphy's law would have it, who should walk in at 10:00 a.m. but our old friend from city hall, Stewy, the proper, pedantic English health inspector, with his lightsaber flashlight and nifty notebook. This time he brought a young Chinese trainee in tow, who, judging by his subservient demeanour, was mightily impressed with Stewy's quest for scrupulous cleanliness and strict adherence to the code of hygiene and sanitation. The Chinese Sancho Panza to the British Don Quixote would ensure that no Chinese restaurateur could get away with feigning language ignorance. Stewy's mission was to rid the world of rodents and pests, starting, it seemed, with us.

The excuse that the previous day, our last 50 Percent Discount Wednesday, had been an extremely busy night did not impress Stewy, nor did it soften his hawkish stance. He found mouse droppings wherever he pointed his unerring light beam and then properly admonished me and Aldo like we were two schoolboys caught cheating on our exams.

"This place is not properly managed. There is no up-to-date sanitation plan as I requested on my last visit, and there is evidence of mouse activity all through the restaurant and the kitchen. These are intolerable conditions and I will have to make a report on this," he said with his clipped, proper Oxford English.

We grovelled and agreed to anything and everything he demanded. Stewy then handed us his report, written in miniscule but perfect English print.

"I will be back soon," he said, holding up his index finger like a schoolmaster reprimanding the class. "Next time you will leave me no choice," he added ominously, turning on his heel and vanishing as quickly as he'd entered, Sancho Panza following behind him like a shadow.

The minute they left, we cleaned and scrubbed, vacuumed and washed for the rest of the morning, eradicating all traces of vermin and grease.

That night's service was a relatively normal shift, meaning about forty to fifty people. I was on my way out the back door, past the kitchen, when Billy hissed at me and pointed to the floor. There it was, darting out of the kitchen, between tables and chairs, toward the front of the restaurant. Behind me I heard a woman gasping. She'd obviously witnessed the mouse. I reacted instinctively, seizing the nearest weapon — the phone book — and, wielding it like the rock of ages, I smashed it down with an almighty thud, flattening the unlucky intruder and splattering the floor and wall with splotches of bright red blood. Maybe I also issued a blood-curdling primeval scream. I don't remember, but witnesses swore that I did indeed yell. I think it was the woman at table seventeen who screamed even louder. In all the ensuing confusion, the facts got a little bit blurred. Suddenly a dead-quiet pall fell over the restaurant, and I felt everybody's eyes boring into my back. I quickly picked up the phonebook with the flattened cadaver glued to the underside and scurried out the back door. I waited a few minutes before I snuck back in. By then, the sordid episode was forgotten and everybody was back to eating, drinking and having a merry good time.

I was nicknamed the Great White Hunter by Big Bad Bob, who'd thoroughly enjoyed the spectacle.

"This was by far the funniest thing I've ever seen," he kept repeating, telling the story in ever more elaborate detail to all and sundry, pointing his big fat finger at me, his whole body shaking like a gigantic pudding and laughing with unconcealed glee.

I opened the door at exactly 11:30 a.m., and in strode Paddy, right on time, after having just walked the ten kilometres around Stanley Park. He steered straight for his usual table, number seven.

"Paddy is here!" I immediately put the kitchen on high alert and made sure we had a bottle of his favourite rosé in stock.

Everything needed to be precise for the old Irish codger, who, in his seventies, was still as strong as an ox. He shook my hand once and almost crumpled it like a pack of crackers. For Paddy, the table, the food and the service had to be perfectly choreographed. First off, he had to recognize the server, and when it was Gino or Melinda or Roy, and BBB in the kitchen, then the world was in synch and the rest would fall into place. Roy knew Paddy from way back when he'd served at the West Vancouver Golf and Country Club, and Paddy loved that sort of connection. To lighten the day, Roy of course had his joke at the ready: "How do you get a Highlander onto the roof? Tell him the drinks are on the house."

Paddy slapped his knee with delight, and right on cue his bottle of Houchart rosé in a bucket of ice arrived. The wine had to be placed on the left of the table, bread without butter on the right, water without ice. Without fail, Paddy would order the mimosa salad, a rare steak with peppercorn sauce on the side and definitely no greens. He hated cooked greens. Something to do with his childhood in Dublin. The fries had to arrive at the exact same time as the steak. The TV needed to be set to the golf channel, his British tabloid folded on his right side.

When all of that fell into place, Paddy was a happy customer, but woe if any of these settings were flawed, he didn't recognize the server or the cook, or the sauce was on the steak or the fries were late. He once walked straight out the door without a word when he didn't recognize Alex, who tried to seat him in one of the window seats instead of table seven. It took a couple of phone calls from Roy and Aldo to placate the old codger and coax him back into the bistro with promises that all would be perfect the next time.

If all was well, Paddy would eat, drink, watch his golf, and read his paper, and when he was in a really good mood, like that day, he insisted on a game of Birds in the Bush with Aldo and me. We each had three coins, and the aim of the game was to guess how many coins altogether were in our fists on the table. Maximum: nine; minimum: none. Every time we played Birds in the Bush, Paddy jokingly offered the special three-day seminar with limo pickup and drop-off, and he regaled us with stories of the rich and old, who all were champs at this game, played in the venerated halls of golf, country, and men's clubs. Paddy insisted on buying a round, and then we played, slapping fists down on the counter, locking eyes, and guessing the amount of coins. Aldo and I always made sure that Paddy ended up as champ, which pleased him immensely and made his day.

"Nothing is more fun than winning," he said, slapping us both on the back like we were on the same team.

Catering to people like Paddy went against my grain and was a constant struggle for me. Fawning and pussyfooting around the wealthy doesn't sit well with my proletarian, equal-opportunity upbringing, my hippy adolescence or even my midlife revolutionary fantasies.

"He's a rebel at heart," Clare told Aldo with a twinkle in her eye at the very beginning of this venture. "Meaning he despises authority or superiority, especially when it is imposed by wealth and position, unless it's by his wife."

Aldo laughed and said, "Kowtowing to the old and rich is part of the game in a restaurant. We have to cater to everybody — as long as they pay, we'll bring them their food and drink and not question their ideas, convictions or political leanings. We're not in business to discriminate or to judge; we're here to serve and make money."

"Amen," I said, not at all convinced that I could be that detached and tolerant.

As Aldo predicted, we had to let Alex go due to his unrelenting tardiness. Another ad on Craigslist for a server brought over twenty responses in a couple of hours. Some of the skills these applicants cited were truly remarkable, but there was one that stood out. This girl listed her favourite hobbies — shopping, going out with friends — and then as her strong point, stated, "I am able to stand for long periods of time without sitting down." If she had been a Lab or a fox terrier, those would be desirable skills.

We hired Randy, who on his very first shift lamented the loss of his wedding band on the beach, how upset his husband was going to be, and that he was afraid to go home and confess this unfortunate loss. Clare and I, who were trying to enjoy a rare dinner together at the bistro, duly commiserated, and Clare told him that it was just a ring, not the relationship that he had lost.

Randy turned out to be a regular whiny drama queen. He was a capable but highly volatile server, always griping about something or other, like the fact that he found it unfair to pay a percentage on liquor to the kitchen staff, since the kitchen added no work to the liquor. I explained to him that this was not up for discussion — it had always been the restaurant policy that the servers pay 3 percent of their daily total sales to the kitchen staff. On top of that, I had to point out that he needed to leave his matrimonial and financial troubles at home and concentrate on the job while on the job. He lasted a week and then just disappeared, along with a $200 advance.

"Why don't you try to be a waiter? At least you'd be making some tips," Clare suggested when I bemoaned the latest calamity with the delinquent Randy.

"It's not my thing, Clare. I just never wanted to be a waiter. Maybe a bartender, but not a server." On the other hand, Clare had a point. I was spending most of my time at the bistro anyway. Why not make a bit of money? I saw what those waiters pulled in on a busy night. More than we took in for the dreaded HST.

"What about Alia?" I asked. "Except Aldo isn't going to like it. He thinks her English isn't very good and she's too shy."

"Aldo picked some highly problematic chefs. You can at least promote your best and most reliable busser. Don't worry, she'll be great, just watch. She is highly motivated to succeed, more than can be said about your last few waiters."

Alia was delighted when I asked her, but apprehensive at the same time. "What if I don't understand what the customer wants?"

"Just give them one of your dazzling smiles and ask them to repeat the order."

Not only was Big Bad Bob an intolerant dictator and a white supremacist redneck but he had also taken himself on holiday during the busiest time of the year. When I tried to argue with him, pointing out that this was not in the best interest of the bistro, he just sneered at me. "That's too bad, but since this is not my restaurant, it's not my problem."

While the chef was on holiday, he scheduled in the sous-chef, Colin, for nineteen days straight during the busiest, hottest time of the year. Either he was trying to break Colin or he really didn't give a damn. I suspected it was both. I had really had enough of BBB and his subversive, self-serving, uncooperative behaviour. I believe he wanted the bistro to fail and was doing everything he could to make that happen.

Since he'd come back from his "camping" trip, he'd been feeling unusually generous. That day he'd given everybody the day off, thinking that since this was a Tuesday, it would be slow and he'd be able to handle it with only Billy, his garde manger, and Maria, the third in the dish pit.

Then we got slammed. A party of four, then one of six, and another of ten arrived within minutes. That was what we wanted, and as it always happens, a busy restaurant attracts more customers. Before we got to 7:30 p.m. we had a full house. Gino and Roy were racking up the orders and BBB was sweating and cursing, trying to keep up. At one point Gino was putting his empty hand in the pass through, asking for the steak for table four. Instead of an answer, BBB whacked his hand with the hot prongs. Gino pulled his hand back, more surprised than hurt, but since there was no time to waste, he carried on through the busy night, silently swearing retribution.

At another point, the kitchen was so badly backed up that Gino had no choice but to refuse customers and temporarily close the front doors. This only ever happened when the exhaust fan broke, or on that one crazy Wednesday, not on a normal weekday when we had less than sixty people in the restaurant. This was anathema. The chef had had a brain fart when he sent everybody home, and now we had to turn away customers. This didn't sit well with the servers, and it really pissed me off.

At 10:00 p.m. the rush was finally over, and when Gino went back to the kitchen to protest the whacking of his now-swollen thumb and the fact that we were hardly in a position to turn down money at the door, the chef launched a dinner plate at Gino's head like it was a Frisbee. The plate narrowly missed the flabbergasted Gino. It shattered against the wall into shrapnel, and a large, jagged piece of crockery just missed the unsuspecting Roy by inches. We all stood there as if we'd turned to stone, while BBB stood in the kitchen doorway in a cloud of steam, hunched forward like King Kong, a knife in one hand and a frying pan in the other. For a moment, nobody knew if he was actually going to throw the knife or the frying pan, and that's the moment Roy chose to launch another silly Scottish joke on us.

"Guess what? Nowadays the Scots don't play bagpipes to frighten their enemies, they do it to annoy their neighbours."

We all looked at Roy, who always laughed loudest at his own jokes, and somehow his irrelevant aside defused the moment. Like a marionette, BBB jerked upright, lowered his knife, and turned around, mumbling a veiled apology. Gino was going to pursue the matter further, but I held him back, fearing more violent escalations.

We were no match for BBB's 300 pounds of uncontrolled fury. BBB turned around one more time, glaring at all three of us. "What happens in this restaurant, stays in this restaurant. I hope I make myself clear."

At the time I didn't know how to respond, but when I related the incident to Clare, she had no such qualms. "The guy is nuts and what he's done is criminal behaviour. Does he think that if he commits an atrocity in the kitchen it will have no relevance outside the confines of the restaurant? That argument is very popular in torture chambers and Nazi death camps. Fire the man before you have to call the police or somebody gets hurt."

The next morning, the chef's day off, I called Aldo for an emergency meeting at Starbucks, our off-site office. First off, I informed Aldo that I was not going to hire another waiter, since we'd had nothing but grief lately with the fly-by-night punters we ended up with, and that Alia and Margo would take over the vacant shifts. We'd hire another busser.

"I think you should pay yourself." Aldo said. "You put in too many hours for free."

I didn't fight back on that issue. Actually, I welcomed the chance to make a bit of money, even if we could ill afford it. The second issue was a bit more contentious, but I was going to stand my ground this time. I told Aldo of the shenanigans the chef had pulled the night before, attacking Gino, throwing dinner plates, and making us turn back customers because he understaffed the kitchen. "He's got to go, Aldo," I insisted. "His behaviour and personality are intolerable and no longer compatible with the staff or with me. In fact, we have people threatening to quit because of the way he treats them, and we can't get good people to stay. We've had a couple of solid, well-trained cooks we tried out over the last couple of weeks and each one of them lasted less than a week. 'Can't work with that monster,' one of them said, and the other, the Indian woman with French cooking experience who would have been a great asset to our kitchen, just walked out in the middle of her shift because of a racial slur that I'd rather not repeat. Look, Aldo, we have plenty of reasons to fire Bob."

"That would only lead to further confrontation and maybe even a labour board hearing," Aldo said. But he finally conceded that BBB had to go.

"Let's not fire him but lay him off, stating shortage of work. No explanation necessary, just two weeks of severance pay and goodbye."

"He's not going to agree," Aldo said, shaking his head. "He's going to make trouble, just wait and see."

I had wanted to fire the bastard back in May, but Aldo always argued that we needed him and his skills for the busy summer. Maybe Aldo had a point then, but now the scales had definitely tipped the other way.

This was supposed to be Melinda's shift, but somehow Mandy, our spunky underage Filipina busser, reappeared out of the blue. Back from Manila, apparently, her broken arm mended, to take Melinda's place. I was surprised. I had long given up seeing her again. She informed me that Melinda had sprained her ankle and called her to fill in. "And I'm nineteen now. You want to see my ID? You promised to give me real shifts when I turn nineteen, remember?"

I sort of remembered, but still she surprised me with her sassy attitude. She left me not much choice, since Melinda was out of commission.

"Welcome back," I said lamely. "And how was Manila?"

"Oh, you know, family and everybody asking me for money. They all think I'm rich because I live in Canada."

"But you are rich, Mandy. Just look around the world. You live in the best part of it."

She gave me a big coy smile and said, "You're right, I love it here."

Now that I had just promoted Alia and Margo to servers, up turns Mandy, also wanting to be a waitress. I couldn't possibly demote anybody without creating a hornet's nest, so I casually told Mandy that she would have to start again as a busser as soon as Melinda was back on her feet.

I was damned either way. One day we didn't have enough servers and suddenly the next day we had one too many. I checked myself in the mirror and could see myself aging.

Aldo and I arranged to meet Colin for coffee at our "office" at Starbucks before his shift. "I think I know what this is about," he said, sitting down nervously.

As usual Aldo was late, so it was just Colin and me sipping our cappuccinos.

"You probably guessed right," I conceded. "We can wait for Aldo, but I might as well ask you myself." I skipped the preliminaries and blurted right out, "Would you be willing to be the chef at the bistro?" The question hung in the air for a moment while we both stared at the table.

"I've been thinking about it," Colin said. "I know that Big Bob can't possibly last much longer. Our kitchen is a toxic environment and no fun to work in. In short, the answer is yes. I'm ready and I have some great ideas and I can bring in a great sous-chef, a good friend from cooking school."

At that moment, Aldo joined us, out of breath, mumbling about the traffic. He fell right into the conversation like he didn't miss a word. "What kind of great ideas?"

"Well, I would like to change up the menu, put my own stamp on it, offer a few modern dishes like ribs and maybe a pork dish."

"Colin, I'm sure you have great skills and ideas, but if you want to be our chef we need you to cook our menu first and foremost. You'll have a chance to create some fall specials, maybe some wild mushroom dishes or venison," Aldo said.

"We need to steer the course for now and offer consistency first and foremost," I reiterated, and Colin nodded in agreement.

"Absolutely, I agree. I was just thinking out loud. When do you think the, uh, changeover happens?"

I looked at Aldo and said, "We're trying for the end of the month, but we need to keep this absolutely confidential because we expect BBB to put up a fight. We'll keep you posted."

We encouraged Colin to stay strong and keep working as if nothing was amiss.

We all left separately, just in case somebody observed us. I looked around furtively, feeling a bit foolish, like I was a bit actor in a cheap conspiracy movie.

Sanchez, our TV-star bartender and Cesar Millan lookalike who'd suffered a breakdown the month before, right behind the bar, limped into the bistro on a stick, with a baseball cap pulled low over his brow. At first I didn't even recognize him. His whole body was bloated, his angular face drooped on the left side, and his speech was slurred and slow. He was not the same jovial man, always ready with a joke and a loud bellowing laugh, always positive about the future, which in his case was anything but certain beyond the next meal or rent cheque. We all thought he had suffered a stroke, but with a mumbling voice he explained that he had been diagnosed with a glioma, a benign brain tumour, the size of a lemon behind his right ear.

"I'm on steroids to shrink the tumour," he said with a lopsided grin, and put a whole arsenal of pills on the bar. "This keeps me going."

At least he hadn't lost his sense of humour. I felt truly sorry for Sanchez and promised him a meal anytime. His unfortunate condition brought home the truth of how fragile our existence can be and how suddenly it can all change.

Colin called me on my cellphone and said he needed to talk.

"The chef threatened today that he will take you two down if you tried to fire him," he whispered.

"Did you say anything to him?" I asked, wondering if Colin had spilled the beans.

"No, I swear, man, I never said a word, but he knows something is up."

"Don't worry, Colin, keep calm. We'll deal with it. Just carry on as if nothing has changed."

I'm not sure he believed me, but we needed help. I called Aldo and he agreed to seek advice from a labour lawyer. He contacted Morris, our lawyer, who gave us the prestigious address of a law firm that specialized in labour disputes.

"They're not cheap, but they're the best," Morris said. "And good luck."

We sat down with the best (and most expensive) labour lawyer in his fancy office on Burrard and Georgia on the twentieth floor. Looking at the genuine Chagall on the wall, we laid out our dilemma. I handed him a list of offences I'd documented during Big Bob's reign of terror. The young lawyer listened to our case and then put his hands together in a perfect A with the fingertips and the two thumbs touching.

"To simply give Mr. Bob two weeks of severance pay and a layoff could still be classified as wrongful dismissal and leave you two open to a multi-thousand-dollar lawsuit if your chef can make the case that he can't find another equal job and that his redundancy, as part of your future business plan about reducing hours, had nothing to do with him."

"Okay, that's why we're here. What do we do now?" I asked.

"We cannot function with him in charge of the kitchen any longer."

He looked at us for a couple of beats and told us to sit tight for a few minutes, then he disappeared through the ornately sandblasted glass doors. We sat in our comfy leather chairs, looked down twenty floors onto the soundless traffic in one of the city's busiest intersections and quietly took stock of our surroundings. Black walnut floorboards, twelve feet of floor-to-ceiling glass on three sides, an oval glass table surrounded by half a dozen white Danish-looking swivel chairs, four orange leather armchairs against the windows, two of which were occupied by Aldo, biting his lower lip, and me, aimlessly leafing through a glossy architecture magazine.

Our young gun didn't waste any time and returned with two letters, both embossed with the law firm's seal. He handed Aldo a letter and the other one to me.

"The first letter," pointing at the one in Aldo's hand, "contains an offer to Bob to take your generous severance package and sign this form," showing us the enclosed form letter, "releasing you from any future claims or litigation. Hand him the letter when he comes in for his shift and tell him he has until midnight to return the signed form."

"Okay, what's in my letter?" I asked.

"If he refuses the generous offer in the first letter, you fire him on the spot and hand him the second letter, which outlines the grounds for his instant dismissal: the varied racial discriminations, insubordination, and physical intimidation of co-workers. If he threatens to take the case to the labour board, you can tell him that we, your lawyers, will collect sworn testimony to substantiate your claims. You can also inform him that he will receive no severance pay and will therefore not be eligible for an EI claim. Either way, you will be rid of your adversary. Good luck, fellows, and I'll want to try that famous steak 'n' frites someday."

We shook hands, thanked him for the swift work, and left, barely an hour after we'd walked into the steel, glass and marble lobby, feeling like we had just been part of a TV crime show.

Later that night I caught up with Colin, who was taking a smoke break out back.

"The coup de grâce is about to happen," I confided, after checking furtively that nobody else was within earshot, still reeling from the afternoon's lesson in legal brinkmanship.

"What's a coup de grâce?" Colin asked, equally paranoid. "Sounds like an ice cream dessert."

"It's the death blow to end the suffering in our kitchen. Be ready, Colin, and on the first of the month you're the chef, and remember, scout's honour, mum's the word."

Aldo and I waited for BBB to show up for his afternoon shift in order to head him off before he could walk into the bistro. He parked his mammoth truck and when he saw us lurking around the back, he knew that something was up. I asked him to come with us to Starbucks next door to discuss his dismissal. Failing that, I tried to hand him the first letter with the generous offer.

"I'm not interested in any stupid letter." He snarled and tossed the letter on the ground. "If you're going to fire me then I'll make you pay. I'll go to the labour board and claim wrongful dismissal and point out all your infractions by not paying proper minimum wage or overtime. I'll take you two down."

BBB pointed his meaty fingers at both of us, telling us how he'd never trusted us and that he would make life a living hell for us. I picked the letters up and tried to point out that he should at least look at the dismissal letter and give our offer some serious consideration.

"It's to your advantage," I said. "You have until midnight to sign the release form or else face the consequences, which are outlined in this other letter, photocopied from the real thing," I said, while thrusting both envelopes at him. Since he didn't take them, I tossed them through the open window of his truck just before he roared off, tires squealing.

Aldo and I walked back inside and encountered Colin, who had witnessed the dramatic incident from the safety of the hallway behind the door.

"BBB's reign of terror is over and he is no longer the chef at the bistro."

Finally. It was long overdue, ever since he'd called Aldo the N-word back in May. His racial slurs and physical intimidations had carried on unabated. He saw himself as a supreme dictator who ruled by fiat in his own fiefdom. His aggressive, confrontational manners didn't win him any friends; in fact, most of the staff were afraid of him. When he'd Frisbeed the dinner plate at Gino and whacked him on his thumb with the hot steak prongs, he'd impaled himself on his own sword.

Flanking Colin, we told the kitchen staff that Colin would now be their new chef and that BBB had left the building. They all clapped and whooped and thanked us. We felt like we'd freed the slaves. A discernable air of relief wafted through the bistro, as if somebody had opened all the windows at once, and suddenly the place felt fresher and altogether more pleasant.

Colin ran a competent evening shift and the food looked very appealing, sculpted and presented in a modern fashion with Colin's personal touch.

Aldo, Gino and I sat at the bar long after everybody had left. I called Clare and ran by her what had happened from the time we went to see the lawyer, and said that now we were waiting for BBB's surrender.

"You did the right thing. Just hang in there — he will deliver the letter. He may be an uncouth oaf but he's not stupid."

At 11:30 p.m., we heard the roar of a big truck out back and then Mirka, his Russian girlfriend, brought us the crumpled but signed release form. I handed over the envelope with his last cheque, the record of employment, and a cheque for two weeks' severance pay. Together with the lawyer's bill, this was our most expensive personnel change to date, and hopefully our last.

A Memorial and a Hobo

Every restaurant is for sale. This is not a cliché but simple fact. A money-making restaurant just has a higher price than a money-losing restaurant. As I said before, a restaurant is much like a boat, with the two happiest days being the one when you buy it and the one when you sell it.

Yes, the bistro was for sale, always had been, always would be, but these were not good times to sell anything. According to a commercial realtor we solicited, there were at that time 900 restaurants for sale in the Lower Mainland alone. That figure didn't include the ones that were not officially listed or advertised. As I said: Every restaurant is for sale. Show me one that isn't and I'll just up the price. In the meantime, we had to make it work, reinvent the wheel, up the ante, maximize our potential, go for broke, cash in our chips.

When I showed Aldo our most recent bank statement, he didn't really want to see it.

"I know we're in trouble, but what do you want to do about it?"

"It's quite simple," I said. "We need to put more money in. We can't pay the bills. Either we skip the rent, don't pay the HST or ask the staff to work a month for free."

Aldo chewed his lip and sat down with a sigh. "I can't believe it. More money. I don't bloody well have any more money."

"I don't either," I said, "and the bank won't give me any more. I probably have to borrow from Clare's mother, God forbid. Bottom line is we each need to put in an extra ten grand. Simple as that. We're 10 percent short once again, only 10 percent."

Ten percent doesn't sound like much, but 10 percent of one million translated into roughly $10,000 short each month. If we hadn't had to pay rent or taxes, we would have been in fine shape.

We really had no choice. We both grudgingly promised to come up with the money. It was a very depressing reality, but we had to pretend for all the world to see that everything was just fine, that we were in fact the success everybody wanted us to be and thought we were.

"Borrow from my mom?" Clare, said, slowly putting down her knife and fork. She stared at me for a beat, as if she didn't believe what she'd just heard.

I solemnly poked around my plate, eyes cast down, trying to appear casual, as if we were just talking about the weather. "The bistro is in temporary financial distress," I said.

"Temporary? There is no such thing. I can't ask my mom, you know that. She doesn't have any money. She's a senior living on a fixed income, and you should know that borrowing from your parents is not the same as borrowing from the bank. I can't believe we're having this conversation."

"Goddamn," I said, about to lose my mind. "What the hell do you want me do? We have to put some money in. Otherwise we're in default, and once the word gets out, it's only a matter of time until we lose the whole thing. We have to carry on, try and make it work, Clare. It's not something that I just dreamed up." I pushed back my chair and stood up, pacing back and forth, not at all enjoying this.

"There must be another way," Clare said, trying hard to remain rational, unlike me. "Maybe we can cash in some RRSPs. Please sit down and finish breakfast. Let's not waste the few hours we have together fighting about money."

I wanted to point out that money was the root cause of almost every fight among lovers, families, tribes and nations. "We're not fighting, just arguing," I said lamely, but I did sit down, and after breakfast we took up pen and paper and crunched some numbers. But no matter how we rearranged them, we were still losing money. Clare hit on the only solution available to us, and we decided to cash in some of my RRSPs.

It had been a year since Alexandra Gill featured us so prominently in the *Globe and Mail*. That was the major reason why the previous September had been our best month to date. August that year was better than the year before, but when the kids went back to school and the tourists evaporated overnight, we were forced to come up with some new ideas that would both save and make money and yet not compromise our food and service. I was sounding like the government: cut spending and increase productivity, the ever-popular oxymoron.

Whenever we had a bad day, we let the genie out of the bottle with great ideas about changes, from the wall paint to the food, and we usually stuffed it back in before we went home long after midnight. What was missing in all of these late-night fantasies was a concept, a proper business plan, backed by a philosophy. Late-night inspirations born of frustration and too much free booze always lack substance, just like the genie.

"We can't just go and paint the walls charcoal or burgundy and make all the lights into pot lights — how is this going to lure anybody through the front door?"

"That's why all corporate restaurants have young, sexy servers in tight black spandex dresses instead of a couple of old crusty waiters," Aldo lamented.

"Who is crusty and old?" Gino protested. "There is something to be said for experience and knowledge, or is that a thing of the past as well?"

"Experience and knowledge is supplanted with clever marketing and pricing."

"Nothing over twenty bucks and all meals in small portions. 'Tapas' is the new buzzword, so that a full meal will cost you fifty bucks by the time you add it all together. Look at our meals. Nobody orders desserts when they've finished our main course. We're old-fashioned with our full meals," Colin pointed out. And he was right.

"Can't we just cut down on our portions, sculpt them and make them look bigger, charge for our pommes frites, and serve only one basket of bread instead of unlimited amounts of bread and butter?" I asked.

"We need to represent a stable image, portray old-world character and new-world savvy, exemplify the fact that we are, after all, a French bistro," Gino said.

"We cannot compete with the likes of Cactus Club and Earls. We have to stick to our little niche market, a French country bistro with a history, a classy, cozy restaurant where you can take your mom, your lover, or your boss. The atmosphere has to include and reflect the food and the service. That is what brings the customers through our door," I said.

"But we should do something," Aldo lamented, throwing up his arms in mock despair.

"I know, we should bloody well sell the joint. Just changing the look and the atmosphere might well change our clientele, meaning we might lose the small, loyal customer base we've worked so hard to maintain and attract. Can we bring in the young and trendy crowd? With a coat of paint? What about the old and rich patrons? What about the business lunch crowd? They come to the bistro for what they know, just as it is. Will they be back if it suddenly doesn't look familiar anymore? Is this a risk and an expense worth the gamble, or should we just stick to the tried and true: food and service?" I argued. I knew Clare thought so. "Maybe instead of the décor we should focus on the food, service and price — the holy trinity of any food establishment." I concluded the conversation, drowned my beer and called it a night.

One day we attended the memorial service for Mauricio, or Sanchez as we called him, for his portrayal of a dictator for all of thirty seconds in a local TV series. He'd died suddenly a week before, at home on his couch, due to his brain tumour. It didn't seem that long ago that he'd told us it was benign. One moment he was joking and shaking cocktails, the next instant he'd stumbled, started drooling and slurring his words. When I saw him the next time, which turned out to be the last time, he was bloated and lame on the right side of his body, his face lopsided, his right arm dangling with no control. And now he was dead.

Everybody who eulogized and paid tribute to Mauricio pointed out that he had been a prince of a man in every respect. He looked like a Latin James Bond — charismatic, photogenic and always in a good mood. Everyone who met him couldn't forget his loud belly laugh with his head thrown back, or his kind, upbeat demeanour. Sanchez happened to be one of the most positive people I'd ever met. "Life is beautiful" was one of his standard phrases, and despite his being broke and destitute, he was always looking forward to the moment when that breakthrough phone call would come, when he would step out and become the star he was destined to be. Never a doubt about that. We used to joke with him, yell "Viva Sanchez!" with a high-five salute and laugh about his undiminished, infectious optimism. He always looked like a successful man, dressed and groomed impeccably, with a smile and a laugh for everyone.

The fact that he died so suddenly from a very aggressive, malignant form of brain cancer took everybody by surprise, and we'd never know if Mauricio knew all along that his time was up. We all missed his humour and life-embracing personality. His death left a big hole in the bistro and in the lives of those who knew him.

The rain was steady and the leaves that had been falling from the trees now clogged the drains on the roof, resulting in water pooling and eventually finding its way into the bistro. The landlord had no intention of fixing the roof, a quilt of patches old and new, so either Aldo or I had to be up there, ankle deep in standing water, plunging the drain every time it rained.

"You call the landlord this time," I insisted.

"I'd like to give him one of these," Aldo said, plunging the drain one more time.

Mr. Lee was cagey and elusive and rich. He didn't spend a penny unless held at gunpoint or compelled by a judge, and even then, he found ways to dodge his responsibility. In other words, we didn't expect the landlord to fix the roof unless it collapsed into the restaurant. Then the insurance would pay for it and make him even richer.

It was Harvest Festival time at Le Bistro again, and a chance for Colin to show his mettle. I brought in a full paper bag — at least two pounds — of chanterelles that I'd purchased from a German farmer on the Sunshine Coast on the weekend for only twenty bucks. Colin looked suspiciously in the bag, and he had to admit that they were authentic chanterelles — needles, bugs and all. He handed the mushrooms off to Billy to clean.

"That will be perfect for my special. Nothing tastes better than sautéed wild mushrooms over venison scaloppini," he enthused.

A Memorial and a Hobo

It was Sunday night and since nobody wanted to work Sundays, it was me as the token adult and the ever-eager Mandy working the floor, with Alice hanging out, a faraway look in her eyes. Sundays can go either way — busy, or nobody at all.

A couple walked in and Mandy took them to table twelve, an alcove by the window. They looked well-to-do, probably in their sixties, he in a fine tweed jacket with a silk tie, she in a bright red wool coat, a dark blue blouse and a grey pleated skirt. The kind of customers we need, I thought to myself. Mandy spent an inordinate amount of time getting their orders and then went straight to the kitchen to confer with Colin. She returned to the table and I could hear raised voices, even eclipsing one of Piaf's pained songs coming out of the bistro speakers. I started to wonder what was up, and when a distraught Mandy came to punch in the order, I casually inquired if everything was all right.

"He insists on steak tartare, but Colin said the meat was too old and he won't make it. I tried to explain to the customers and now they're pissed off."

"Oh boy," I said. I asked Colin if those were the facts.

"Yeah, this is Sunday and the meat is from Thursday. I don't want to risk it."

"Can't you just trim it on all sides?"

Colin shrugged his shoulders. "You're the boss."

I sauntered over to the stubborn customers, jovial and wearing my not-worried-and-in-charge face.

"How can I help you? I hear you were advised against the steak tartare."

"I've been coming to this restaurant for the last thirty years," he bellowed, his trimmed moustache quivering, lips compressed, nostrils flaring, "and I always have the steak tartare. In fact, that's the reason why we're here. I was going to order a nice bottle of wine to go with it but since you can't supply the food, we'll skip the wine as well."

His companion said nothing, just kept poking at her piece of bread with the butter knife, eyes downcast.

"I tell you what," I said, "you promise me two things and I'll be happy to serve you steak tartare."

"Oh yeah, what's that?"

"Promise me you won't get sick and you won't sue me."

He looked at me, taken aback, his purplish lips pursed, and there was a split second when I thought I had overdone it. But then a big grin spread across his ruddy face, revealing a set of large, yellowed teeth, and he clapped the table with a guffaw. "Well done, chap. You have my promise. We'll have two steak tartares on the double and a bottle of your finest Bordeaux, how about the Saint-Émilion."

They ate steak tartare followed by filet mignon, rare of course, and drank two bottles of the Château Rothschild. The bill came to $400. Mandy was ecstatic with the tip. I just hoped we didn't get a call from a doctor or a lawyer. A promise is only as good as the one who makes it.

We had a slow lunch one day, the usual at that time of year, and I sent Alia home early. About ten minutes later, two girls walked in the door with Styrofoam containers, wondering if they could sit down and eat their bagged lunches. I was flabbergasted. What nerve! Would you like some water and fries with that!

"Sorry, girls, we've just closed until dinnertime."

I had to let them use the washroom. I'm not inhuman.

For a couple of days, we had also gained a new resident on our bench on the alley side of the bistro. His name was Peter. He had a full beard, was the size of a grizzly bear and smelled like a skunk — because he'd cuddled and petted a run-over skunk the previous night until Gino told him to move the carcass to the other side of the street, away from the restaurant's front door. Peter bedded himself down every night on the bench. He carried his old sleeping bag in a suitcase, had a small transistor radio and even an alarm clock. He always shouted a hearty "Hello!" when he saw me. I tried to avoid him, but he was hard to ignore, practically at the front door.

Shortly after I denied the two girls their impertinent request, Peter walked into the restaurant without shoes, only his filthy woollen socks on his large feet. I could tolerate him sleeping on the bench, but now he had overstepped his welcome.

"You cannot come in here, Peter," I admonished him.

"I just need some water," he pleaded. I filled up his old Pepsi bottle with water. "Where are your shoes?" I asked.

"Some bum stole them off me last night."

I couldn't believe it. One bum steals from the other. I went into the staff room and retrieved some shoes left behind by one of our former cooks, probably BBB, from the size of them.

"Here you go, Peter, but you cannot come into the restaurant. Go up to the community centre for your water, please."

Peter thanked me profusely for the shoes and tried to give me a bear hug, which I firmly declined. He shuffled out to his bench and turned up his transistor radio to the classic rock station.

Some days were just like that.

We hadn't heard from Jean in a while, and although I didn't want to sound desperate, I wanted to know, so I called him. When he finally answered, I asked him straight out if he was still interested in buying the bistro and if so, what kind of a price and time frame did he have in mind.

"Absolutely," he said, not committing himself. "I'll send you an email."

"Okay, Jean, we really need to know so we can adjust. Should we sign up for Dine Out or not, should we go ahead with some of the advertising for next year, and all of that. I don't want to pressure you, but we would like to have a better idea." I didn't want to sound whiny, but I probably did. Aldo would not have approved.

A protracted silence ensued, and for a moment I thought the connection was lost. Then Jean was back on the line and said, "All right, I hear you. I'll get back to you."

"When?"

"Today, I promise. Gotta go."

Jean did send me an email in the afternoon with his offer, which was insultingly low. When I showed it to Aldo, he almost had a fit.

"What does he think, we're giving it away? Is he crazy? He has to do better than that. No way we'll agree to this."

"He's the only fish on the hook, Aldo, and a slippery one at that. It's all we got. Let's think about it."

Since we'd cancelled the infamous half-price nights, the bistro fell quiet again on Wednesdays. It was somewhat bittersweet. Only the kitchen crew was happy, since they weren't crazy busy and still got the same pay. But the waiters and the owners felt a bit cheated. The fact is that everybody loves a bargain, or at least likes to think they're getting a deal. And because there was no 50 percent lure, most people didn't realize that our food was a great deal even at full prices.

The service was over by 10:00 p.m., and instead of a hurricane, as on other Wednesday nights, tumbleweeds were blowing through the restaurant. Instead of 150 people, we counted twenty-eight covers. Everybody left except Gino and me. I poured us a couple of pints and sat at the bar and we philosophized and proselytized about the failings, the ups and downs and the reasons for the missing patrons.

"Give me back the crazy Wednesdays — at least we made some money," I complained, and Gino agreed.

"Tell me about it. It was good for us servers too. We made 15 percent of the sales, no matter at what discount we sold them."

"Here's the thing," I said, feeling better, pouring another pint. "It's quite clear to me that the generation between eighteen and twenty-eight, let's call it the H generation, H standing for herd, is blissfully ignorant about French food. Their mothers had no time or no motivation to impart basic cooking skills to their offspring, and from what I know, most of generation H orders out, eats in chain restaurants and warms up pre-cooked food in the microwave."

"Most don't know the difference between a Béarnaise and a béchamel sauce, or between halibut and cod, but that's why we explain the food to them and earn our tips," Gino said. "But first they have to get in the door and into a seat."

"The H generation knows basically five food groups," I said, working up a head of frustration. "Burgers, pizza, pasta, Chinese and sushi. That's it. I've had people ask me what filet mignon is and when I explain that it's from the tenderloin, I get a blank look.

"'It's really tender steak.'

"'Oh, it's steak, like T-bone?'

"'It doesn't have the bone, but it's the triangle part of the T-bone steak.'

"'And it comes with gravy and fries?'

"'Sort of. It's peppercorn sauce and pommes frites.'

"It drives me crazy. I'm constantly surprised by the vast ignorance about food, cooking, dishes or recipes among generation H. It is awesome in its scope, only matched by an equal absence of knowledge about world history and geography. But who needs all this education when you can just ask your smartphone or google any question? They're all masters of miniature keyboards, and their nubile dexterity is evident in speed-texting, and their superficial knowledge of instant trivia is unique and unequalled by any preceding generation."

"And nutrition fits somewhere between the weight loss, diet propaganda and workout world," Gino said. "Nothing to do with science or common sense."

"They haven't even heard of the evil trinity: fat, sugar and salt."

"Moderation is the cardinal rule," Gino pointed out, taking a swig. "That goes for everything: food, drink and sex. Well, maybe not sex."

"Who watches all those cooking shows on TV?"

"Probably only lonely housewives and the unemployed. They're a good thing, I guess. At least it entices people to cook and try out new foods."

On that hopeful note, we called it a night, checked that all the burners were off and the coolers closed, and turned off the lights.

When I weaved home in a maudlin mood, I didn't see the glistening sidewalk, reflecting the early Christmas lights, or the other late-night figures hurrying somewhere, wrapped in greys and blacks, heads turtled inside upturned collars and wrapped in scarves, with hats and umbrellas. I kept thinking instead of the herd mentality of this or maybe any generation. It was evident everywhere, from clothing to hairstyles, from the way the under-thirty crowd walked and talked, and of course from where and what they ate. A full restaurant like the Korean noodle place next door attracts customers, whereas the empty gourmet palace, like the bistro, stayed depressingly empty. People go where others have gathered. I do it, you do it, we all do it. Maybe when we get old and cranky we tend to avoid the crowds and opt for the empty restaurant. It was this kind of customer we still catered to. I was afraid I would be one of them in the foreseeable future.

It was close to midnight when I finally got home, and I couldn't go to sleep, worried about money and the future. Clare got up and made me a soothing cup of tea.

"Owning the bistro is like having a kid," I said to Clare again. "It's always on the brink of trouble, always in need of more money, calling daily with issues and demands, happy when there is a party, sad when left alone, unwilling to grow up and change, and incapable of taking care of itself. It's a constant worry, just like a child, with all the growing pains, rewards and disappointments."

"You need a holiday," Clare said, and I agreed.

"But this is the wrong time of year."

"Is there a right time of year?" she said.

We were deep in the pre-Christmas hole and appreciated every customer who came through the door. A good-looking guy with a long forelock falling over his eyes, in his late twenties I guessed, came in from the damp, cold day and sat down at the bar. He ordered a lovely lunch of steak 'n' frites with several beers and a couple of tequila chasers, chatting amiably to Alia, who served all the weekday lunches by herself. She was also the only waitress who cared about the restaurant as a whole. She cleaned it, took wine inventory, kept the kitchen on their toes, and expressed genuine concern about the quality of the food and service. She never missed a shift in two years. She never idled like most of the other girls, who would marinate in their own fantasies in front of a mirror or a window.

At least we had one customer, I thought, and dabbed at my right eye, which had developed an irritating flutter. Nobody else could see it, but I felt it. I was rather on edge those days about the missing cash flow, trying to present a jovial, unconcerned front while inwardly seething with worries.

Alia did her best to keep up a polite banter with the increasingly talkative guy. The more he drank, the more he talked. Then he had to go out back for a smoke. Nothing wrong with that. Lots of customers do it. Out back for a puff. About ten minutes later I noticed the guy's jacket still hanging on his chair, the unfinished beer going flat, and him nowhere in sight. I checked the front, then the back of the bistro. Nobody. I immediately examined the jacket, a generic black midget hockey jacket, well-worn, worth nothing, too shabby even for a thrift store. Pockets empty, wearer vanished. I inwardly groaned, trying to placate the upset Alia, who took it personally.

"I should have known," she said, berating herself. "I knew this was too good to be real."

"Alia, there was nothing you could do. You can't ask customers to show us their money or check their credit cards."

Just then I saw Peter arrive at the bench in the alley. His large frame was draped in a Mexican blanket and he dragged his battered suitcase along. After he settled in and made himself comfortable by kicking off the large shoes I'd given him a few days before, he took a clandestine swig from a mickey, which he swiftly hid under his blanket, leaning back all comfy and seemingly content.

For a fleeting moment, I envied him.

The Worry and the Merry Season

I put in another call to Jean from Gino's phone to find out at what stage our negotiations were. For once he answered right away, not recognizing the phone number. I got right to the point. No small talk with this man. "Jean, we received your, uh, offer, and we agree in principle on the deal, but we need to have something in writing, maybe even a down payment, some letter from a lawyer. Something, Jean."

"You sound worried. Don't fret, my word is gold and you shouldn't worry for one second. It's going to happen."

"When, Jean? Is the January first deadline not a little too soon? We need to give the staff two weeks' notice and I'm not sure if we can do that just before Christmas."

"You're right, it's too soon. How about the end of January instead?" he casually suggested.

"Okay, that way we'll get the Christmas business and maybe I should sign up for the Dine Out promotion in January. We also don't want to lay people off for a Christmas present," I said. "But we still need something in writing, Jean. I'm happy with an email outlining the basics. Something we can show to our lawyer and accountant."

"You're much too worried, did I ever tell you that? Believe me, my word is like the Pope's honour. No worry, my friend, I'll put something in writing. Gotta go."

I'm not sure why I still didn't feel very confident, but I had an uneasy feeling that it would all go sideways, just like the bizarre offer Rudy had brought us the previous September.

When I told Aldo of my conversation with Jean, he just shook his head and solemnly said, "It's not enough money. It's just not enough."

Gino had a new favourite customer. Lukas was a middle-aged, overweight German stockbroker who'd started to honour our establishment with his bulky presence a couple of months before. He came in two or three times a week, always with different female company, usually half his age. He liked to drink his champagne, the real stuff, not the cheap bubbly. He always ordered a bottle of Moët & Chandon Impérial before dinner and usually two bottles of Clerc Milon Pauillac with his meal, and he liked to finish off with multiple shots of XO Rémy Martin. We had to order in special stock of these expensive spirits, but at $25 a shot it was definitely worth it.

The previous day, Gino had agreed to take over the lunch shift for Alia, who had things to do. I showed up just when Gino staggered in the door, looking rather ghoulish with large bags under his red-rimmed eyes. "What happened to you?" I queried.

"I stayed here until 5:00 a.m. with Lukas."

"You're kidding! Until 5:00 a.m.? What the hell were you doing?"

"Serving him and his new girlfriend drinks, and after midnight he insisted on me joining them. His bill came to $1,200."

"You didn't have to do that. Just tell him we're closed at midnight," I said.

"Well, it wasn't really all that hard, drinking champagne and cognac until the sun came up, but it's rather painful right now."

"Sorry, I'm right out of sympathy," I said on my way out the door, "but thanks for the extra cash."

One day we had a meeting with Ray and Jim, two young local Chinese entrepreneurs. They wanted to sell us a promotional deal akin to Groupon, the latest craze in marketing techniques.

Here was the setup: Ray and Jim would sell as many half-price coupons of a particular item via social media as they could. A $30 item Ray and Jim would sell for half the price at only $15. The two entrepreneurs would then take 20 percent of this for their effort, which left us $12 for a $30 item.

"If we sell a thousand coupons, that would translate into $12,000, 50 percent — or $6,000 — of which we will hand over right away," Ray said. "The remaining 50 percent we'll pay out in increments depending on the redeemed coupons, which we can track on our website. Sound good?"

Well, better than Groupon, which would take 50 percent of the deal, in our case leaving us with only 25 percent, or $7.50, of the original prize. The upside of Groupon was that they handed over all the money up front, which would be $7,500. That was the lure, but the catch was that we would have to give away 1,000 filets mignons in the following three months (the redeemable time period). To sweeten the pot, both Groupon and Jay and Jim pointed out that up to a quarter of all coupons would never be redeemed. That was the deal. Aldo and I promised Jay and Jim that we would mull it over. After they left, we both exhaled visibly and scratched our heads.

Yes, $10 would cover our cost, and if they sold 1,000 coupons that would bring in an extra thousand people to the restaurant. During the slow time of year, let's say January before Dine Out, that would put some bums in the seats — but we still didn't like the unknown factors. We could have been swamped by coupon redeemers on any day, which meant that we would have to staff and stock for this eventuality. This might work for haircuts or bike rentals, but not a restaurant.

Instead, Aldo and I opted for our own West Coast Promotion Deal. We decided that after the holidays, we would publish our own coupon in the *Georgia Straight*, offering 50 percent off any entrée, every day, per coupon. The ad would cost us $450 and would certainly bring in customers. And at 50 percent we would still do better than with Jay and Jim, and certainly much better than Groupon. The only drawback was that we wouldn't get a fat cash advance.

One day, Melinda, our Quebecois waitress, came flying in the back door, dishevelled and fifteen minutes late. As usual, I expected her to blame the rain, the traffic, the bus, the alarm clock or the boyfriend. But today she blamed the French prime minister, Monsieur Sarkozy, or more precisely, the French news media. "Guess what is big news today in Paris?"

I declared my ignorance.

"You would not believe it. It's Monsieur Sarkozy's zipper," she declared with passion, accelerating her voice into almost a screech.

I looked at her, bemused, shaking my head. "His zipper?"

"Yes, his ziiipppper was down when he met the Chinese premier at the Palace d'Élysée in Paris, and everybody talk about that and nobody mention the billion-dollar deal in nuclear reactors. It's all about his stupid zipper. I cannot believe."

She didn't wait for a response from me and stormed off to fix her hair and get ready for her service. I guess Mr. Sarkozy and his embarrassing zipper was to blame for her tardiness today.

Inadvertently, I checked my own zipper.

I don't know why or where Walt Disney got his inspiration to cast vermin as heroes and elevate mice and rats into the pantheon of fantasy superstars for millions of children the world over. Mickey Mouse and his brood of offspring were nothing but a curse on the bistro, and many other food establishments for that matter, infesting the walls and the ceilings and finding ways into the restaurant, even right during service.

We were always diligently armed with glue boards, bleach for the floors and kitchen surfaces, and steel wool for the holes, and yet they found their way in. Our nemesis, Stewy, always went through the place with his laser-beam flashlight, picking out every little mouse turd and hole in the wall, to our consternation.

We had a good table of four, a sixtieth birthday party, and Alia was just about to serve the main course when a shriek tore through the tranquil evening, turning everybody's head in the direction of the outcry. I was in the back and I knew instinctively what the problem was. The next instant the spry birthday boy leaped from his chair with a napkin in his hands, pounced on the floor, and with a guttural hunter's cry of "I got him!" stunned his audience into motionless suspension. I turned up the music and walked over to the table to confront the issue straight on.

The birthday boy proudly handed me the rolled-up napkin like an offering. "It's just a mouse. Please don't kill him?"

I'm sure in his mind this mouse still represented Mickey, forever engraved on millions of young minds as the funny, big-eared hero of Disneyland.

"Of course not," I assured him, lying with the ease of a seasoned politician.

As the Christmas lights illuminate the city nights, the restaurant business picks itself out of the doldrums of dreary November and toward the festive season. People take each other out for lunches, office dinner parties start to book in, the general mood is elevated, and worries about unpaid Visa bills are relegated into the post-Christmas future.

Aldo and I had the same seasonal argument as we did the previous year. He likes Christmas music and I can't stand it. We reached a perfect compromise thanks to Colin, our young, savvy chef, who showed us the Yule log on TV. Channel 256 displayed the perfect crackling fireplace in real time, accompanied by tasteful jazzy Christmas music, twenty-four hours a day. We clapped like little kids when we saw the hand placing a new log in the fire about once every hour, and we left the virtual Yuletide fire burning every night, to the delight of the staff and customers.

After having been missing in action for a couple of weeks, our old friend Peter reappeared on the bench at the side of the bistro and once more made it his own. It was a coveted spot for street people for the fact that it was sheltered and out of the direct weather, thanks to our overhanging awning.

But now that Peter had come back, I found myself saying "good morning" to the large, bearded man who looked and smelled like a bad Santa. I felt the same social disconnect as when I had a conversation with a scrawny guy standing in our Dumpster, telling him to watch out for broken glass and rats. Peter made himself comfortable on the bench with an underlay of cardboard, a fluffy pillow and a gigantic red parka that also served as a sleeping bag. Beside the bench, he parked his carry-on suitcase, on top of which perched his small transistor radio and, of all things, alarm clock.

"The cops called yesterday, wondering if Peter is bothering us," Gino informed me one day. "Apparently some resident on the twenty-second floor has a perfect view of the bench and has complained about Peter."

Everything about Peter was large: his tremendous bulk, amplified by the several layers of clothing, his big head, framed by a wild, unruly beard, his long, curly hair, poking out from a hand-knit woollen tea cozy, his large bulbous red nose and his booming, baritone voice. I pieced together various bits of information from Gino, who talked to him, as well as from some of our customers, who seemed to know about Peter. Apparently, he originally came from Hungary as a young man, then drifted across Canada and parts of the US, like New Orleans and San Francisco, taking various jobs but mainly working as a baker and pastry chef, as he proudly pointed out to me.

"I'm a master patisserie chef and I make the best sourdough this side of San Francisco," he proudly stated, rubbing his large belly. He ended up in Vancouver, on our bench, because he couldn't go any further, due to the Pacific Ocean, and because "It's the best weather for an outdoors person like myself," as he proclaimed with a large, bellowing laugh.

One of our regular customers ordered a crêpe Suzette for Peter and had it served to him on his bench by a reluctant Alia. When Peter walked into the bistro to return the empty dish, I had to admonish him once again.

"Peter, we have an agreement! You cannot come into the restaurant and certainly never during service." And especially not in your smelly woollen socks, I wanted to add.

Peter's residency became problematic when he started holding court with some of his cronies, who came equipped with various forms of cheap booze. These gatherings started to impact our business, as prospective customers opted for the other side of the street, avoiding passing by the group of smelly, bearded merrymakers. I confronted Peter, telling him to take the party down the alley, away from the restaurant's front door. He assured me that he'd take care of it. "If they show up, I'll kill them all," he bellowed in his best operatic voice, which I was sure could be heard blocks away.

"Please, no killing, Peter. Just tell them to go somewhere else," I pleaded in a calm voice. I had visions of removing the bench, but that would cause more bleeding-heart pushback from the odd customer and even some of the staff, who all thought it quite novel and entertaining.

The next day, half a dozen of Peter's buddies gathered again around midday. Obviously, Peter's bench had become a regular jamboree.

"Just call the cops," Gino advised me, "or even better, call Aldo." I was reluctant to involve the authorities and I knew that

Aldo would make short shrift of Peter and his buddies without any consideration for the delicate social intricacies this situation required. Instead, I took it upon myself to reason one more time with wild man Peter.

"Peter, you promised me just yesterday that this would not happen again. You leave me no choice," I said to him, while the group of guys immediately pocketed their bottles and moved off, not wanting any sort of public confrontation.

He glared at me as if about to eat me for lunch, and then broke into a wide grin, showing off his decaying teeth. "You call the cops, I call the newspaper."

"I'm sorry, Peter, but I'm trying to run a business. It's nothing personal, you know that."

"Okay, that does it," Peter yelled, indignant. "I'm moving out!"

"Peter you're not moving out," I pointed out to him, "you're moving on. This is not your home — it's just a bench."

"Look at this," Gino greeted me, stabbing the front page of the *Vancouver Sun* with his index finger. "Peter is a celebrity."

My heart dropped into my stomach. And there he was, front-page news, Peter getting a hug from a social worker, lamenting the lack of proper housing in the city, citing the poor and displaced like himself who were falling through the frayed and tattered safety net and especially vulnerable at this time of year. Lucky for us, Peter didn't cite the bistro's bench as his last place of residence. It looked like he still wore the old chef's shoes I gave him. I breathed a sigh of relief and wished him good luck.

It was no surprise that the holiday season brought in all manner of fascinating customers, those who count on the owner's seasonal goodwill and charity. At exactly 12:00 noon, a nun in full head garb and with a large wooden cross dangling from her neck entered the bistro. She looked every bit like a penguin in distress. She demurely handed me an amateurish-looking indigo postcard with a disproportioned angel holding a baby engulfed in a yellow halo, mouthing "Merry Christmas" in a speech bubble. Her other hand clutched what looked like a rosary. "I'm Sister Ophelia from the Holy Rosary, collecting alms for the poor," she said with her head bowed in submission.

"Well, Sister Ophelia, uh, . . . we're kind of short on cash, but would you like a bowl of soup instead?" I offered, while Alia rolled her eyes in exasperation.

Sister Ophelia accepted without hesitation and planted herself in a nice window seat, fiddling with her rosary and mouthing wordless prayers. I wondered where she got the costume. The large wooden cross on its heavy chain that dangled around her neck looked more like it belonged to a punk rocker than a nun, and her headgear had seen better days, probably in a theatre company.

She finished her soup, two baskets of bread and a jug of water, and then blessed us all in lieu of a tip, making the sign of the cross — the wrong way around, Alia thought.

"May the force be with you," I mumbled when she glided out the door, "and a Merry Christmas to you."

At this time of year, the poor seem poorer and the rich buy presents and take each other out for lunch and dinner at French restaurants. The homeless line up at soup kitchens for free turkey dinners put on by unions and volunteer organizations.

Christmas highlights the material gulf between the haves and have-nots, but the lights and sparkles add an air of festive unreality to the gloomy, dark days, and it does bring out the best in most. Neighbours and strangers smile when they hustle past each other on their way to a blow-out sale or Christmas party.

December is a good month for restaurants like ours. Office parties, family gatherings and business lunches filled the bistro. The closer it got to the twenty-fifth, the more people seemed to throw fiscal and dietary caution to the wind, order a better bottle of wine or indulge in a decadent dessert.

During the afternoon lull, I called Jean on the spur of the moment. The excuse was to wish him Merry Christmas, but I really wanted to know if the darned sale was going through and when. As expected, he didn't answer his phone, and I left a fake but cheerful holiday message.

Just before closing one December night, who walked in all glittery and coiffed but Rama, with a beautiful young girl on his arm. They planted themselves at the bar and ordered a bottle of Dom Pérignon. We carried only one of those at any one time, since they cost us $240 to replace. Oh boy, I thought, this was going to be a long night. I hoped Rama had money this time. I snuck out back to check what car he was driving. If it was the Ferrari or the Rolls-Royce, then we were okay; if it was his mom's Honda Civic, we might be out of luck. The black Ferrari was parked right behind the bistro, even though Rama lived only two blocks away.

"How is the Italian luxury park in Bangaluru coming along?" I asked, trying to make small talk.

He didn't need any prodding and launched effortlessly into his promotional spiel. "We're just about to put the shovels in the ground," he said. "We had nothing but grief with the changes in government, having to bribe new functionaries for the third time around, but we're there now. This would be a good time to invest, because in another six months the stock will be worth ten times what it is now."

"Sorry," I said, "I'm right out of investment capital. Actually, I'm looking for some capital right here in the bistro. Pocket change for a guy like you who deals in gazillions," I said, trying hard to keep the cynic lurking inside of me at bay.

"Let me make some calls," Rama offered, while Margo refilled their flutes.

He casually gave Margo a $100 bill for a tip, but asked me with a wink to put the bottle on his account. Which account? I wanted to ask, feeling rather frustrated, but I didn't want to embarrass him in front of his new girlfriend and just days before Christmas.

"Here," Rama said magnanimously, handing me the keys to the Ferrari. "We'll cab it home. I'll pick it up tomorrow."

I guess a Ferrari quattrovalvole would do for collateral. When I dangled the keys in front of Roy the next day, his knees visibly buckled. "Oh my god!" he cried, "I want to drive that baby so bad."

"What the hell," I said. "Merry Christmas, Roy. Just remember: It's a racehorse, not a mare." A moment later the powerful engine roared to life and the squealing tires told me that Roy was either going to hell or was indeed in heaven at this very moment.

Half an hour later he was back, with a look of bliss on his face like he had had an epiphany.

"That's the best Christmas present anyone ever gave me," he gushed.

I was surprised by how many people preferred to go to a restaurant on Christmas Eve. I suppose the West End, and for that matter the whole world, is full of people whose families are either gone or too far away. Add to that the atheists and adherers to faiths other than Christianity who just wanted dinner out. We were happy to serve anybody, and Christmas Eve, just like the previous year, turned out to be a decent night. We served turkey as a special, carved by yours truly in a Santa hat in front of the Yuletide log on TV. We closed the doors by 8:00 p.m. to give the staff a chance to go home at a reasonable hour and have a belated evening with their respective families. That left me, Clare and Aldo to close up, but not before we cracked a nice bottle of bubbly to celebrate the season. One of the benefits of owning a restaurant is the readily available wine stock. It can be both a curse and a blessing. That night, it was the latter.

Jean finally called back and wished us a good season, and when I asked him if we were on track, he reiterated, "Of course we're on track. Did we agree on the end of January?"

"As it turns out, Jean, that's in the middle of Dine Out. How about after Valentine's Day? Let's go for February 15. That would be the best date for everybody."

There was a pause at the other end. For a moment I thought I'd lost Jean again. "All right then, February 15 it is," he said, to my relief.

"I'll send you a sales agreement indicating the date and the amount so you can sign it and we can then pass this on to our respective lawyers," I said.

Jean laughed and said, "You're still worried, aren't you? Hey, I told you my word is better than gold. When I say I will, I always do. Just ask my ex-wife. Trust me. Happy New Year. We'll talk next year, my friend."

Aldo wasn't impressed by Jean's assurances. "Without a piece of paper, we have nothing. Just words."

The biggest night of the year for most food and drink establishments translated into a lot of work for everybody. Just like a theatre or dance performance, once the curtain goes up everything has to be perfectly choreographed and performed seamlessly. No matter what chaos reigns in the kitchen, in the front of the restaurant everybody must have a good time, customers and servers alike. The servers love it because they make great tips; the kitchen staff hate it because they don't get to party like everybody else. Colin, on the other hand, was excited, and created a fabulous gala menu, planned out to the very last detail.

Only Clare, Aldo and I knew that this might be our last New Year's Eve at the bistro, and to mark the occasion we invited everybody we could think of to come and join us for a night of celebration. We planned ahead despite the ludicrous predictions of some self-styled interpreters of the mysterious Mayan calendar, who proclaimed the end of the world by December 21, 2012. If anything, this folly added an extra degree of excitement to this year's celebration.

Here is Colin's New Year's Eve menu for 2012.

NEW YEAR'S EVE FIVE-COURSE DINNER

Palate Teaser
Chef's hors d'oeuvre

Appetizers
Five oysters on the half shell, vodka cocktail sauce
or
Foie gras crème brûlée, gratinée of Asiago
or
Chili and lime ahi tuna tartare in Belgian endive

Soup or Salad
Classic lobster bisque, brandy crème fraîche
or
Greens, goat cheese truffles, honey balsamic vinaigrette

Main Course
Served with seasonal vegetables

Tarragon and dijon-crusted rack of lamb
Chambard reduction with garlic pommes purée
or
Magret de canard
Fraser Valley duck breast, cassis reduction
Thyme-roasted Yukon potatoes
or
Eight-ounce grilled rib-eye steak
with Syrah and wild mushroom sauce
Roasted garlic pommes purée, truffle drizzle
or
Fillet of black cod & king crab legs
Pine nut beurre noisette, saffron rice pilaf

Folly Bistro

Palate Cleanser

Lemon sorbet, champagne drizzle

Dessert

Madagascar vanilla bean crème brûlée

or

Chocolate brandy monton, raspberry coulis, Chantilly cream

or

Lemon sabayon in tuile cup, Chantilly cream

Bon Appétit

6

The Beginning of the End

After New Year's everybody had two days off, except for Aldo and me, who were in on January 2 to hammer out some new strategy. We agreed to roll out our new promotion with the 50-percent coupons in the *Georgia Straight*.

"That should bring in the punters," Aldo said.

"It's our going-out-of-business special," I said wryly, "the last desperate attempt to attain the impossible, fill the restaurant in January."

"Nobody knows, I hope," Aldo said. "Jean better keep his French horn under wraps. We don't want anybody to know until two weeks before the turnover. Otherwise, we'll lose our staff."

We also opted not to take a year-end bonus as we had originally planned, since we couldn't afford it. But we did take each other, Aldo's wife, their two kids, and Clare out to dim sum in China-town. We marvelled at the army of servers, cooks and bussers and ate our fill of mystery food.

It was our first day open in the new year, and we assumed it was the post-holiday blues that left the restaurant somewhat deserted. We would all rather have been in a warm place with our toes in the sand, enrolled in margarita therapy, but we needed to get our engines cranked up again after the previous busy two weeks. As Clare put it, "It's better to dream than to mope," and Alia, always pragmatic, thought it was better to hope for more customers than to close up early and go home.

On January 4, we still hadn't heard from Jean. No response to the agreement-of-sale draft that I emailed him. It was driving me crazy to be in this limbo with only his "golden word" to hang on to. We needed to have that elusive piece of paper, something more tangible than mere words.

I called from Clare's BlackBerry, a number he wouldn't recognize. He answered on the second ring. "Oh, it's you. I was going to call you. I was incredibly busy, but we're right on track. When did we agree on for the takeover?"

"February 15, the day after Valentine's."

"Oh right, how could I forget? Sounds perfect. Can you send me over a kitchen and restaurant inventory of all the chattels, et cetera? And also maybe you should write out a sales agreement which I'll then show to my lawyer, and we can go from there."

"I already sent you a sales agreement, but I'll send another one. Also an inventory list, the one we kept for the insurance. It will be in your email today."

"You sound anxious. You need to relax more. How was the holiday season?"

"Well, yeah, the season was great. Better than last year," I said.

"Great, I'll call you as soon as I run the sales agreement past my lawyer."

"And some sort of a down payment," I reminded him.

I handed Clare back her phone. "I think we're moving forward," I said. "He wants an inventory and a sales agreement."

"You're doing all you can," she assured me.

On January 5, our 50-percent coupon appeared in prominent tricolour in 120,000 issues of the *Georgia Straight*, promising anybody who presented it half price on all our entrées, every day, for up to six people per coupon.

"If that doesn't bring them in, we'll try 'all you can eat for free,'" I said. We were running out of ideas.

"You guys are crazy. That's like Wednesday night every night," Gino said.

"Not exactly. People still have to read the ad and bring it along."

"Or show the picture on their cellphone or google it right

here in the restaurant. If only one in every thousand brings in the coupon, it will still be 120 people plus guests," Gino pointed out, shaking his head.

"Bring it on," Colin said, rubbing his hands in eager anticipation.

Gino had a point, but I doubted he was right. We overstaffed in anticipation, and when the stampede didn't materialize by 7:30 p.m. we started to send people home. In total, we counted eighteen redeemed coupons at the end of the night. Not exactly the tidal wave some expected.

We'd been packed with coupon redeemers since the previous Friday, and it felt like we were a very successful restaurant. Except the bottom line looked rather depressing, considering the amount of covers we served. Deduct from that the extra staff and food replacement and the cost of the ad, and we didn't really make any money. We decided to skip running the ad for a week. But for anybody walking by Le Bistro, it looked like the most popular place in town.

"What makes your restaurant so popular in January?" a curious diner asked me, blissfully unaware of our promotion.

"Excellent food and service," I replied without blinking.

On January 10, Aldo finally received a call from Morris, our lawyer, that his uncle had contacted him with regards to Jean, our prospective buyer.

"His uncle?"

"Turns out that Morris's uncle Fritz is also a lawyer and just happens to represent Jean."

"What a coincidence," I marvelled. "This should smooth the process. What did he say?"

"Morris has received a written offer and is drafting a purchase agreement as we speak," Aldo said.

"This sounds like the beginning of the end."

Many questions remained, like what exactly was Jean buying, and did the amount we talked about include everything, from the cutlery to the pictures and posters on the wall? Up to that point, we had only talked informally, Jean in sweeping gestures, I a little more detail-oriented, which to him came across as "worried."

That evening Jean surprised us with a visit to the bistro. He planted himself at the bar and ordered a glass of Côtes du Rhône. "Just coming to have a good look at my future," he whispered to me with a wink. "Don't worry so much, my friend," he said, reiterating his mantra. "My word is better than gold, thicker than blood, solid like the Pope's. The lawyer's papers and contracts are just window dressing. The real contract between two men is made here," he said, dramatically thumping his chest for emphasis.

I nervously looked around to see if any of the staff were paying attention to us, since the whole transaction was still a well-guarded secret. "Of course, you're right, Jean," I said, leading him to the back of the restaurant, out of earshot, "but the paper and the contracts are for the liquor control board, the city's licensing department, the bank, the suppliers, and last but not least, the landlord. By the way, have you spoken to Mr. Lee?"

"We have already talked and are like old friends. It will not be an issue."

We shook hands, the European way, which should have reassured me. Now that we had an actual paper trail started with our lawyers, I felt a whole lot more confident that the deal would actually go through. Still, we had to keep everything under wraps and confidential. If this information got out too early, we would have a mutiny on our hands and the staff would leave the sinking ship in droves. We still had Dine Out and Valentine's Day to get through, both potential money-makers.

"Aldo, if this gets out, we're in trouble," I said to him when I told him of Jean's clandestine visit.

"It's not going to get out. Nobody knows about it but us, so don't fret so much."

"You sound like Jean," I said, feeling a bit miffed.

I got home that night and told Clare the good news, but despite the fact that everything seemed to be on track, I felt kind of low and not very optimistic.

"The *Titanic* can't sink, the Canucks can't lose, the roof will never leak. So many sure-fire precedents to count on," I said.

"What's the worst-case scenario?" Clare said, and answered

it for me: "That the whole deal doesn't go through, in which case you have a better restaurant now than when you started two years ago."

Had it been two years already? Unbelievable. "I guess you're right. I just want this deal to go through. I really want out of it. Like that CEO from BP Oil said after the Deepwater Horizon oil spill: 'I just want my life back'!"

"Honey, you didn't spill 200 million gallons of crude and kill eleven people, you just tried to run a French restaurant. You are doing the best you can, and I really enjoy my weekly French onion soup with the mimosa salad and all that free wine. It's one of my weekly highlights. It will be sorely missed."

I desperately wanted to tell Gino or Roy or even Alia of the impending sale, the end of the bistro as we knew it, but I couldn't. I wasn't even sure myself that it was all going to happen. Every night Clare had to listen to me speculate and reiterate what we already knew.

"You're going to have a nervous breakdown," she said, genuinely worried about my state of mind. "Just relax and go with the flow. Run the restaurant like nothing is happening. Lower your expectations and you will not be disappointed."

"Yes, nurse. If we sell, or better yet, *when* we sell, I want to sit on a beach in Zihuatanejo or Caye Caulker and worry about the next margarita."

"Now you're talking. We'll take that trip that we postponed two years ago when you bought a restaurant. But meanwhile, you need to focus on the present."

We were packed on January 14, and the fifteenth looked full as well. Even though we didn't run the ad that week, we didn't turn anybody away who had the ad from the previous week. Some just showed us an iPhone picture and we honoured it.

Filling the bistro is what we wanted this time of year when the weather was cold, wet, dark and grey. Clare believed that the whole city suffered from SAD — seasonal affective disorder — and the cure was a holiday in the sun. I fully agreed, but for most of us who were stuck in the losing race against the banks and the government up here in the rainforest, the answer was vast amounts of vitamin D. I swallow 2,000 milligrams every morning, but it never feels like sunshine on a rainy day.

I know we served great food: full meals prepared from raw ingredients in our small, hot kitchen. We were proud of what we presented, and over that couple of years I had became a food snob.

One night, we went to the new Cactus Club, and apparently I bitched and complained about the food and the service the whole time. "This sauce is out of a can and the steak is overdone," or "Two spears of asparagus and a sprig of mint does not make a side of vegetables," or the worst sin, "These fries are frozen from a plastic bag."

"Can you please hold back your words of wisdom so I can enjoy a dinner out?" Clare asked, annoyed. "I like my Szechuan rice bowl."

"I'm sorry," I said, feeling bad.

I had no right to ruin my wife's dinner, but it wasn't easy to accept overpriced food that came out of a microwave and hadn't seen a proper kitchen, coming precooked from some warehouse in Surrey. I knew what these chain restaurants sold was a chic and cool atmosphere, with all the waitresses looking like the cast from *True Blood*.

I admit I felt anxious and disappointed. All I really wanted was my former life back. No responsibilities. No debts. No health inspectors. No licensing. No HST bills. No restaurant, period. On the other hand, I was convinced that if we'd had the kitchen crew we'd had with Colin, our fifth chef, we would have been in better shape. We might have been a real success instead of just appearing and pretending to be one. Looking back, I could only see the many mistakes we made and how we could have done things differently. And yet deep down I was proud of what we had achieved. If we failed, it wasn't for lack of trying. Maybe we were just twenty years too late with our concept, swimming upstream like salmon toward the inevitable fatal climax.

"I've got two guys here who are willing to write a cheque right now for the bistro," Aldo said, talking heatedly into his phone, out of breath.

"Are you all right? You sound as if you've been jogging."

"I'm just running over to the bistro now to meet these two guys. Maybe you should try to be there as well."

"Aldo, we have a deal with Jean in the works. How can we sell it to somebody else?"

"We don't have anything in writing — yet. No paper, no down payment, no deal."

Technically, he was right. "Okay, I'll see you there in a few minutes." I felt rather sceptical about this new development. It sounded more like a dope deal than a serious offer for a restaurant. Where did Aldo find these guys?

"They're friends of Rama," he confessed. I should have known.

Even though it was only 10:00 a.m., I was afraid there would be people in the kitchen already. This could be awkward. So far, we'd been able to keep the impending sale under wraps. There was no need to tell anybody until we had a firm deal. To have these two punters, whoever they were, go through the restaurant as potential buyers could seed the kind of rumours we didn't want. I was actually quite pissed off at Aldo, which didn't happen often even though we'd crossed some rough patches in the past two years.

I jumped on my bike and in less than five minutes I was at the back door of the bistro. Aldo was already there with two Indian guys, Gil and Usal. Luckily nobody was in the kitchen yet except Kana, who was always first in. She was the one person I could trust not to start any rumours. The two guys talked loudly in badly accented English and used sweeping gestures, and with large steps crisscrossed the restaurant. Gil sat down at the bar and theatrically waved a chequebook in the air. "I'll write a cheque right now, how much?"

I told him, and he instantly put his chequebook back into his jacket and started asking stupid questions like "What kind of restaurant is this? How late are you open each night? How many customers each day? How much money per day?"

Instead, they could have asked questions like "How much rent per square foot? How long is the lease? What is the average dinner bill?" which would have given them a good idea of how much money they needed to make in a month.

I already knew that this was going nowhere, and I looked at Aldo, tilted my head, and raised my arms palm-up in a gesture of "What the fuck is this all about?"

"Okay, we have to think about it," Gil, the mouthpiece, said. "We make you an offer tonight. We have two other Indian restaurants and we think we can turn this into an Indian restaurant right away."

I ushered them out the back door and thanked them for their interest.

Of course they didn't call, and on my prodding, Aldo contacted them. They made such a ludicrously low offer that Aldo just hung up. What a waste of time.

The next day, we finally did get a draft of a sales agreement from Uncle Fritz via Morris, our lawyer, and Jean did come to an agreement with Mr. Lee, our landlord. As far as I could tell, it was now a straightforward affair. We had one fish on the line and, very patiently and carefully, I reeled him in. Over the previous six months, Jean and I had actually become very friendly with each other and he gave me lots of good advice about maximizing the seating, changing menus and managing our wines — "Too big a wine list, cut it in half," or about advertising — "It's a waste of money."

There were still a lot of details to work out, but basically, he would buy the restaurant as-is with all the chattels, artwork, posters, dishes and glasses, etc. If we wanted anything, we would have to let him know what it was and remove the item. I looked around and couldn't think of a thing I wanted.

I asked Clare and she just shook her head. "I've got everything already because I ate and drank it. No need to bring home any trinkets or French liquor posters," she said.

I felt the same. There was nothing I wanted, except maybe the fondue pots we'd never used. They'd make good presents.

There was less than one month to go.

The winter's saviour of restaurants in Vancouver is the annual Dine Out promotion put on by Tourism Vancouver. We posted a fantastic four-course menu and the reservations started pouring in.

Interestingly enough, 80 percent of the bookings came from Asians. Wong, Chen, Yeng, Yu, Wu and Liam were the predominate names popping up on the reservation system. I'm not sure why that was, but we were happy to have them. They were the same customers who would fill the bistro on those crazy half-price Wednesday nights, which seemed already in the distant past. The other fact we learned was that most of these diners didn't drink. Just water, please. And we had to stock up on tea.

Maybe it's generational, maybe it's part of the herd mentality, the H factor. Probably both. They all suffer from an advanced form of smartphone addiction, completely dependent on their electronic communication devices. The girls more so than the boys. These young women continuously text and tweet, bent over their small screens.

Once in a while, they look up and take in their surroundings and interact, like when they actually have to order. The boys snap pictures of each other and all the food, from the soup to the dessert. Some then go home and blog about their dining experience on restaurant websites, along with close-ups of food and who and how their servers were, how loud the music was, how long it took for the main course to arrive, and on and on in nauseating detail. I'm not sure who reads these blogs but it's safe to say that probably nobody over thirty has either got the time or the desire, unless of course they own a restaurant.

A friend of Clare's from her Toronto days was in town and staying with us. Jane now lived in Winnipeg — "Winterpeg," as she called it — and made her living as a TV producer for children's shows. They ate dinner at the bistro, a bonus for all our friends. I was busy at the door, and the next time I looked over, the two of them were giggling like little girls.

"What's so funny?" I had to ask.

"Nothing, honey, just dredging up some old memories. You know, girl stuff."

I was mystified and felt left out, like they were speaking in a foreign language. They left soon after, still whispering and giggling like schoolkids.

Folly Bistro

I asked Clare when I crawled into bed what the hilarity was all about. "Girls giggle," she said, "and when girls giggle, it means they are the best of friends. Good night, honey,"

What do best guy friends do? I wondered. Drink and holler? Aldo and I were best friends, but we were never that intimate. Come to think of it, it had been a long time since I'd had a good laugh.

It was a typical January Monday in Vancouver. Drizzle and grey clouds hung so low that people hurried along with their heads bent down and tucked into their collars. I was in dire need of some distraction, and this was a perfect day to sneak into the Denman Cinema for the afternoon feature, *Jiro Dreams of Sushi*, a movie about an eighty-five-year-old Japanese sushi chef, Jiro Ono, and his ten-seat restaurant in the Ginza station of the Tokyo subway. It was the only sushi restaurant that had been awarded the three-star Michelin rating. As the saying goes, if a restaurant has a three-star rating then it's worth flying to that country just to eat there.

As Jiro points out in the film, there are five basic laws to good food:

1) Ingredients. You cannot make good food with substandard ingredients.

2) Knowledge. Without proper training and supervision, you can ruin the best ingredients. Every day is a striving for perfection, and the learning never stops.

3) Cleanliness. An absolute law in any kitchen and food establishment.

4) Consistency. A customer returns only for one reason: to have the same dish, service and environment he remembers from the last time.

5) Passion. Last but not least, a chef has to have passion for his craft, his food and all that goes with it. His reward is the satisfaction of a pleased customer. Nothing less will do.

I recommend this little movie to every aspiring cook and chef. It's an inspiration and lays it all out simply and truthfully. It's also a bit humiliating, owning a French restaurant, which is supposed to serve the highest class of food, just to find ourselves in a race to the bottom, caught in a spiral of forever lower prices without compromising our food quality. It's impossible to serve organic duck breast or Kobe tenderloin for the price of a hamburger, but strangely enough that's just what people expect. For two years we had been handing out free fresh bread and butter to every table, and until the summer before, every table got a free basket of our signature pommes frites. We started charging for the frites and we cut back on the amount of bread and butter. Our prices were reasonable for the kind of food we served and, yeah, I was proud of the quality of fare we offered. Our prices were equitable, but we were in direct competition with corporate restaurants that served up fast, fancy-plated food by servers dressed like nightclub hostesses in homogenous, chic designer environments where everything from the music to the menus and even the way the servers talked was choreographed down to minute details.

We were still waiting for the signed purchase agreement and the time was getting short. I was irritable and nervous, anxious and walking on eggshells, evermore playing a role in a charade. I was not the same jocular guy who took over the bistro two years previously, but I wanted to reclaim that man who could dance through the rain and laugh at his own jokes. Life had become very serious and worrying, full of sleepless nights and moody solitudes. I knew Clare would have liked me to stop beating myself up. She also wanted that other guy back.

"You've created a successful restaurant. Everybody praises what you've accomplished, and you should be proud of it. That is what people will remember, what will stand up over time," she said, while I was moping over breakfast on Sunday, wishing the umpteenth time for the final curtain.

I was reluctant to call Jean again, but we really did need to have that piece of paper in hand in order to move on. The whole situation reminded me of when we bought the bistro. Waiting for pieces of paper, licenses, permits and contracts. Very unnerving. I put in a call to Morris, our lawyer.

"Fritz is not available until after the weekend," Morris said, which brought us awfully close to the end of the month.

Folly Bistro

"We need to let our employees know two weeks ahead of time to avoid paying severance. Not only that, it's the right and fair thing to do," I said, trying hard not to sound desperate. Getting out of this business was a lot harder than getting into it.

Jean called first thing in the morning on January 30. "How are you? How was the weekend?"

"Great. I wish it would always be this busy," I answered, trying to swallow the lump in my throat. Why was he calling? Was he pushing the sales date or was he pulling out? So far, we hadn't seen a penny in down payment, nor the elusive sales contract.

"I know you're still worried, but don't fret. Today I'm meeting Fritz for lunch and then we'll send everything over to Morris. This deal should be all inked and A-okay by the end of the day. That, of all things, should make you happy."

"Great. We'll wait for Morris's phone call," I said, barely containing my excitement. In fact, I wanted to jump and scream. Yes! I could see the light at the end of the tunnel, and it wasn't a train coming head-on.

The phone call never came.

After Clare left for work the next day, I scurried on down to the bistro. It was a rainy, gusty, grey morning. Winter people in their greys and blacks hurried back and forth, guys with their hands plunged into their pockets, the women with their umbrellas held sideways against the rain. Everybody had somewhere to go: the bus, the coffee shop, work or the store. I let myself in the back door, sat down at the bar without turning on any lights, and looked out at the empty restaurant and the world beyond. If all went according to plan, this chapter in my life would soon be over. No more worries about the bills, the food, the payroll and all of the people whose lives and loves I seemed to have somehow become involved in.

My cellphone rang loudly in the empty restaurant. Aldo. "We've got it!" he yelled over the noise of the traffic. (Aldo always does all his phone calls while driving. "It saves time," he says, waving my objections about legality and safety aside. "I'm a multitasker. I can

266

talk, steer and watch at the same time. I used to smoke as well, but I gave that up, didn't I?")

"The down payment, Aldo?"

"Yes, and the agreement."

"That's it, then. We need to tell everybody."

"I'm on my way. I'll be there in ten minutes."

I sat down, feeling kind of suspended and in limbo, letting it all sink in. Was this really it? Did it all come down to a feeling of huge relief with a bit of emptiness mixed in? Was this really the end — and a new beginning, perhaps? A big weight was starting to slip off my shoulders and there was nobody to celebrate with. I stared at the fully stocked bar and decided to allow myself a shot of XO cognac, even though it was only 9:00 a.m.

Aldo flew in the door an hour later, reasonably late even by his standards. To break the news to everybody was not going to be an easy job, telling everybody that they were all going to be out of work after Valentine's Day. I didn't want to carry the load all by myself, no matter how many cognacs I had in me. "Please don't give the speech about beginnings and endings and that all good things come to an end. Nobody wants to hear that," I said.

The first one in that morning, like most mornings, was Kana, who looked at Aldo and me with a puzzled expression. She didn't say anything and proceeded with her work. I'm sure she sensed that something was in the air. Next in was Colin, and then Billy arrived shortly after, in a hurry about nothing, as was his usual manner. We asked all three to come to the front. They knew that this was different from other briefings, since both Aldo and I were there, with me looking at the floor, fidgeting and procrastinating, Aldo drumming his fingers on the bar and licking his lips.

"What's up?" Colin asked. "I've got stuff to do."

I let Aldo take the reins; he was better at this than I. He launched right into the heart of the matter. "We just found out that the bistro has sold and will change hands after Valentine's Day. This is good news and bad news. The good news is that the restaurant will continue on under new ownership and he will gladly accept applications from all of you. The bad news is that as of the fifteenth, we are all out of a job. But we need to make these two weeks the best time possible and we want to go out with a bang, not a whimper." Aldo looked over at me to see if I had something to add.

"We want to thank you for all you've done, and I'm sorry," I said, feeling all emotional and probably a bit drunk.

"No need to be sorry. I understand," Colin said after a brief pause. "And we'll do our best for the next two weeks. I already have the Valentine's menu in my head."

Kana just looked at the floor, not saying a word, while Billy fidgeted with his apron, wringing his hands.

"Kana, are you okay? And how about you, Billy?"

Kana looked up and said, "Thank you for giving me this job. Nobody else was going to hire me. It is good. Now I can spend time with my son."

Billy just shrugged and said, "Maybe I go back to accounting again. I still have some contacts. I'm actually glad this job is over. It's hard work."

When we told Gino, he indicated that this would be his chance to go home to Italy for a couple of months. Kay said that he had long harboured plans to visit his mom in Taipei, and Margo, looking like the cover of a magazine, indicated that she wanted to go back to Prague for the summer. Alia came in with a new fab haircut and announced that she was going into modelling, while Alice mumbled something about going back to school. And Selena, well, I had no fear for her. She would probably end up at a Cactus Club or Earls. Only Melinda broke into tears, but she recovered pretty quickly. She was going to take the opportunity to go back to Quebec, while Mandy would also have no trouble finding another server position. "Maybe I'll go back to Manila and become a nurse," she said. Our third Maria took the news stoically. She was used to being hired and fired. Roy said he knew all along that something was in the air and he too seemed happy to take a few weeks off.

It was the hardest on me, it seemed. We had such a great crew now and I practically considered them all to be friends, in stark contrast to Aldo, who wasn't about to make friends with people he had to pay.

"We have a two-week window," I told everyone, "where we can have some fun, make some money and launch our future. And everybody will get a layoff for EI."

The Beginning of the End

Colin was very quiet for the rest of the day. It was a big blow to him. He'd been a young up-and-coming chef at an iconic French restaurant, and now it was suddenly over. I caught up with him out back during his smoke break.

"Colin, you're twenty-seven and have the world by the tail. Don't worry, this job will look good on your resumé and you will find another, probably better." I said. Like throwing a handful of light into a bucket of darkness, I thought, not sure how else to turn bad news into good news.

"I guess you're right, and believe me, I understand your situation. I was going to ask for two weeks' holiday after Valentine's. Now I can take a whole month, or the rest of my life," he said, butting out his smoke.

"I know it sucks, Colin, but we had no choice. I wish you could have been with us at the beginning and we might be in a different position."

"You don't have to explain anything. I have a pretty good idea, and I am glad I had the opportunity."

We shook hands.

That afternoon, Aldo and I went to see Morris to sign the papers. That night after the last customer left, everybody discussed the news among themselves, and one by one they thanked me, expressing their understanding of the situation and promising to do their best to make the next two weeks a roaring success. It was very touching, and confirmed to me that being personal with employees wasn't all wrong; there is value in trust and respect, which in my mind rates higher than simple obedience and doing one's job.

I had told Clare earlier in the day that it was now official. When I got home after midnight, Clare offered to make us a cup of tea. I told her what everybody had said and that they all thanked me and would do their best for the next two weeks.

"I think their respect and gratitude is the best compliment, and it affirms what I told you before. You resurrected a great little restaurant and you should be proud of your achievement. You did the right thing and your honesty was rewarded with respect. It's not all about money."

Folly Bistro

This was the first night in a long while that I actually slept all the way until the morning without the usual wacky dreams or worries worming through my brain.

On the last day of Dine Out, the restaurant was fully packed. By now the news about the demise of the bistro had gotten out, and I didn't deny any of it. It added a dramatic dimension, a place for fantasy to prosper. Like politicians, we answered all the questions without divulging any secrets. I opted to follow Clare's advice: "Tell the truth — it's always the easiest position to defend." Everybody wanted to know who the new owner was going to be or what the restaurant was going to be called and when would it reopen and what were our plans, a new restaurant?

I stayed late those last few nights, as did some of the staff, who took advantage of the fact that I opened the spigots and offered free drinks from the bar. All of those opened liquor bottles had to be emptied, and there were lots of eager volunteers. We talked about the past and what we could have done differently, but mostly people were concerned about their future.

Gino looked forward to some time off, maybe even a career change, like working for the post office. "Working every night and sleeping every morning till noon. How am I ever going to meet a girlfriend?" he mused.

Roy, who couldn't let this go by, quipped, "You know the old saying: If it flies, fucks or floats, rent it — it's cheaper."

Alia, who was still drying cutlery and stacking dishes, sadly shook her head. "Men are so shallow, ATNO."

"Meaning?"

"All talk and no action."

Roy liked that. "You are a funny one, Alia. I'll miss you."

"I'm gonna miss this old bistro. We had some good times here," Colin said, uncharacteristically meditative. He was usually upbeat after a long shift and liked to sit at the bar and enjoy a beer or two. I never saw him eat, but that's not uncommon among chefs and cooks. "I usually eat something at home or order out for pizza or some Chinese," he said when I asked him

"How can you eat that crap?"

"If you're around food all day, it simply becomes a necessity to eat, not a pleasure. Fuel for the machine. I need to have some days off before I can enjoy food the way other people do. I'm not fussy at all and I like it best when somebody else cooks, but most people are intimidated by the fact that I'm a chef. In other words, only my mom cooks for me," he said with a shrug. "How about a refill, boss?"

I promised myself to enjoy these last days at the bistro and told all our friends to drop by one more time for their "last decent meal." Naturally I plied them with plenty of free wine. I spent as much time as I could at the restaurant, mostly as moral support for the staff but also because I wanted to make sure that there were no last-minute mutinies, revolutions or other upheavals. Not everybody was happy about moving on, and there was some grumbling in the kitchen. Not from our long-timers like Kana, Billy, Kay, Colin or Chase, but some of our recently hired kitchen help felt cheated. Maria the third, the Italian dishwasher, moaned that she would never find another job and had two kids to feed, while Colin's sidekick and part-time sous-chef Leon, who I never really liked because he spent all his time fiddling on his iPhone, bitched to everybody that the management owed everybody severance pay. I pulled him aside and told him that he was wrong, since the two-week advance notice was what the labour law required. "Get the facts straight and stop these rumours!"

Closer to home, one of the casualties would be Clare's regular Tuesday dinners: mimosa salad and gratin Lyonnais with a glass of Côtes du Rhône, usually served by Roy, and unfailingly accompanied by a Scottish joke or much-repeated detail from his recent trip to Paris. He kept showing us a video clip on his new iPad of driving up the Champs-Élysée and through the Arc de Triomphe in a Lamborghini at 120 kilometers an hour. "Cost me a hundred bucks for half an hour. Saw Paris at high speed. The most fun I ever had, not counting my wedding night."

On many nights I had joined Clare for her dinner, and yes, I would certainly miss those. It was a privilege to be served like aristocrats and fed like kings

Swan Song

We had one more major affair to stage at the bistro. Valentine's Day was traditionally the second-biggest day in any restaurant, after New Year's Eve, and since this was going to be our swan song, I wanted to make it extra special.

"Colin, pull out all the stops this time. Let your creative juices flow. This is going to be our pièce de résistance and your masterpiece. We need to go out with a bang."

"I'll have a draft for you later today. We've been working on some ideas. It's going to be a challenge because we don't really want any leftovers, do we."

He was right, but I sensed something more than just worries about the menu. "I know you're disappointed, Colin, but I have no doubt that you will make your way."

"I know. I'll have to and I will. I just liked it here. It's a real restaurant, just the right size, and a fantastic opportunity for any aspiring chef. I don't want to go back to a corporate kitchen where every dish is exactly regulated and standardized. No creativity allowed, just cook according to the preordained recipes and do your job from the neck down. Basically warm up pre-prepared food. It's hard to find a small restaurant where everything is created from scratch with fresh ingredients. My job isn't just cooking; it starts with sourcing the ingredients, the best meats and fish, the best prices, the freshest produce. It's interacting with all the people from the fishmonger to the baker to the farmer. I'll miss that as much as creating a dish that only exists here at the bistro."

Colin's passion for his job was evident, and it made the whole unraveling of the bistro that much harder. I tried to placate him by being positive, constructive and forward-looking, but I'm no psychologist. "You're right, Colin, and it's ever harder to make it in this highly competitive environment. All the resources are squeezed to a point where the difference between success and failure is a couple of percentage points."

I don't know why I tried to explain myself to Colin. I guess I thought I owed it to him, and explaining it one more time helped me as well. "The fact is, we needed to fill the place every night, not just on weekends or special occasions, in order to justify the staff we carried and the kind of food we presented. Believe me, Colin, we tried, and you're right, we could probably make it now with the present crew, but we've been bogged down with the luggage of two years of revolving chefs and crews. If you ask me what the one thing that can make or break a restaurant is, I repeat over and over: It's consistency, consistency, consistency, in the staff as well as the food."

"I understand all that and I'm not blaming you at all. I think you showed guts to even enter into an eclectic food venture like a French restaurant without having any prior experience," Colin said.

"I'm not sure if it was guts or just plain folly. I had a dream and then it took me a while to wake up. But I'm glad we did it, and now that it's coming to an end, I'm sad. But I have no regrets."

I believe Colin knew what I was trying to say. "You don't need to worry about me," he said, "and don't you worry, we'll finish on a high. The Valentine's menu will be the best this side of Paris."

Mandy, our savvy computer expert, sent out Colin's Valentine's menu to our database, which had grown to over 1,200 strong by then. It was the best way to reach our clientele, since we were on neither Facebook nor Twitter. Alas, it's a digital social world, where a click can do as much damage or good in a nanosecond as a public broadcast of old. It's not only a brave new world but also a virtual and instant one.

We had less than one week to go. We tried not to broadcast that the restaurant was about to change hands, but of course the rumours were rife and the news of our impending demise had already gone viral thanks to the endemic proliferation of smartphones. Every day the serving staff were pestered by customers about the future of the bistro. I told them all to be casual and positive, emphasizing that it would be newer, possibly better, and still French, and that the new owner had every intention of welcoming all the regulars back. In a strange way, this turn of events filled the bistro every night. I almost felt like maybe we'd made a mistake, and when I mentioned this to Aldo he almost physically slapped me to jolt me out of my fantasy.

"What are you, a masochist? You like losing thousands every month and working for free? Give your head a shake."

Folly Bistro

Even Clare wanted to eat at the bistro every chance she could get. "I'm the one with the most to lose," she said. "I had all the benefits without any of the headaches or responsibilities."

"You're very kind, my dear," I said, "to disregard the depressed and stressed-out psycho you have been living with."

"Oh that. We women are used to living with battle-scarred men, and for that matter, you weren't all that bad. At least you talked to me and included me in your misery," she said with a smile. I knew she was like me, relieved and sad at the same time now that the bistro was coming to an end.

And so we dined every remaining night at the bistro, working our way through the favourites on the menu. Mine were always the bouillabaisse or the boeuf bourguignon, but mind you, I also enjoyed the magret de canard — Fraser Valley duck breast — and at the end of the day a plate of charcuterie with a glass of Bordeaux always did the trick. Eating daily at a French restaurant can be quite challenging, and both Clare and I made up for it by riding our bicycles around Stanley Park or going for a swim at the Aquatic Centre every chance we got.

Not wanting to turn anybody away, we overbooked the Saturday of the Valentine's weekend. The kitchen was under pressure to produce, but unlike Colin, who remained fully committed, some of the other kitchen staff didn't care any longer. How to motivate them? Point out that their personal integrity was at stake, their self-respect? Not so much. But how about a bonus? Now that's a good motivator. Money always talks.

"That's like bribing them," Clare pointed out.

"It's more like blackmail," I said.

"Same thing. It will cost you."

"Don't give them any money," Aldo said adamantly, refusing to play that game. "I'll tell them that if they don't want to work they'll be fired instead of laid off, and no letters of recommendation. I can play that game too. You're crazy, offering them a bonus for work that they are already getting paid for. Don't worry, I'll handle it."

Of course, Aldo was right. Clare tried to make it even more clear to me with a food analogy. "You're bocconcini while Aldo is parmesan. You're a warm pudding while Aldo is hard, frozen gelato," Clare said, with more than a hint of irony.

"You're calling me a marshmallow?"

"No, a marshmallow is soft all over. You're more like a cream puff, solid on the outside and soft on the inside."

Jean and a female companion paid us a surprise visit for brunch. "In all the time you've been open, I've never eaten here," he said, holding the chair for his friend, a woman in her thirties. Her black hair was tightly pulled back into a ponytail, and she had pencilled eyebrows, pale skin, and thin lips without lipstick. She looked severe and businesslike. Jean introduced her: "This is Caroline, and she will be the maître d' when I take over," he said rather loudly. Luckily, it was just me in the front, and Melinda was in the back on her cellphone, as she had been all morning.

"Can you just kind of be discreet?" I asked Jean politely, not wanting to overload an already charged atmosphere.

"Don't worry, there's nobody here. Where's your staff?"

"Melinda is supposed to be our server, but she's busy yapping on her phone. Boyfriend trouble, I guess. Now that she's losing her job, he might have to go to work."

Jean laughed. "There will be a killing!" he prophesied. "By the way, just to make it clear, everything in here stays as it is."

"Absolutely, just as we agreed, as is: posters, paintings, glasses, tables, chairs and all that you can see. It's all yours. Are you gonna keep it all?"

"Don't know yet, but if you want anything, let me know now."

"How about the posters in the bathroom? The Toulouse–Lautrec and the Freudian cartoon?"

"You can take the Lautrec, but the Freudian poster has been here since day one. It's perfect in a men's bathroom. You should go and check it out, Caroline," he urged his companion.

She raised an eyebrow, and I offered to show her the iconic poster.

She stared at the black-and-white drawing of Freud's visage in the shape of a naked woman with the caption "What's on a man's mind" and said, "This is so 1970. I can't believe he wants to keep it."

"Maybe he wants to hang it in his own bathroom at home," I said, grinning, but she didn't share in my humour.

Jean enjoyed his brunch — on the house, of course. "This is delicious and much too cheap. Not sure how you can make any money on this."

Nice dig, I thought. I should charge him double.

We entertained a busy crowd that night, and after everybody had gone I wandered through the empty restaurant by myself, making sure that everything was turned off and under control. When I checked the men's bathroom, I felt that something was not quite right, something was missing. I looked around, and instead of Freud's poster, a blank wall stared back at me. What the hell? Where did Freud's head go?

Ah fuck, I thought, somebody ripped it off. Jean would be pissed off, thinking that I took it. He specifically mentioned it as one of the original treasures that had been there since the seventies. I needed to have it back. Fucking thieves.

Valentine's Day and the last day at the bistro. The swan song. The fat lady sings. First off, I wanted to know if anybody had seen Freud's head. Since we had a full crew in, I asked everybody personally, but nobody knew the whereabouts of the missing poster. They all looked at the empty wall and were as much taken aback as I was. It looked as though I had to explain to Jean that somebody had stolen the silly print and that I would somehow replace it. I'm sure I could get it off the Internet or from the poster shop up the street. I couldn't let this unpleasant incident cloud the mood of the day, since this was supposed to be a happy, festive occasion. I pushed the missing print to the back of my mind and told everybody to carry on. "Let's have a good time, people, one more kick at the can." I felt like the coach in the locker room before the last game of the season.

We didn't expect a large turnout for lunch, but we were ready for anything. Because Valentine's fell on a Tuesday, some did take their significant others out for an extended lunch. For dinner, we had 120 reservations, all of them deuces, which translated into a full house. The restaurant looked festive, with glittery hearts in the windows, a gorgeous bouquet from My Florist at the entrance, all the tables set and the crew ready to roll.

Valentine's is the one time boyfriends and husbands opt for a better bottle of wine, and it's the one time when the guys can make it up to their wives and girlfriends and show them their love by way of a five-course dinner at a restaurant of their choice. It's not cheap, but well worth the price, and the beauty of it all is that there is no age limit. Love is a timeless muse and today it passed through the five senses (or five courses).

It's a fantastic day to be in the restaurant business. Hearing the menu described by your server or read aloud by your partner. Seeing the fabulous presentation of the food. The touching of hands across the table, the heavenly aromas, and finally the orgiastic stimulation of the taste buds when that first bite crosses your lips. There is a saying in German which translates to "Love goes through the stomach," and that is Valentine's Day at a French restaurant with the one you love. Here is Colin's masterpiece.

Folly Bistro

VALENTINE'S
FIVE-COURSE CELEBRATION DINNER

Amuse-bouche
Chef's hors d'oeuvre

First Course
Ahi tuna tartare
Chili citrus marinade, cucumber nest
§
Five oysters on the half shell
Shallot mignonette, vodka cocktail sauce
§
Foie gras crème brûlée
Olive oil crostini, balsamic reduction

Second Course
Classic lobster bisque, brandy crème fraîche
§
Watercress and melon salad, lime vinaigrette

Main Course
Rosemary and confit garlic rack of lamb
Yam purée, Chambord reduction
§
Grilled eight-ounce rib-eye
Yukon Gold mash, wild mushroom and Marsala
§
Pan-seared Arctic char fillet
Lemon thyme risotto, pine nut beurre noisette, king crab legs
§
Cinnamon and anise-infused duck confit
Yukon Gold mash, Calvados sauce

Swan Song

Palate Cleanser
Lemon sorbet with champagne drizzle

Dessert
Madagascar vanilla bean crème brûlée

§

New York cheesecake, triple berry compote, Chantilly cream

§

Brandy espresso chocolate mousse with chocolate-drizzled
strawberries

HAPPY VALENTINE'S FROM LE BISTRO

Folly Bistro

The first seating started at 5:00 p.m., and from then on it was a full-court press. We gave each pair of diners two and a half hours before the next seating, and as always, some stayed longer and some diners came too early. We managed as best we could, putting some up at the bar with a glass of Veuve du Vernay on the house, which kept everybody happy. When we ran out of menu items, we had to substitute, but that was Colin's plan all along, because ideally we didn't want any leftovers. We needed to clean out the kitchen as best we could. As of the next day, only the mice would be left.

It was all over by 11:00 p.m., and only some inebriated stragglers remained. This was the time for the staff to have their well-deserved staff meal — the last supper, as Gino called it. It consisted of everything left over from the menu, including unlimited desserts and all the open bottles of wine. This turned into the mother of all after-hours parties at Le Bistro. Somebody swapped their own iPod of head-banger techno-hip-hop with ours, which consisted of 250 songs of French bistro mix that everyone was sick of. We closed the doors, put Chevy on the bar, and pulled the curtains. The only people still working were Maria the third and Billy; Maria was still cleaning the kitchen with Billy, who didn't drink. It looked like Leon, the sous-chef, had already left the premises without saying goodbye to me, unlike Kay, our valued Taiwanese pastry chef, who thanked both Aldo and me and took his leave in style with a bow and a hug. I would miss him.

Colin joined in the party with a full mug of draught, but he didn't eat anything, even though he must have been starving after the day. He wanted to talk to me in private. "I know who took the poster," he said, staring into his beer.

"Who in hell would do that?"

"It's Leon. Three people saw him leave with it yesterday. They want to remain anonymous. I knew this afternoon, but I didn't want to tell you and put extra stress on the service."

"Why the hell would he steal that? Why didn't he just get his own damned poster? Thanks, Colin. It's not the way I wanted it to end. The fucking thief, picking over the corpse before it's dead!"

Colin was very distraught himself and shook his head in disbelief.

"I trusted him. I brought him along when you hired me, and now he betrayed me. I've already taken him off my Facebook and Twitter accounts, and I posted the fact that he stole and betrayed my trust."

I looked at Colin with awe. That was indeed the worst punishment for Leon, because now all his friends would know what he did and probably shun him. This was twenty-first-century justice at its best. Worse than jail for a cyber crackhead like Leon. I thanked Colin for his service and loyalty and offered him all the free beer he could drink. He declined, and quietly left out the back.

I immediately called Leon's cell but only got his voicemail. "If the poster is not back in its place by tomorrow at noon, I will report you to the police. I have three witnesses who saw you take it."

When I told the remaining gang — Gino, Aldo, Alia and Billy — who the thief was, nobody seemed surprised.

"The little weasel. I knew it was him," Gino said.

Alia also had no high regard for Leon. "He was never nice to me, always treated me like trash. I will certainly take him off my Facebook."

Amen.

I refilled everyone's glass and we carried on for a while longer, talking about all the fun and crazy stuff that had happened over the past two years. Gino was reminiscing about the good old days when this kind of after-service party had been a regular event which would go on until the wee, wee hours. He also told us that he was through with serving and would move on to other things.

Roy, on the other hand, had no such qualms. "I'll work to play," he said. "It's not a chore, it's a pleasure, and all that cash gets me and Shirley" (his wife) "out of town. I want so see more of Europe, maybe Barcelona, Prague, and also go to a sunny clime during the rainy days in Vancouver."

Alia was more worried about her future. "No way I'm going back to Latvia. It's a dead-end place with no opportunities, and all the young people are leaving or have already left, just like me."

"But that will only make matters worse. Who will rebuild their country and their future?" I asked.

"Well, not me. I have my own future to worry about. I need another year before I can apply for immigrant status. I do send money home to my mom. I guess that's a big part of Latvia's economy, the support payments coming in from abroad."

We drank and talked and laughed, and yes, there was the odd sad moment, like when Mandy, our feisty young waitress, broke down in tears when she took her leave. "I will miss this place. You were so nice to me." She gave me a big hug and ran out the back door.

For me, the end of the bistro was both a happy and a sad event. I was happy to be rid of it but sad that it was all over.

I stayed to the end. It was around 2:00 a.m. when Gino and Aldo were finally done and staggered out the back door.

"Is it over?" Clare asked sleepily when I came home.

"It's all over," I said and fell into bed.

At 11:00 a.m., I met Leon, who was practically in tears when he brought back the stolen poster. As to why he did it, he mumbled something about a bet and a prank, but I couldn't care less. I was just happy that the darn thing was back in its place.

At noon, Aldo shuffled in the door, suffering from the alcohol flu. We both had a job to do: clean the coolers and get rid of all the leftover food. Also, we had to take all the unopened wine to the liquor store for a rebate. There were a few bottles I didn't want to return, a 1994 one-and-a-half litre Beaucastel and a couple of others which were worth more now than when we paid for them. Aldo likes the whites; I prefer the reds. We divided them up equally, and like everything over the past two years, we did it fairly and amiably. We reflected on the fact that we had both steered this venture into a safe harbour without scuttling the ship or having any fights. Yes, we'd had our disagreements, as in any partnership, but we always found a solution, we always moved forward, and we always knew that we could trust each other implicitly, which is the number-one commodity in any relationship. We were proud to have come through some crazy times and still maintained our friendship, which endured long past the bistro.

What to do with all the open liquor? Easy: sell it to Jean at a price he couldn't refuse. Again, I took home some cognacs, while Aldo opted for the sweet dessert wines.

Now all we had to do was wait for Jean. For once, he was worrisomely late. We had agreed to meet at noon and exchange the cheque for the keys. It was 2:00 p.m. and still no Jean. I called his cell but only got the answering service. I started to fiddle and worry, but not Aldo, who knew all about being late.

Then at 2:30 p.m., Jean drove up in his Citroën and, without getting out of the car, gestured for us to come over. "I'm really late and I'm sorry. Had to meet the lawyer, the designer and the architect. Here is the cheque. Hope all is well, and if you don't mind, I'll be on my way. We'll chat later."

I took the cheque and gave Jean the keys. With a quick wave, he backed up and drove away. Aldo and I were left standing there, looking at the ordinary cheque, which seemed fine. And that was that. A bit anticlimactic, but what did we expect? Fireworks and dancing girls, popping champagne and cheering crowds? We laughed, shared a long hug, and called it a day.

While I walked home, people looked at me funny, probably because my feet were skipping and I had a big, goofy grin on my mug. I felt like flying, feeling suddenly as light as a feather, and a woozy, euphoric feeling engulfed my head, replacing the fuzzy hangover clouds from the night before. Slowly it dawned on me that my future did not include the bistro, which was already part memory and part legend, and freedom meant that my phone didn't ring for the rest of the day.

THE END

Epilogue

Epilogue

It's been almost ten years since we took over the bistro, and still I meet people who remember it fondly, especially the pommes frites. "I've never tasted fries like that since" and "I wish I could have some of those frites right now" are common reactions when the subject of the bistro comes up. The question that I always get asked is "Did you lose a lot of money?", as if it's a foregone conclusion. My answer is always along the lines of "I didn't lose my shirt, but my socks, on the other hand . . ." Or I give them the boat parable about the two happiest days, the first and last day.

A restaurant is much like a theatre production. The stage (the front) has to stick to the script, all the actors (the servers) have their roles to play, and the audience needs to be seduced, pleased and entertained, no matter if backstage (the kitchen) is a raging chaos — none of that can transfer into the front, where the server who just screamed at the chef, calling him a freaking lunatic, is all smiles and amiable. That's why I divided the book into acts, just like in a play, because that's what it felt like a lot of the time.

I also maintain that if we'd had the crew at the beginning that we had at the end, we might still be there. Yes, I did lose money, but it's not the money I mourn but the fact that the demise of the bistro almost felt like the end of an era, a time when properly cooked and prepared meals were something to look forward to, like a feast or a celebration. It was when people took the time to eat, savoured the spicy and delicious sauces, and lingered over a glass of good wine and maybe even tried a delicate dessert with a glass of cognac. Now it's all tapas and craft beer, quick food with no provenance and no history. We tried to swim upstream with our eclectic French menu, tried to serve up a classy dinner that you wouldn't cook at home and at a reasonable price. Granted, the free pommes frites and fresh baguettes with butter usually precluded dessert but, hey, we aimed to please.

There are no regrets. It was a fantastic time, and we entertained all of our friends; and my wife — "Clare" in the book — loved the bistro: the atmosphere, most of the staff, and especially the food and wine. Aldo and I are still the best of friends. We hark back to the bistro days with some nostalgia, like for a wayward relative that always was good for a lively story. And there were plenty of stories, most of which made it into this book, but once in a while a new nugget surfaces and we have a good laugh. "Remember when Mandy advised Big Bad Bob to use castor oil because she thought his constant bad mood had to do with indigestion?" Aldo reminded me just the other day.

I laughed. "Yeah, that's when he threatened to toss her into the deep fryer. But the big bad baboon could never scare the sassy chick from Manila."

Today the building complex that housed the bistro, a bicycle rental, a sushi bar, a pizza franchise, a Mongolian grill and Ciao Bella, the best Italian family restaurant and piano bar in Vancouver, is all gone and a tower is rising in its place. It's the new replacing the old, and the iconic French restaurant that served three generations of customers is now nothing but a memory and a treasure trove of stories, some of which I feel are my privilege, my pleasure and an honour to pass on.

B.H. 2019

Acknowledgements

I want to acknowledge and thank everyone who worked at the bistro and all the patrons who enjoyed themselves there. Without them there would be no story to tell. Also, I'm grateful to all my supportive friends and to both my kids, Sandra and Brian, who loved the bistro and urged me on to write about it.

A special thank you to everybody at Granville Island Publishing, for your insights, advice, patience and book-making skills. It takes more than a writer to create a good book.

Bruno Huber was born and raised in Zürich, Switzerland. In 1977 he won the Höhnharter Wanderpreis, a literary prize for the best short story in German, and subsequently Ullstein published a book of his short stories, *Das Gelübte*.

He immigrated to Canada in the seventies and settled in Nelson, BC, then moved to Gibsons, BC, on the Sunshine Coast, where he still lives with his wife Elizabeth. For the past twenty-five years he has made a living as a lighting technician in Vancouver's film industry. During this time, he owned and operated a bookstore in Gibsons and later an iconic French restaurant in Vancouver's West End. His humorous behind-the-scenes account of that adventure is currently being adapted for the stage. He divides his time between Gibsons, Mexico and the Caribbean.

You can follow his blog at www.brunospointofview.com.